MW00412418

An Odd Steelers Journey

By
Andy Russell

Sports Publishing L.L.C.
www.sportspublishingllc.com

Director of production: Susan M. Moyer
Developmental editor: Stephanie Fuqua
Dust jacket design: Kerri Baker
Project manager: Gregory Hickman
Copy editors: Ashley Burum/Cindy McNew

ISBN:1-58261-492-x

Printed in the United States of America

Sports Publishing L.L.C.
www.sportspublishingllc.com

Dedication

This book is dedicated to my good friend and mentor, Walter Bent, a wonderful family man and a successful entrepreneur who passed away last year after a valiant struggle against cancer. Walter was always an inspiration, pushing me to work harder and chase my dreams. He significantly enriched my journey, and I am forever indebted.

Contents

Foreword

By Jack Ham

In the world of business, sports and life, I'm not known to be a sentimentalist or one who walks down the memory lane of the "Steeler Dynasty." So when Andy asked me to script the foreword of his new book, it forced (encouraged) me to reflect on the history of a friendship that has spanned some thirty years— a relationship that has developed from teammates to friends to businessmen. Actually, the years that we have known one another outside of football are fivefold of those that took place within the football arena.

Our friendship goes back to my earliest days as a 1971 second-round Steelers draft choice. Thinking that I would be a first-round choice of the San Diego Chargers, I was not sure how I felt about being a Pittsburgh Steeler. I was a scared, confused rookie about to play for one of the worst teams in football.

Being a Penn State graduate, however, I was excited by the fact that my linebacker coach, Dan "Bad Rad" Radakovich, was now an assistant coach with the Steelers. Bad Rad was fundamentally the best technique coach in the league and had helped me and players like Ted Kwalich to develop into All-Americans. To say that I respected his opinion would be an understatement. So it was natural for a rookie to seek the sage advice of someone so trusted and familiar.

On my first trip to Three Rivers Stadium and the Allegheny Club, I was about to sign my contract and conduct the obligatory press conference. Bad Rad was there to give me some much-needed support. I took the opportunity to ask him, "What does it take to be a professional linebacker in the NFL?" Being a man of few words, he pointed to Andy Russell, who happened to be working out in the stadium, and said, "Watch number 34 and do what he does. You'll be just fine."

Those of you who don't remember football previous to 1971 may not realize that the Steelers were an abysmal team. But somehow, Andy Russell was able to play great football on a bad football team. There were few years that he failed to make the Pro Bowl.

Today, most players back into the Pro Bowl by playing mediocre football on good football teams. Andy played great football on a worse than mediocre team. Why? Because Andy was always the consummate professional. His personal pride and drive for excellence allowed him to stand out on even the worst of football teams. It would have been easy for him to give up or be sucked into the mediocrity that he saw all around him, but he refused to do so. That attitude was clear to me from my first day of training camp to Andy's last game as a Steeler.

One of the first plays that I witnessed was a sign of things to come. I observed Andy on a "37 Power," perhaps one of the hardest plays for a right outside linebacker to read. On this play, the right guard pulls to the outside, trying to kick Andy outside and away from the play. He tries to create an inside alley between Andy and Dwight White. Andy's job is to read it immediately and close that alley so the running back can't run off tackle and bounce to the outside. The key is a quick read and then to close the play and make penetration.

Andy read the play and closed the off tackle, making the running back bounce to the outside, and yet he was still able to make the tackle. All of that and he made it look easy. No big deal. He helped the running back get up and went back to the huddle. Business as usual. As Joe Paterno would say, "Act like you've been there before."

"Damn," I thought. "This guy is good." I wanted to do it just like that: diagnose the play as it developed, close on the running back and knock him out of the play—then get back into the huddle and do it again. And Andy was more than willing to become my tutor. He was in no way intimidated by my presence;

he welcomed an addition to the team—one who would push him to work harder. Push him, perhaps the best outside linebacker in football at the time? He was happy that I was there to push him to play better!

And the amazing fact was that I was about to replace one of his best friends and teammates for many years, Jerry Hildebrand. But in Andy's mind, if it was better for the team, it was best for everyone. It had to be business as usual. This set the standard of what I began to expect of Andy, but more importantly, a standard that I expected of myself.

As per Bad Rad's instructions, I continued to watch Andy, and I became ever more mesmerized in what I witnessed on and off the field. I began to take mental notes in both arenas. I guess that you could say that Andy became my mentor. It was a smart choice on my part. It became a symbiotic relationship, one in which we began to feed off each other's talents. We became bookend linebackers, known for our intelligent choice of play.

In a few years, Jack Lambert was drafted to play the inside linebacker spot to complete the trio. And what a trio it became. Ham, "the thinking man's linebacker," Lambert, the gruff bohemian or "Dracula in Cleats" as he was known around the league, and Andy, who was, of course, always known as "the businessman's linebacker." He ran his position the way that he ran his business: quiet and professional. He made it look easy.

Somehow that chemistry of the linebacking trio worked just right. There were a lot of things that went on behind the scenes and on the field that few people ever knew. To really know the person who is Andy Russell, you have to understand some of what did happen.

In most situations, Andy (being the right outside linebacker) played the weak side, which means that the opposing team's tight end lined up on my side of the field, or the strong side. Most teams are right-handed teams, meaning their tight end lines up across the defensive left outside linebacker, who was me. That left Andy to cover the running back out of the backfield on passing plays.

One play that epitomizes how Andy would use his intelligence to outwit the offensive player occurred in a game against the Houston Oilers. Fred Willis, a running back, was lining up opposite Andy. Andy had a free blitz to the quarterback, a designed defense. Andy, being the cerebral player that he was, realized that Willis had blitz pickup on him.

Now Willis was a bright young Boston College graduate and one who would not "bite" on an obvious bluff. We all heard Andy yell to Lambert, "I have Willis on man to man." Willis, believing this, thought that he was now free to run his route and didn't have to pick up the blitz since he thought Andy was not running a blitz. Willis came out into the flat, and Andy blew by him. Mike Wagner, playing free safety, picked up Willis man to man, allowing Andy to blitz the quarterback, Dan Pastorini, and cause him to fumble the football. Willis just laughed and shook his head, knowing that he had just been bluffed out of his jock.

It was all done without physical skills or quickness or strength. It was all done with guile. He outwitted an opposing player with his brain, and it was a beautiful thing to see.

Those are the things that Andy taught me. I saw all of this from the other side of the field, and I marveled. Lambert would just shake his head, put his tongue through the hole in his mouth where his front teeth used to be, and yell a few expletives. I guess that was his way of saying, "Nice play, Captain."

Perhaps the greatest game he played was against the Raiders in the 1974 AFC Championship game in Oakland. Anyone who remembers those years knows that the rivalry with the Raiders was historic. And this was to become the game that would begin to set us apart from other teams in the NFL.

As I have mentioned, most teams are right-handed, but the Raiders were the anomaly. Because their quarterback, Ken Stabler, was left-handed, Dave Casper, their tight end, lined up to their left—opposite to Andy. Ernie Holmes and Dwight White had the responsibility of covering two Hall of Fame players, Art Shell and Gene Upshaw.

The Raiders had a devastating running game. Controlling the line of scrimmage to stop that running game was the ultimate challenge and the key to winning or losing the game.

I played the open end against Fred Biletnikoff and Cliff Branch, which meant that I played pass for most of the game. This put Andy into a position that he did not necessarily like to play. That is, he had to rely on pure physical strength against Dave Casper. There was no "tricking" or "bluffing" those Raiders. They were much too intellegent and experienced to fall for such tactics.

So Andy had to adapt to a much more physical game, and he was able to do it to perfection. Whatever it took, Andy was able to deliver. I can summarize the right defensive line's play by citing just one statistic: the Raiders had 29 rushing yards. When I saw him play that game and witnessed how the entire defensive line just fell into place, I knew that we could beat anyone. And beat them, we did.

When Andy decided to retire, it was a devastating blow to our defense. The linebacker trio would never be the same without "Captain." In the last game of his career, the Steelers wanted Andy to be replaced on the field so that he could receive the standing ovation that he so richly deserved. It was the last home game of the season against the Tampa Bay Buccaneers and a Steeler blowout, so earlier in the game Loren Toews had replaced me. Then I was asked to return to the game as Toews replaced Andy.

This gave Andy an opportunity to walk off of the field before the game ended. The crowd loved it and rose to its feet and gave a roaring ovation like only Steeler fans can do. In the glow of what was a wonderful moment for the team and the fans, Andy walked to my side of the field. He looked at me, and I realized that a large part of my football career was about to come to an end. I knew only too well how very much I would miss this man who had come to become so much a part of my life, not just in football.

To this day, I can still feel the emotion, love and admiration that I had for Andy at that moment. As I hugged him, I said, "Good luck, Captain. I loved playing with you."

So many images of Andy went through my mind as I watched him leave the field for the last time. Seeing him on countless occasions taking a shot in the groin to ease the pain so that he could play with a torn groin muscle. Watching him play with a broken hand. Seeing him pick up a fumble in a Baltimore playoff game and taking what seemed like twenty minutes to run it back for a touchdown.

But the consummate image is of Andy at training camp, walking from the dorm to practice, carrying an umbrella and reading the Wall Street Journal. This was so much the image of the man that was Andy Russell, an all-business football player, thorough and prepared for anything. I am not alone in my thought that the Hall of Fame is a lesser place because his bust does not reside within.

People are surprised to find that when they come into my home there is no evidence that a football veteran resides within. I like to tell them that I am a "today person, not a yesterday person." It is only when they are in my most private spaces that they see a photo that is most precious to me. It is a picture of Jack Lambert, Andy and me, taken after a playoff game; the three of us are still in uniform and sweaty. We have our arms wrapped tightly over each other's shoulders, and we're sporting smiles a mile wide.

To the outside world, it would appear a victorious trio celebrating a win. But to us, it was the epitome of camaraderie, of a successful accomplishment achieved in a large part by the talent, skill and focus, and yes, love and respect of each other. And we understood that this was a moment that only the three of us could ever appreciate or understand. For only we knew what it took to get there and how many fates played a part. An intimate boys' club where only we three knew the secret handshake.

Each time I see that photo, I am immediately transported back to that moment in the locker room, where we three were such a large part of An Odd Steelers Journey.

Introduction

This book is not just about football. It is about some of the life altering experiences that we all go through as we make our life's journey—the valuable lessons we have learned from our mentors, some of the mistakes we have made, and the challenges we have faced that make our lives more meaningful. Of course, I can't write about your journey, only mine, but I suspect that we all can relate to the similarities of someone else's life experiences: the choices made, the sometimes serendipitous nature of important incidents, and the way fate seems to impact our lives.

I refer to myself as an "Odd Steeler," because unlike my teammates, I was dividing my time between business (going to early morning and late night meetings) and the NFL. It was a very hectic and, yes, odd experience.

Unlike my first book, A Steeler Odyssey, which focuses on the personalities and accomplishments of my teammates, I have attempted to write a number of chapters that will give the reader a sense of what it is like to be on the field and how it feels to compete at the professional level, to really play the game. I realize these opinions are mine and may not be shared by all or even some of my teammates. I suspect that the game meant something different to each of us. This book is certainly more autobiographical than Odyssey, telling more about my journey through high school and college and the challenges I faced in the early years.

Having played five of my 12 NFL seasons in the 1960s (seven in the '70s), and having played with wonderfully eccentric players of the '50s as well as many of my '70s teammates who went on to play in the'80s, I have also chosen to write about some of the wonderful players and characters who played in those early years, as well as those great teams of the '70s, who all helped forge the NFL into the league it is today.

I will explain, perhaps in more detail than some will want, the intricate complexities involved in football, impossible for viewers, including myself now, to actually see—the interactions, techniques, thought processes and even deceptions that go on constantly throughout the game.

The game of football is very up-front and personal, and the athlete must attempt to combine his passion and his emotional need to succeed with his intellect. You can't just go out there, as I suspect a lot of fans (and, I'm afraid, some players) think, and run around like a crazy man, trying to hit somebody.

You must stay intensely focused, concentrating on your assignment and how the opponent is trying to cause you to fail in executing that assignment. Sometimes you have to be patient and willing to wait, resisting the impulse to charge, to react too quickly or to overreact, a tendency I fought to overcome my whole career. At the same time, the player must still have the passion for the game, an almost neurotic need to succeed, to do whatever it takes (always within the rules, of course) to win.

In this book, I will try to pass on some of the values and lessons I have learned from teachers, coaches, teammates and mentors that I've had the privilege of working with. Other stories are about some of the good people I have known and what they have taught me. I will also explain some of the lessons that I learned all by myself. Life has a way of teaching us whether we want to learn or not.

Writing this book is also just for me—a need to tell some eclectic stories that have absolutely nothing to do with football, stories of wilderness adventure and stories that attempt to define my life and get straight in my own head some of the good and some of the bad, and give many other people credit who made my journey infinitely more interesting, challenging, fun and rewarding.

Life has shown me that in the vast majority of meaningful experiences there are no short cuts. There is no easy way. You must play hurt, make a huge commitment to time and effort, and then sit back and enjoy the experience.

CHAPTER ONE

The Early Years

W hat is it that drives someone to become an athlete, or, for that matter, to become anything—a violinist, an artist, a business-man, doctor, lawyer or the best parent one can be? What causes some people to have an unrelenting desire, an almost neurotic need to succeed, and a drive so powerful that it overshadows nearly any other interest? Is it a fear of failure? Is it fear of not realizing one's potential? Or is their success more about God-given talent, ability or IQ? Maybe it has to do with insecurity or an anger caused by how one was treated early in life. The world is full of very talented people who do not fulfill their potential because they are not willing to pay the price.

Some people seem to believe that athletes are born, not developed. My own belief is that attitude and commitment are overwhelmingly the most important factors—assuming, of course, that you were born with a cer-tain level of genetic physical talent.

Here's my story, not that it is any more important than anyone else's. After all, my brother had no interest in sports and focused his intensity on becoming a good student and a short wave radio operator. Electrical and mechanical things fascinated him, whereas I was a kid (like many others, I'm sure) who lived for sports—wanting to compete, to win, and to beat all the other neighborhood kids in whatever game we chose to play.

Why was I like that? I have often wondered what caused me to want athletic success so badly. I can remember lying awake all night worrying that I might lose the Cub Scout footrace or some other relatively meaningless event. Most of my friends didn't really seem to care that much.

I wasn't really encouraged by my parents, who seldom saw me compete as a youngster—the total opposite of the classic "stage parents." We didn't own a television set until I was ten years old, so I didn't see any college or professional games until long after I'd become obsessed with sports. No one in my family had been a particularly gifted athlete, and no one mentored me in sports at a young age.

I do remember walking to a movie theater in Evanston, Illinois by myself when I was seven years old to see a film about Jim Thorpe's life. I was thrilled and inspired by this Native American's amazing athletic achievements. I was also given a book about Olympic track and field events and dreamed about winning the decathlon someday.

Maybe most kids constantly dream about winning, about climbing that ladder of success, but are not encouraged to chase those dreams. I give my mother a lot of credit, because she always encouraged me to pursue my goals and assured me that I could accomplish anything if I truly made the effort.

Part of my attraction to sports was that I discovered early on that I could run faster and jump higher than most other kids in the neighborhood. Perhaps we just focus on what we do best—have a little success, get a little attention or praise, and then want more. If you have a gift, you want to use it and try to develop it.

By age twelve I had won every running race I entered, was victorious in most of the games in grade school, and had outswum the other kids on the country club swim team. I never really experienced losing and didn't know what it was like to be beaten, except in Ping Pong, a game in which my Dad beat me like a drum. I would soon, like all of us, have to learn to deal with the bitter taste of defeat on a more regular basis.

The summer before I entered the seventh grade, while living in Pelham Manor, New York, I got very sick with a disabling disease. I was in bed for almost two months, and my musculature just disappeared, leaving me a virtual skeleton with no strength whatsoever. My parents told me later that the doctors weren't sure what the disease was, but they feared that it was polio, which in those days could be devastating.

Then one day, after weeks of throwing up every day and not being able to eat, I felt a little better and got up and went to school, still skinny as a rail, slightly dizzy and very weak.

That same day one of my classmates challenged me to a footrace, and stupidly, I accepted the challenge. I couldn't run. My strength had disappeared, and a kid I used to beat regularly defeated me quite easily. Things had changed. I no longer had the good stuff. I knew I would have to figure out other ways to succeed in athletics.

But looking back now, I think I still had the idea in my head that I was an athlete. That mental concept, which to me was everything, caused me to expect athletic success (positive imaging), and bred more and more confidence by pushing me to try harder than most of the other kids to achieve that success. It became an obsession.

Shortly thereafter, we moved to the St. Louis suburb of Ladue, and I entered the seventh grade at Horton Watkins School. On the first day, the only class I worried about was gym class, concerned that these new kids wouldn't know I was any good and would relegate me to the bench.

Worse than that, they played a game I had never played, soccer, and they put me where I couldn't get in the way—as the goalie. It wasn't too long, however, before they realized that I could run and jump and play. My speed never fully returned, but I did get my quickness back. My strength came back and improved every year, but I would never again feel that powerful sprinting speed that I had felt before the illness. Of course, some of this feeling could be attributed to the fact that as you get older, you naturally start running into other more gifted athletes as the competition stiffens. It's easy to be the best in grade school, but it gets tougher at every level, as you move up to high school, college and the pros.

Like many high school athletes, I played football, basketball (my favorite sport), and ran track. In fact, our track and football coach Bob Davis, wanting me to improve my speed, forced me to run the 100-yard dash, an event that embarrassed me badly as I took last in every race, except one in which I tied for last. My best time was a wind-aided 10.7 seconds. The track probably sloped downhill, as well.

Coach Davis was a counselor at Camp Lincoln, a summer football camp in Minnesota, and he encouraged anyone with any talent to attend. The three-week program was very strenuous, with two workouts a day and lots of scrimmaging against older kids. The coaches—Bud Wilkinson of Oklahoma fame (48 straight wins), Murray Warmath of the University of Minnesota, and the Elliot brothers from Michigan—had brought some of their star players to be counselors. I learned a lot about technique at that camp and came back to Ladue with a keener sense of commitment to the game. I wanted to be the best I could be.

Upon returning to St. Louis and preseason practice as a sophomore, Coach Davis started me at end, a position I had never played. I had good hands, but in those days the offenses were built around the running game, and we seldom passed unless it was third and long. Since we rarely threw the ball, I mainly tried hard to learn how to be a good blocker and throw downfield blocks, a skill at which, frankly, I wasn't very good.

I played reasonably well but certainly didn't stand out in any spectacular fashion—just got the job done as best I could. I actually had more success my sophomore year playing basketball, leading the team in scoring. My junior year, I was switched to fullback and as the season progressed I got more and more carries, finally scoring four touchdowns in the season's final game against our big rival, Clayton.

But still, my favorite sport was basketball, a game that to this day seems to demand the most of an athlete. Clearly the best athletes in the world are the NBA players—the game demands the most of its players: speed and stamina, the toughness to deal one on one, jumping ability, refined hand-eye coordination, and dealing with extreme pressure. I loved the game and certainly practiced it far more than I practiced football techniques.

In fact, during the summer between my junior and senior years, a number of my Ladue teammates and I would drive over to Webster Groves, the top basketball school in the area, and challenge some of their top guys to a three-on-three contest that would often last late into the night, despite the humid heat of St. Louis. My buddies and I tried our best and often gave the Webster guys a good battle. But when it came down to our ability to beat them during the year, when it counted, they always won.

One of my most humiliating moments in an athletic contest came when we faced Webster the following season, during which we played them twice. The first game, I was guarded by one of the fellows we had played against in the summer. He was a person I admired, because he worked all summer on his jumping, and, despite being only 6'3", he could dunk the ball from a standing jump. Fortunately, he wasn't very quick, and I was able to beat him to the baseline and make a lot of easy baskets, scoring more than 20 points. We still lost, but at least it was a close game, decided by only a few points.

In the second game, a playoff, John Russell guarded me. Russell was super-quick and very smart. He later became the captain of the Vanderbilt University team. John, knowing from our summer contests that I could only go to my right, lined up way to the right, just daring me to move to my left. John knew that I wasn't a particularly good dribbler with my left hand. He was also forcing me drive into the paint where their 6'8" center was waiting to block my jumper.

It was a very long night, and I managed only two points. On the rare occasion that I had to shoot foul shots, the Webster fans chanted, "Come on, Horse, hit the wall," and I obliged them, shooting a number of air balls. I guess every athlete has humiliating moments. Hey, if you haven't choked, you haven't played.

During my senior football season, Davis gave me most of the carries, and we beat everyone in our league by some 40 points or more. I averaged twelve yards a carry because my teammates opened huge holes that anyone could have run through. We went undefeated and won the league championship. Coach Davis, who recently passed away, was an outstanding coach who made us concentrate on technique and attitude.

Sitting on my office credenza is a plaque sent to all my high school teammates in the '90s by Coach Davis that reads, "MENTAL TOUGHNESS AND SECOND EFFORT WAS YOUR TRADEMARK," still reminding us, after all these years, of what it took to be successful.

That year I made high school All-American and received a scholarship to the University of Missouri, where I would play for Dan Devine, one of the most successful college coaches ever.

I quickly learned that being a successful athlete in college is far more difficult than excelling in various games on the neighborhood playing fields or standing out in high school

I'll never forget getting a phone call from my mother after only a few weeks into that first semester.

"Son, your Dad has just been named the head of Monsanto Overseas, and we are moving to Europe. We'll be gone about ten years. Don't call more than once a month, and no more than two minutes, because long distance is very costly. Good luck, sweetheart. Bye," my mother said as she hung up the phone.

Despite being just a wet-behind-the-ears 17-year-old kid (I was young for my class), I realized that it was time to grow up. Gone were the days when I could count on my parents to make my decisions. Of course, that's what they always wanted—for me to become independent and make my own way. It didn't really seem like a big deal at the time. I had a scholarship, and as long as I produced on the field, made my grades and followed all the rules I figured I'd get along just fine. After all, college is the place where you're suppose to grow up anyway.

Coach Devine treated me in a fatherly fashion, perhaps feeling that I might be somewhat homesick with my parents being so far away. Shortly thereafter, Coach allowed me to keep an old family Buick in his garage since freshmen were not allowed to have cars on campus. Of course, he didn't let me use it very often.

That was a rare rule violation. In fact, it is the only one that I'm aware of that the Mizzou athletic department allowed. There were no shenanigans going on with alumni slipping us money, loaning us cars, or setting us up with phony jobs for play money. Missouri's tough old athletic director, Don Faurot (a former coach who invented the "Split T" formation), was a real stickler for proper behavior within his department, and there were no under-the-table deals going on under his administration. In fact, after our final season was over my senior year, I was required either to turn in an honorarium fee to the athletic department or lose my scholarship. As soon as I received my Steeler signing bonus, I was taken off scholarship.

Coach Devine, however, wasn't exactly what he appeared to the media—a sweet mother-hen type, appealing to the mothers of new recruits. Make no mistake about it, Devine was a very tough taskmaster and ruled his teams with an iron hand. He was a strict disciplinarian, expecting total attention and no rule breaking.

He often refused to play very good players, even guys who might have been stars otherwise. Players who did not perform in the classroom or were caught breaking his rules (such as no carousing or drinking) were relegated to the red-shirt squad.

Devine once cut a *Parade Magazine* All-American high school standout from Chicago, Bob Newman, from the team for yawning during the coach's pregame speech. Fortunately, Bob was able to retain his scholarship as a member of the track team.

Devine was so tough, and his practices were so full of exhausting scrimmages, that he was incredulous when the team voted against the opportunity to play in the Bluebonnet Bowl (1961) in Houston my junior year, after being the runner-up to Colorado in the Big Eight. I'm sure the majority of the players remembered the previous year, playing in the Orange Bowl against Navy, when we were forced to run wind sprints on the grassy strip between the Miami Beach Boulevard until some of the guys vomited.

The players just would not voluntarily agree to go through more of those grueling practices, regardless of the potential rewards of a fun trip and the excitement of a bowl game. The following year, again being the runner-up (this time to Oklahoma), we were not given the opportunity to vote and went to the Bluebonnet Bowl, where we beat a good Georgia Tech squad. I'm glad he forced us to go!

My first year as a starting linebacker (1960), we played Penn State at Happy Valley in their first game in their new, sold-out stadium. The Nittany Lions, surprisingly, had beaten Mizzou, the Big Eight champions, the previous year, and Devine was very psyched about getting revenge. Penn State, coached by "Rip" Engle, fielded a fine team.

One player in particular, Dave Robinson, also a sophomore linebacker, would eventually emerge as a quality pro with the Green Bay Packers. The quarterback was Dick Hoak, a very gifted athlete, whom I would later play with on the Steelers.

The game was mostly a defensive battle, as both sides, almost wearing out their punters, played the game entirely within the thirty-yard lines. Finally, it appeared as though we had gotten the break we needed when Penn State fumbled and we recovered. Unfortunately, the refs ruled that ball dead, a very bad call. As the refs were setting the ball for the Lions' offense, I noticed the fans getting excited about something. I glanced over my shoulder, and there, only yards away in the middle of the field, was Coach Devine, who ripped his sport coat off and angrily slammed it to the turf, completely out of his mind with anger over the bad call.

As assistant coaches pulled Devine off the field, I was struck by his over-reaction to this bad call and his willingness to make a complete ass of himself in front of all those angry Penn State fans. Somehow that moment seemed to inspire us, and we went on to win the game, beating them 21 to 8 and moving into the top ten in the country.

Devine's temper tantrums were legendary. He would often become so outraged that he'd throw his clipboard, and the team enjoyed keeping a record of the length of each throw. Once while we were playing at Oklahoma State, Coach became so angry that he twirled around like a discus thrower and lofted his clipboard far up into the stands. It was clearly his best throw ever, nearly fifty yards. Of course, we were a bit worried that the students might give the clipboard to the State coaches.

Looking back on my years at Mizzou, a number of things stand out as pivotal in my career. I'll never forget the shock I experienced at my first spring practice with the varsity as a freshman. I was trying to make a team that had lost in the Orange Bowl to Fran Tarkenton's Georgia team. Devine called out the rosters of eight teams (there were over 88 players on the field that day), starting with the eighth team and moving up. Expecting to hear my name mentioned at the third or fourth team's fullback position, I was incredulous when Devine called me out as the first team's fullback. He literally gave me the first-team job without making me earn it. Granted, the starting fullback, senior Ed Meher, was playing baseball and was not available for spring ball.

The following fall, my sophomore year, I would end up starting at linebacker and backing up Ed at fullback. I thought I could run the ball better than Ed, but the fullback was mostly used as a blocking back, and I was a lousy blocker.

My junior year, playing both ways, I led the team in rushing, but

Devine made me a defensive specialist my senior year, only playing line-backer. Now, looking back on my professional career, I am very glad that Devine made that decision. I must admit that at the time I was less than thrilled, because I still found carrying the ball totally exhilarating—it definitely draws a crowd in a hurry.

When you play fullback, you have to be the best fullback on the team to start. If that was true for linebackers, both Jack Lambert and I would have been riding the bench watching Jack Ham play all the downs.

But I should also give Coach Devine credit for having a sense of compassion. Once I flew in a private plane with Devine and the other cocaptains (Tom Hertz and Jerry Wallach) to St. Louis for a television interview prior to a big game late in the season. Wallach decided to tell Devine about a little deception he pulled while trying to get recruited. Wallach had been a marine in California, where he had apparently made his name as a pretty good player in military football.

"Coach, I've got to tell you something—level with you after all these years and get it off my chest," Jerry said.

"Sure, Jerry, what's on your mind?" Devine asked.

"Well, you remember how I sent you all those articles about what a terrific player I was at Camp Pendleton?" Jerry asked.

"Sure, you were quite the star."

I watched Jerry as he cleared his throat a number of times and squirmed in his seat, looking very uncomfortable.

"Well, Coach, those were bogus articles. I was also working for the base newspaper, and I wrote those articles about myself. They were totally fake, and I had them printed up and sent to you. I didn't have any money, and I needed that scholarship or I would never have gone to college."

I watched Devine closely as he shook his head, trying to understand the repercussions of what he had just heard. After all, Jerry was one of his cocaptains and an outstanding student, getting the top grades in his Shakespeare courses. What should he do?

"Jerry, I've always believed in the power of forgiveness, but we should just keep that little story to ourselves, because you've sure turned out to be a fine player and a tribute to this program," Devine said.

"Sounds good to me, Coach," Jerry agreed.

I learned a lot of things from Dan Devine. He taught us how to be a team, how to work together without ego and politics. He would also teach us something far more important: that the sporting world is one of the few places in our society where everyone is equal. It doesn't matter what race you are, in what religion you worship, who your parents are, what school you attended, what country club you belong to, or your socioeconomic background. The sporting world is a totally level playing field. Prejudice, presumptuousness, bigotry, social snobbery, egotism, money— none of it was important; the only thing that mattered was the game and how well you could play it.

But I also learned that Devine could be very stubborn, often refusing to take what the other team was offering and instead continuing to force something that wasn't working. Perhaps the greatest example of his bull-headedness came when we played Kansas during our final game of 1960.

The previous week, we beat a very good Bud Wilkinson-coached Oklahoma team in Oklahoma University's renowned "Snake Pit." It was a game in which our famous wide-side-of-the-field sweep was executed to near perfection. The play made huge gains time after time. After that game we were ranked No. 1 in the country with one game to go, a home game vs. our archrival, the University of Kansas.

Kansas had a decent team with a couple of star players—John Hadl at quarterback (who went on to pro fame) and two good running backs, Curtis McClinton and Bert Coan—but the team hadn't done as well as expected. We were picked to win big.

With the No. 1 ranking on the line, Coach Devine made sure that we didn't take the game for granted during the preceding week and worked us harder with scrimmages to stress the importance of the game.

Early in the game, the Kansas strategy became obvious. They would have five or six players and have them penetrate upfield on the wide side, hoping to stop our vaunted wide-side sweeps. It was very effective and threw many of those sweeps for sizeable losses. Devine, angry that his favorite play wasn't working, refused to admit that we couldn't execute it against Kansas's penetrating defense. He ran the play over and over again with no success. Kansas was just daring us to run it up the middle or to the short side of the field.

Getting a chance to play some fullback that day, I only had the opportunity to run up the middle a few times. There was nobody there, and I picked up good gains each time. In fact, a couple of times the hole was so wide, and I was leaning so far forward expecting to be hit, that I fell down without being touched. Had I been a better running back I probably could have scored a couple of times.

We lost that game, and in doing so forfeited the national championship, which in those days was picked before the bowl games. As the winner of the Big Eight, we went to the Orange Bowl and beat a good Navy team. Had the No. 1 team been picked as it was for most of the '70s, '80s and '90s (prior to the BCS), we would have won that elusive national title.

I'm not saying it was Coach Devine's stubbornness that caused us to lose—that was just one factor. Our poor performances were another. In fact, being stubborn, refusing to give up on your best play, is probably a good coaching trait. Vince Lombardi certainly forced his players to run their sweep even when it was occasionally stopped in the first quarter, and Coach Noll hated to have the defense dictate what he would call.

That Orange Bowl game against Navy was a real thrill for our team; playing prime time on national television against Joe Bellino, the Heisman Trophy pick, with Jack Kennedy up in the stands watching his beloved Navy. Some reporter had made the mistake of saying that Joe Bellino was so elusive that it was virtually impossible to tackle him one on one in the open field. Devine, of course, picked up on that quote and badgered us all week in our Miami preparation, inflaming the defensive squad. In the game, Bellino barely gained a yard, and we blew them out.

Those Missouri teams had truly become teams without petty jealousies—groups that worked hard to help each other get better and always played better, through intense effort, than the collective talent would have indicated we should. I left the game many years later with tremendous respect for my teammates—their character, values, honesty, and talent. Coach Devine was a tremendous motivator who always had his teams ready to play.

Devine has to be considered one of the greatest college football coaches of all time. Coaching his Missouri Tigers, he has the distinction of having the best win/loss percentage for all Division I schools during the '60s. He went from there to the Green Bay Packers, replacing the legendary Vince Lombardi, and took Green Bay to a playoff game his first season. Later he became the head coach of Notre Dame, where he won a national championship, got his ring, and always had a winning season.

I last saw Coach Devine at a Devine Players Reunion, where we were honored at halftime at a Mizzou game. It felt strange to walk out on that field after so many years, and I was flooded with positive memories. I stood there thinking about where it all began, trying to beat the other kids in the neighborhood, the footraces, and the challenges. When Devine gave me a hug, as he did all the players there, I almost cried, recognizing how lucky I was to have played for such a fine gentleman who taught me so much.

CHAPTER TWO

Making the Team

I am often asked, "What was the biggest moment of your pro career?" I think most people assume I'll recount a story about a big play that I made. Actually, I made very few big plays because I was often too cautious, careful not to make a mistake that might cost us the game. Other times I would be too aggressive, too impatient, committing myself too soon. Finding that elusive middle ground frustrated me, and I rarely found it.

I think most people guess that just being a member of a Super Bowl team might be the most exciting moment, or being team MVP, or being selected to the Pro Bowl. Actually, for me, the most exciting, critical and life-changing moment I experienced in pro football was just making the team. Let me explain how it felt.

I was drafted in the sixteenth round by a team whose head coach, Buddy Parker, was known for hating rookies. "They lose games for you," he had said. I really hadn't expected to play professional football because I had promised my father that I wouldn't play. He didn't want his son to be so frivolous as to play a game for a living. I also had a two-year military commitment through the ROTC program at Missouri. Most of the teams in the league sent me the standard questionnaire requesting information about speed, strength, honors, etc., and I had answered the first question—"Are you interested in playing pro football?" with a resounding "no." The Pittsburgh Steelers had not sent me a questionnaire.

But in truth, another reason that I hadn't considered a pro career was that I hadn't been all that good in college. In fact, I'm sure that when I decided to accept the challenge it surprised many of my Missouri team-mates since I hadn't been too successful. I hadn't made All-American—not that I expected to. I hadn't even made All-Big Eight—I wasn't All-Anything, and deservedly so.

I hadn't been a total flop, however. I won the award for being the top sophomore, led the team in rushing my junior year, and in my senior year, led the team in interceptions (nine) and was named a team captain. I had also been lucky enough to make two interceptions in each of our bowl games —the Orange Bowl vs. Navy in 1960 and the Bluebonnet Bowl vs. Georgia Tech in 1962.

Having been taught by my parents to always set my goals high, those achievements seemed pretty insignificant. I thought I'd become better and always felt as though I was as good as or better than most of the players I had played against. I just hadn't gotten the job done; I made too many mistakes and didn't make enough big plays. Deep down I was dis-appointed but still proud to have played a meaningful role in a good college program.

Of course, I had all my excuses lined up. I had sprained my ankle badly early in my sophomore year. The sprain wasn't bad enough to cause me to miss any games, but it nagged me all season in a year when Missouri should have taken the national championship. I started that year at line-backer and backed up at fullback.

My junior year was more of the same: concussions, broken fingers, and then, something unusual—a bad hit to the chest during a game against California that resulted in a bruised lung (I was coughing up blood). A week later, after not practicing at all, I started against Oklahoma State. I was blindsided, a clip that wasn't called, early in the game and got another bad ankle sprain. They shot it up with Novocaine at halftime, and in the second half, I got lucky and intercepted a deflected pass and ran it in for a score on the deadened ankle. I was plagued with a painful ankle and an aching bruised lung for the rest of the year.

My senior year, I arrived at training camp with severe lower back pain caused by sleeping on my stomach on a hammock-style mattress at Fort Sill, Oklahoma where I spent two weeks going through military training for ROTC. Right before that senior season, I had seen my first chiroprac-tor, and after a series of X-rays, he told me in all seriousness, "You can never play football again. Forget about it!"

Feeling that football was everything, the most important thing in my life (other than my family and friends, of course), I threw the X-rays away, ignored his advice and showed up at training camp really hurting, barely able to bend over to tie my shoes. After a hard practice the first morning, we had to run a mile race in full pads in 100-degree heat. Being in pretty bad shape and the back giving me a lot of pain as I ran, I wondered if I could possibly make it to the first game. I was the last running back to finish. Coach Devine was not happy and criticized me in front of the team—the Captain hadn't paid the price to get in shape. I decided not to tell him about the bad back, figuring he might bench me.

But you know what? Deep down I knew that those excuses were just that—excuses. Everyone's got one, right? It doesn't matter if you're hurt; your job is to perform well—and I hadn't. Period.

Obviously my college career wasn't pretty—not nearly as good as I had hoped it would be. So when the Steelers drafted me, I was secretly thrilled, although I acted as though I had no interest in playing and couldn't possibly play anyway because of my ROTC commitment and my promise to my father. I was reconciled to leaving the game and putting a positive spin onto my college career.

I didn't realize, of course, that the Steelers really didn't expect me to make the team and that Coach Parker had traded his first seven draft choices for veteran players and drafted Frank Atkinson, a defensive lineman, from Stanford. Number eight was really the Steelers' first draft choice.

Frank and I would become good friends, often choosing to talk about our future business careers instead of football. Frank also started his first year, but only played a short time because he considered a career in professional football to be slightly irresponsible—comparable to becoming a ski bum or waiting tables at some resort. He returned to school, got his MBA at UCLA, and ultimately went into the venture capital business in San Francisco before anyone had even heard of venture capitalists.

The Steelers' draft in 1963 was also unique in other ways. Many years later, I heard this story about how I was actually drafted. After drafting Atkinson, Coach Parker was getting impatient, believing strongly that it didn't matter who he drafted because he would cut them anyway. He apparently only hung around for a few more choices and then departed for his favorite Manhattan watering hole.

"You boys can draft whoever you damn well want to, because they've got no prayer. I'll be cutting all of them before the first game."

As soon as he left, the assistants, feeling less pressure to perform, ordered a case of beer and some pizzas. Hours later, when it came to the sixteenth round, even the assistants were getting bored, and no one had a clue who to draft—they had run out of their scouting reports.

"Anybody got any ideas?" Jack Butler, the head scout and former Steeler great asked.

The room was quiet, no one wanting to go out on a limb in front of their peers. Finally, a scout named Will Walls raised his hand.

"There's a linebacker at Mizzou who's not bad—he's usually around the ball—some kid named Russell."

"OK, draft the linebacker. By the way, where the heck is that pizza we ordered?"

That huge endorsement included no information regarding my accomplishments or stats, such as 40-yard dash times, my bench press, squat press, or vertical jump, information routinely offered and required today and knowledge that would have probably caused them not to draft me. Walls's only recommendation was that I was usually "around the ball," meaning, I guess, that I seldom got faked out. Thank God for Will Walls, because his offhand recollection would alter my life forever.

I left my young wife at home, not knowing if I would make the team. Getting on the plane in St. Louis, I was extremely psyched, completely wired, and ready to give whatever effort was needed for me to be successful. I had worked harder than ever before, running wind sprints, climbing the stadium stairs, and even lifting weights for the first time in my life. Since I played college ball at 198 pounds, the Steelers asked me to gain 32 pounds, wanting me to report to camp at about 230, the weight it was thought was required to play linebacker in the pros. I ate like a horse, supplementing my diet with various sports drinks and gaining 27 pounds.

I arrived at training camp by team bus at West Liberty State College, near Wheeling's Oglebay Park. I was surprised when I was given a room on the first floor, where the veterans were housed, with Bill Nelson, a quarterback from USC who was the No. 10 choice. The majority of the rookies were up on the hotter second floor (no air conditioning, of course). The only other rookies on the first floor were Frank Atkinson and Jim Bradshaw. I wondered why we were assigned the first floor and whether it had any relevance, but I concluded that it was probably just a coincidence.

Looking back on my first professional football training camp, I am reminded of the extreme contrast between college and pro. First of all, the facilities were totally substandard compared to college. At Missouri, as I'm sure is the case with most major college programs, we had a brand-new locker room, training room, and four or five quality fields on which to alternate. West Liberty State had an old, antiquated locker room, a minuscule training facility, and only two fields, one of which was so bad that Parker made the rookies pick rocks off the field between practices.

Another difference was the attitude of the players. The Steelers in 1963 were a bunch of talented old-timers (many in their thirties), guys who had been in the game for a long time and had grown more than a little cynical. Men like Ernie Stautner, Tom "The Bomb" Tracy, Lou Michaels, Buddy Dial, Preston Carpenter, Red Mack, John Henry Johnson, Myron Pottios, John Reger, Brady Keys, and Clendon Thomas were certainly not intimidated by the coaches. They had seen a lot of coaches and athletes come and go. When you coach a man in his thirties, it's a lot different than coaching a kid in college who is only nineteen or twenty.

Players would talk back to the coaches, saying things like, "Buster [our defensive coordinator, Buster Ramsey], that might look good on the blackboard but it sure as hell won't work on the field." They didn't show coaches the same kind of obedience that was expected in college, and there was clearly a different kind of rapport.

There also weren't as many rules. I was astounded when Lou Michaels, sitting in the front row of our meeting room, lit up a big cigar (most colleges have no-smoking rules) and proceeded to blow smoke into Buster's face while he diagrammed plays on the blackboard.

Meanwhile, two other guys off to the side were keeping score on another blackboard, giving themselves points (on a 1 to 10 scale) for whose farts were the best. I grew up with coaches, Devine in particular, who demanded total respect, complete silence, and intense focus. It took a little time to get used to this more relaxed discipline.

Conditioning was also more lax than it had been in college. For example, to demonstrate our level of physical preparation, the first thing we were asked to do was to run a two-mile route that wound its way through the woods just off the main practice field. We all got in a big line with the veteran players up front. I noticed that many of them had a sizeable bulge in the front of their shorts and concluded they were unusually well-hung.

The first 100 yards of the route took us down a steep hill off the field, through a small gully, and then into the woods. As we entered the gully, hidden from the coaches' view, I was astounded when many of the veteran players dropped out of the run, pulled packs of cigarettes out of their jock straps (so much for their prodigious genitalia) and lit up, while the gung-ho veterans like Stautner, who was clearly intent on leading, and the rookies continued the run. After a difficult up-and-down run through the hot woods, I tried to pass some of the vets and move up behind Stautner, but I was told, "Back off, Rook," with vets barring my way as I tried to pass.

As we reentered the small gully just below the field, the older vets who had dropped out earlier put out their cigarettes on nearby rocks and jumped back into the lead group. As we ran back up onto the field, with the coaches checking their stopwatches, the older vets who had done nothing but sit and enjoy a good smoke for the last ten minutes, surged pass a tiring Stautner.

Parker yelled, "Some of you old farts are looking pretty good. Must have worked real hard this summer. Good going, boys!"

Training camp went by very rapidly, but certain memories will stand out forever. This was my big chance to redeem myself for not being as good in college as I believed I should have been. More importantly, I needed to find out how good I could really be without excuses. In college I just hadn't gotten the job done often enough, and if you are out there, injuries or not, there are no excuses. If you're willing to play hurt, and I was (as were all my teammates), you've got to make the plays. There's no one to point the finger at but you. We were taught accountability early in football—don't blame other factors, and certainly don't blame other people.

During my first Steelers practice we did a series of agility drills, and I immediately recognized that I had more agility and quickness than any of the other linebackers, veterans included. I had always been good at drills. Playing the game was a lot more challenging. I remember thinking that since I had superior athletic ability, if I could be as smart and as tough as the vets, I should be able to make the team. The "tough" part, I reasoned, should be the easy part because it was something I could control, a function of the effort I made. The "smart" part would be a more difficult challenge, because I figured that would have a lot to do with experience, and I didn't have any.

The other rookie linebackers, a couple of whom had been drafted above me, were too slow, and despite being very tough guys, they lacked the agility needed to get into position to make the tackles. After watching a few practices, I realized that it really had little to do with how tough you were and was much more about how quickly you read something and then how fast you reacted to get into position to make the play. So in this case, success wasn't just about attitude. Concentration, focus, and physical talent were the keys; if you couldn't come off or avoid the block because you lacked agility or quickness, you'd be in a lot of trouble.

Don't get me wrong. I'm not saying that I had some kind of super talent, the kind of talent it would take to make the team by beating out guys like Jack Ham or Jack Lambert. No way I could outperform them. Ham was quicker and just better. Lambert was super tough and had all the tools—quickness, strength, and brains.

But I realized I was in the right place at the right time. The veteran outside backers had been good players, but having ten or more years in the league, they were nearing the twilight of their careers. The other rookie linebackers, who were certainly trying as hard as I was, just didn't have the physical ability or, in some cases, the proper technique.

John Reger, a Pro Bowl linebacker, was in his twelfth year, and I watched him avoid blocks in a way that I never even considered. My high school and college coaches always told me to fight through the pressure, never to run around the block. Watching the previous year's game films, I was astounded when I saw Reger, working to avoid a pulling guard's block, fake to the outside and then jump inside around him and make the tackle for a loss. "Wow," I thought, "You mean we're allowed to make a move that creative in the pros?"

The next time Reger faced that same play, he faked inside and jumped outside, again not even dealing with the guard's block. Believe me, it's tough to take on a 265-pound pulling guard (strength to strength), stop him in his tracks and then still have time to separate yourself from the blocker and make the tackle.

The final time the opponent ran that play, Reger neither jumped inside or outside, but instead drilled the guard, who had slowed down, expecting Reger's fake, right in the head with his forearm, stopping the guard in his tracks and easily gaining the space he needed to make the tackle, right at the line of scrimmage. Guess what? That was the last time they ran that play. Reger would not allow the opponent to dictate the action. I figured I'd try his tactics as soon as the opportunity presented itself. Of course, fighting against pressure is still the best way to find where the ball is going.

Later, when we were into the exhibition games, I realized that my inexperience was causing me to make too many mistakes and that my hesitance, lack of anticipation, and confusion were eliminating whatever athletic edge I had. Coach Parker was right. Rookies cost you games.

I played passably on the special teams, not making any really outstanding plays—just surviving, not getting burned by the devil ego by being patient and staying in my lane. In the past, I would occasionally get so impatient to make the big play that I would ignore my responsibility and freelance, a move that would usually bring the coach's wrath.

In the third quarter of a game against the Eagles in Lehigh, Pennsylvania, I finally made the defensive play of my life to that point. Before the snap, when a zone pass defense had been called, requiring me to drop ten yards deep to the hash mark on my side, I heard safety Clendon Thomas shout, "Get deep, Russell—help us out back here." Hearing that and wanting to help out Clendon (someone I had admired since his All-American halfback days at Oklahoma), I dropped too deep (fifteen yards) and looked for wide receivers crossing, but they were all running upfield. When I looked back towards the quarterback, I could see a screen forming to my side and the ball floating towards the halfback. There were three very large linemen out in front, blocking for him. It was a play that could definitely go a long way.

Approaching the lineman, who had formed a sort of wall that the half-back was content to stay behind, but thinking that my football career was on the line with the last cut only a few weeks away, I decided to take a chance and do something unexpected. I would try and split the two biggest lineman by increasing my speed directly into the wall they had formed and attempt to knife my way between them, by diving head first below their waists, at the same time grasping out for the back, guessing that he would still be there, feeling safe behind his big wall of linemen.

Normally, I would have attempted to playoff the middle lineman's block, staying on my feet, but giving ground to do so and then, hopefully, make the tackle a few yards further downfield. We had been taught since high school to never trade one for one against a blocker, to always stay on your feet. After all, you can't be a player if you're lying on your back.

But in this case, I sliced right between these two giants, surprising them with my unconventional tactic, and cut the legs right out from under the runner, for little gain. It may have been the best play of my career. Of course, it was only an exhibition game, not really that important in the scheme of things, but to me it was a quintessential moment. I had proven to myself that I could be tough enough to deal with the challenges of playing pro football.

Unfortunately, at that same moment of realization, I felt a stab of pain in my right thumb. Staring down at it, I could see that it was twisted back in an unnatural position, clearly broken. I stayed in the game until we forced them to punt a few plays later. My brain wanted to show the injury to the trainer, but I also wanted to play, to make another play and to do it again and again. I was psyched, but I knew that an injury could be the kiss of death, the precursor to being cut. I decided to show it to the trainer. He yanked my thumb back into place, wrapped it and told me I was finished for the night. I sat there for the rest of the game, thinking about the irony that my all-time best play would probably get me cut from the team.

The next day, after a night of drinking boilermakers with Ernie Stautner, I flew back to Pittsburgh very depressed. The X-rays confirmed the thumb was badly broken, and Steeler doctor John Best felt that it should be in a cast for three or four weeks. Later that afternoon, I returned to training camp, just in time to watch the game films. I sat there, feeling slightly goofy, full of pain pills, waiting for my big play. When they finally showed the play, it didn't seem as good as I remembered it. They never do. But after the coach ran the play back and forth a number of times, I felt really good when our super-tough middle linebacker, Myron Pottios, reached over and patted me on the shoulder.

"Not bad, Rook. Good effort."

Coming out of that meeting, still on a high, I felt the thumb beginning to throb. The pain pills were wearing off, and I realized that I might soon be asked to turn in my playbook (the dreaded phrase before being cut) and get on the bus back to the Pittsburgh airport. After all, Parker hated rookies, and what good is an injured one?

The next week we played the Vikings in Atlanta, but I didn't play. The following week we were in Detroit, my birthplace, to play the Lions. I was surprised when Doc Best decided to cut my cast off and tape me up, painfully tight, so I could play. I ran down on some kickoffs and punts and didn't actually do anything, just avoiding blockers, trying to get into the flow but never really getting near a ball carrier. My thumb let me know it wasn't pleased. Despite too many pain pills, it throbbed almost unbearably the entire game.

Weeks later, at the close of the exhibition season, having contributed nothing since my big thumb-breaking play, I was still there, uncut. The rookies that made the team were the four of us that had been placed on the first-floor dorm rooms with the vets and one other, Roy Curry, a back from the top floor. No one from the team, either the coaching staff or the management, actually told me that I had made the club; I just wasn't told that I hadn't.

Now that I am about to turn 60 years old, I think the most momentous, most important thing that happened to me as a pro was not a single outstanding play, or any individual honors, or even being a member of a world championship team. No, the biggest moment, the one that gave me the biggest thrill, was just making the team and being given the opportunity to find out if I could someday learn how to really play a very challenging game.

CHAPTER THREE

Inside the Game

One of the aspects of pro football I most enjoyed were the head games we occasionally played with the guys across the line. I also enjoyed trying to figure out what the opponent was going to do by analyzing and memorizing tendencies, noticing presnap clues, and then trying to confuse him as to what I was going to do.

Some more physically gifted players might not have had to focus on so much detail. They just reacted to what they saw once the ball was snapped. I watched my good friend Bobby Bell (the great Kansas City Chiefs Hall of Fame linebacker) make plays that I couldn't possibly make if I had gotten such a late read. Bobby was so gifted athletically that he could just overcome the opponent with his awesome talent. I'm not saying that Bobby isn't as smart as me. He just didn't need to use his brains as much as I did. He could rely more on his physical skills, whereas I had to have a pretty good idea where the ball was going before it was snapped to have any prayer of stopping the play. Because I couldn't rely on superior speed or strength, I was forced to concentrate more on the mental aspect of football to defeat my opponent.

Yes, I made it personal, because that's what football always comes down to, a mano-a-mano battle with the opponent you're responsible for defeating. In the case of linebackers, Jack Ham and I most often had to try and defeat the block of a tight end, a fullback or a pulling guard. Jack Lambert, working inside, had to beat the center's block as well as guards and tackles. Of course, once we got away from the blockers, we still had to prevent the ball carrier from running over us or making us miss an open-field tackle. Football is an in-your-face game, and failure can be very personal, almost like losing a fistfight.

I was fortunate to have outstanding coaching my whole career, coaches who focused on detail. Bob Davis, my high school coach (we only lost two games during my three years), was a stickler for good technique. Dan Devine, my college coach, was a superb motivator, always pushing us to exert maximum effort.

My pro coaches, Buddy Parker, Bill Austin, and the great Chuck Noll, taught us the value of sound techniques and anticipation—the value of understanding what your opponent was most likely to do. Chuck Noll was a great teacher, and he made me a much better player.

Our assistant coaches—guys such as Woody Wodenhoefer, George Perles, Bud Carson, Buster Ramsey, Hank Kuhlman, Charlie Sumner, and Lavern Torgeson—were also invaluable in preparing us, both physically and mentally, to make plays.

Football is a sport that takes a long time to learn how to play. In high school, we primarily react to what we see, not really understanding how to think. It's not until college that players start to get a true feel for the sport—understanding how the opponent's coach thinks, getting ready for their tendencies on certain down and yardages and then reacting instantly to their postsnap keys. But I was a slow learner. It took me until my thirties before I really understood how to play the game.

Some people are surprised that I could survive at all in pro football, because I'm not naturally a very violent or overtly aggressive person. When I first started playing the game in high school, I wasn't a very good open-field tackler, and the coaches accused me of being afraid. Later, I realized that my inability to tackle had nothing to do with a fear of being hurt or being afraid of a violent confrontation. It was more that I hadn't learned the proper technique. Yes, I was afraid, but it was a fear of failing and the resulting humiliation, not a fear of injury. If you really care, you naturally don't want to fail.

Tackling is not rocket science, but you'd be surprised at how many pros miss tackles because they neglect to follow through with the proper technique. Here are all five steps:

1. Reduce your speed just slightly as you approach the runner, thus gaining greater control of your balance. (If you try to take his head off, he'll make you miss.)

2. Continue to move forward. Do not allow the runner to freeze you in one spot.

3. Keep your eyes on the runner's belt buckle.

4. Put your head in front of the runner's knees, or through the ball.

5. Wrap your arms and hold on.

We would all get cocky on occasion and try to make the devastating hit, but too often, we missed when doing so. Even pro athletes sometimes forget the basics and go too high, don't wrap their arms, or get frozen or overextended.

After learning this technique I significantly reduced my misses. When I did miss, it was usually because I got my ego in front of my brain— wanting to make the spectacular, devastating, crowd-pleasing hit and neglecting the technique described above. The devil ego will get you every time. Other times, I would find myself focused on the runner's head and shoulders instead of his belt buckle. Even late in my career, I had to force myself to remember to go through the technique by the numbers.

I never really thought of what I was doing as violent. I would hit the runner, receiver or quarterback as hard as I could, exploding into him with all the strength and timing I could muster, but the feeling I had was never that I had intimidated, overpowered, embarrassed, or crushed the opponent. Instead, I just felt the real satisfaction of executing a difficult technique well against a respected opponent.

In those days we never strutted around, never taunted our opponent, never asked the crowd to appreciate our play, never took our helmets off to show our ugly mugs; we just went back to the huddle feeling that we'd done our job—that's what we got paid to do.

Sometimes, when an opponent made a particularly good block, knocking me off my feet, I would congratulate him, saying something like, "Hey, nice block. Good job." Of course, the very next play I would try my best to defeat him and make him miss that block. If a player took a cheap shot at me (like punching me in the face mask or stomach) I'd try to stay calm, maintain control of my emotions, and politely say something like, "I thought you had more class than that."

The first coach to really force me to focus intently on the opposition's tendencies, based on different sets or splits, was Al Onofrio, the University of Missouri's defensive coach. Despite studying a lot about an opponent's favorite plays, the importance of anticipation didn't really get into my thick skull until my senior year. Of course, sometimes anticipation could backfire.

Coach Onofrio had noticed that the University of California team would always run a certain play, an outside off-tackle run, when the center placed his right foot further back than his left, which apparently enabled him to pull better. It had been an effective play for the Bears, and Onofrio wanted us to notice when the center put his foot back and then react to the point of attack quickly.

Unfortunately, Cal fooled us when we played. Maybe because they had seen us on film reacting so quickly to our opponents' flow, they had designed a counter-play, running back against the flow (the opposite direction of the center's pull). It was a long day, and we never did get it right. So sometimes you can outsmart yourself.

Later that year we were preparing to play against Georgia Tech in the Bluebonnet Bowl. Tech had a good team, having beaten top-five Alabama that year, and we knew we were in for a battle.

Coach Onofrio showed us that if we anticipated the play and reacted immediately (before the offense moved but not so quickly as to be off sides) and penetrated into a certain hole, we would defeat the play even if they knocked us down. Football is all about gaining control of a certain square footage of the field at a precise moment. He who gets there first wins.

You can't get there first if you're slow to react to the play, waiting to be sure what the opponent is doing before you move, over-thinking the situation, worrying about making a mistake, or dwelling on the multitude of possibilities. Al convinced us that Georgia Tech was going to call a certain play when they showed a certain set, splits, downs, or yardage. During the game, my teammates and I overplayed those plays that Al had taught us to anticipate and easily shut them down.

I realized later that our success that day had absolutely nothing to do with being superior athletes to the Tech players but instead with being well prepared mentally. Granted, if the Tech coaches had known that we would overreact to certain plays, they could have adjusted and run counter-plays or reverses that might have hurt us badly.

In the pros, such anticipation is taken to an entirely new level. For one thing, professional teams have all day, from 8 a.m to 6 p.m, to study and prepare for the next opponent.

In college, we would attend our academic classes from 7:40 a.m. to 1:40 p.m. and then practice from 2:30 to 5 p.m., with film sessions afterwards and the mandatory dining hall. We wouldn't return to the dorm or the fraternity house until around 7:30 p.m., giving us only a few hours to study until our 11 p.m. mandatory "lights out."

The non athlete student, who is so often critical of the athlete's academic achievement, or lack thereof, has no idea how difficult it is to return to the dorm exhausted and then try to study, with your thinking confused from your latest concussion or body aching from that last hit.

When I returned to graduate school to get my MBA, I was a much better student, getting nearly straight A's and ending up high in the class rank. The difference was that I was not exhausted and had all day to study. It was hard work, but I had plenty of time and energy to do it.

The pro player has no homework except football homework. During my career, I often took home game films and tendency charts to study the opponent's strategies, running their successful plays back over and over again, often past midnight, searching for something they did that might tip off the play. Quite often I would find some little clue.

Ray Mansfield, our great center, also took films home and discovered— after running the projector back and forth until he was bleary-eyed—that his nemesis, Curly Culp, a Houston nose guard, would line up with his foot deeper and wider on one of his two favorite pass rushing moves. When the foot was up and his stance narrower, Ray knew the other move was coming. Ray, who had dreaded playing Culp prior to this discovery, did very well against him from then on. Knowing what an opponent is going to do is a huge advantage.

For example, when I came into the league in 1963, statistics clearly show that the most frequently injured player was the outside linebacker. This occurred because of a play that allowed a legal crack-back block by the wide receiver—coming from our blind side, below the waist, the block thrown down at our knees. Linebackers were going down right and left with major knee injuries, all because of this running play which allowed the crack-back block.

Today, such a block is illegal. Most players, although we'd never admit it, worried about the potential for a career-ending injury. Wanting to avoid injury, I began to study this play. I figured that this was one play I needed to be ready for.

Watching the films, noticing every detail of how our opponents ran this potentially dangerous play, I figured out a number of ways that most opponents tipped off the play—ways I began referring to as "presnap keys" (clues recognizable before the ball was snapped). First, they would typically run a pitchout to the halfback around end on second and long (rarely on first down and never third and long) into the narrow side of the field (the side closest to the sidelines) between the 20-yard lines. Second, the wide receiver would always look at me on his way out to his position, and he would cheat in three or four yards from his normal lineup (wanting to be closer to me in case I penetrated quickly). "Why," I asked myself, "is he looking at me? He doesn't look at me when he's going to run a pass pattern. He looks at our defensive backs, noticing their alignment." Third, the halfback who was going to take the pitchout would often line up deeper and wider and put very little weight on his down hand and even lean towards the sidelines, cheating a little to get himself into position to take the pitchout and get a quick jump to the outside. Fourth, the offensive tackle, lining up right next to me, was also putting no weight on his down hand, clearly preparing to pull around the cut-back block on me to get at our cornerback. Finally, teams liked to run this play on what's called the quick count (getting ready and running the play on the first sound made by the quarterback).

When I observed all of these tipoffs, it became very difficult to run the quick pitch to my side. If all six keys were apparent, I would ignore the defense called in the huddle and blitz towards the halfback on the snap, penetrating too quickly for the wide receiver to crack back, and would tackle the halfback in the backfield just as he was catching the ball. Best of all was that teams stopped running this play to my side, knowing they might lose substantial yardage.

So once again, I realized that my success in stopping the quick pitch was primarily due to my mental anticipation. Any linebacker in the league could have made the same play had he known it was going to happen and had he made his penetration on the snap of the ball. If you waited until you read your postsnap keys (i.e. you see the ball pitched and the tackle pull), it was too late and you were about to be cracked back upon and possibly badly injured.

Of course, you had to have the guts to go against the defense called and do your own thing (freelance) when you thought you'd figured out what they were going to do. If you were wrong, the coaches would not be pleased and would chew you out for "guessing."

Sometimes, if you were lucky, you could learn something from a fellow player that you would never hear from a coach. Coaches, of course, teach you to be a complete team player, someone who is always there to help his teammates and be involved in every play.

When I got back from the army, I was backed up by a very solid linebacker named Rod Breedlove. Rod had played more than ten years in the league, and he was an extremely savvy old pro who knew how to think and avoid getting out of position. Like most older players, he had slowed a step or two, which was one of the reasons I was starting.

But after I had played a particularly bad game against Cleveland—playing with uncontrolled emotion, reckless abandon, missing assignments and just generally being out of control—Torgy Torgeson, our defensive coordinator, announced that Rod would being taking over my position on first team, and I would be demoted to second team.

Despite realizing that Torgy was right—knowing that I'd made a lot of mistakes and missed too many tackles for being over-extended while trying to annihilate the runner, or being recklessly out of position trying to make an interception or sack—I was still devastated and humiliated by this demotion and felt angry and hurt because I had essentially been benched for trying too hard. It didn't seem fair.

That week I was a fairly miserable person to be around. All week in practice I went full speed, hitting my teammates, getting in scuffles, demonstrating to the coaches that they had made their point loud and clear, but Rod remained the starter.

Since I was not going to start, I found myself back on the special teams. And remembering my rookie training camp, I realized that it is awfully difficult to impress the coaches just playing special teams. It occurred to me that I might be backing up Rod the rest of the year.

That week we put in a punt block where I might have had a chance to make a big play. But I was completely in the tank, thinking I had ruined my chance of becoming a serious player—someone other teams respected and sometimes altered their game plans to avoid.

To make things even more humiliating, the next game was against the St. Louis Cardinals, a game that would be televised back to my hometown, and all my pals would see that I had been benched. Kneeling on the sidelines, watching Rod intently, I realized that he was playing a very good game, making all the right moves, and I became even more depressed. Then, in the second quarter, I blocked a punt, scooped it up, and ran it in for a touchdown.

At halftime the coaches congratulated me on blocking the punt and started me in the third quarter, a starting position that I would hold until my retirement in 1976. I played pretty well during that second half, trying hard to not make any mental errors and to avoid over-aggressiveness, but I walked off the field knowing that I still had a lot to learn. Rod Breedlove had shown me in that first half how well you can play if you use your brain. I wondered how Rod was able to react so quickly to the plays. He seemed to know exactly what they were going to do.

My starting the second half, of course, didn't thrill Breedlove. He watched me struggle in the following games but never said a word. I could tell by his expression, though, that he was often critical of my play, particularly whenever I would make a mental error.

Finally, after I had been suckered by a counter-play to my side, giving up a big first down, Rod had enough. When I came off the field, after the opponent punted three plays later, down on myself for getting beat, not really understanding why, Rod grabbed me and asked, "Russell, don't you pay attention in the meetings?"

"Like what?" I responded, still angry with myself.

"They only used that formation twenty times in the past three years and they ran the ball every time, never passed it—seventeen times to the other side of the field (the left) and only three times to your side of the field (the right), all the same play—the counter-play they just ran against you, rather successfully, I might add. You should have played the counter first. It's a no-brainer. If the ball goes the other way, you've got to have enough confidence in your teammates that they'll make the play. Don't try and be a hero."

Rod paused and looked over at Torgy, probably wondering if he approved of Rod playing coach, and said, "Just overplay the opponent's historical tendency that could attack your position. You were racing over to the other side of the field, which is what they wanted you to do. Dumb."

"So how do I avoid doing that?"

"Make sure that your first step or reaction is to stop the most likely tendency they have from that formation that attacks your position. If you're wrong and they go in another direction, you can always get into your pursuit angle and try to make the tackle downfield if the runner breaks through."

With that he walked away, shaking his head. Rod was a smart guy.

I would remember Rod's advice, making my first move to prevent being beat on key plays to my side, and it would reap huge benefits. Once Chuck Noll, noticing that I had first taken a quick step to my right when the ball had clearly gone left, asked me, "Andy, why did you take that step? You're not reading your keys correctly. It's a wasted motion."

Despite knowing the real reason was that I was positioning myself so that the tight end could not hook me, which is what he had to do for them to run their favorite play to my side from that formation, and thinking he would most likely disapprove of Breedlove's theory, I just said, "Sorry, coach. I was guessing."

"Don't guess. Read your keys," Chuck said.

I needed an edge to defeat the opponent, and the only one I had was to figure out what they were going to do before the ball was snapped. Granted, if the opponent did not attack my position I might be slightly late to react, but in the '70s my teammates were so good that it seldom mattered. They made the tackle anyway.

I would also try to think like the opposing coach. If, for example, they ran a screen to my side successfully early in the game, I figured he would come back with that same play sometime later in the game. I would wait patiently, looking for the moment in the game that if I were the opposing coach, I would call that play again, remembering the down and yardage and field position that they had previously run it. It might not be until the fourth quarter, but I would be waiting, ready to pounce on it. Rarely will a coach, when his team has run a play successfully, not come back to it. Cincinnati Bengals coach Paul Brown was the only one who wouldn't repeat a successful play, and it drove me crazy.

Coach Noll convinced us that success is in the details—precise spacing, quality techniques, total concentration, maximum intensity, and reading all the keys. Once, when playing the New York Giants (when the great Fran Tarkenton was their quarterback), I noticed that the two times we had called a "four-three under" (where I would stack behind the defensive line on the weak side—lining up over the offensive tackle), I could sometimes make tackles if the opponent ran away from me to the strong side. Tarkenton checked off to a running play directly at me—running towards the "bubble," as it is called. Apparently, they had decided that the best way to attack that defense was to run right at me, forcing me to take on a much bigger offensive lineman, a true mismatch.

So when Fran saw me lined up in the "under" formation, he had on both occasions checked off, shouting "Brown (apparently their live color), counter 37." Despite noticing this, I had not reacted quickly enough to the seven-hole, and they made good yardage both times. Fortunately, we had only run the under defense twice in the first half. At halftime the coaches had encouraged me to react more quickly to the tackle's block, stepping up into the hole.

It wasn't until late in the third quarter that the coaches called the under again. As Tarkenton approached the line, seeing him notice my under alignment, I waited until just the instant before he called the audible and I yelled, as loud as I could so all the Giants would hear it, "Brown, Counter 37." I saw Fran freeze, not anticipating my knowing, let alone announcing, the audible he was about to call. But since it was too late for him to change his mind, he repeated what I had said.

My assignment was not to blitz, but there are just some times that you have to commit totally to stopping one play, to play your hunches and if you're wrong, you're going to look pretty silly. I, of course, realized that they could have changed their live color at halftime, in which case Tarkenton's guys would just have ignored the audible and run whatever he had called in the huddle. Knowing I was taking a risk, I blitzed anyway, up through the seven-hole, and threw the play for a two-yard loss.

Tarkenton smiled and wagged his finger at me, as though I had cheated him. I figured I had been lucky and decided to ignore that audible if he called it again.

Tarkenton, not possessing the powerful arm and physical strength of some other quarterbacks, was one of the league's most savvy quarterbacks. He also was one of the all-time best scrambling quarterbacks ever, despite not being particularly fast. I studied his moves and noticed how he would always roll deep, back towards the pressure (sort of against the grain), always pivoting away from his previous direction. He would make this move time and again, getting deeper and deeper, until finally executing a successful pass to one of his teammates or just throwing it away. He was seldom sacked. He made a lot of big plays off the scramble.

I also noticed a number of linebackers, or defensive ends, who had come free from their blockers, thinking they had Tarkenton in their sights, coming from his blind side, sure they were about to get a sack, when he would spin away at the last second, as though he had eyes in the back of his head. How did he know they were there? Could he hear them, or did he just have a sixth sense that told him they were coming?

I decided that if I came free on a blitz I would surely be approaching him from his blind side (because he was right-handed and he usually rolled to our left), so that I should actually aim about two or three yards to his right, expecting him to roll deeper as he reversed to his right. Sure enough, I came free and as I approached Tarkenton, it struck me, for the first time, that if he didn't roll but just stood his ground, that I'd look amazingly stupid running right by him, two yards to his right. But I decided to go through with my plan anyway. Aiming two or three yards deeper and to his right, I was rewarded for my somewhat unorthodox strategy when, at the very last moment, Fran spun right into me.

When we got up, Tarkenton again looked at me, this time with some confusion in his eyes. How had I known he would spin? Again, I thought if I came free again, I should expect him to step up into the pocket and not spin deeper, against my flow. Tarkenton was a very smart guy, and I didn't want to be the victim of one of his tricks.

Another time I found myself on the bottom of a massive pileup of bodies, clutching at the fumbled ball of our opponent, the Cleveland Browns. The problem was that a Brown player, whose back was to me, had a much better grip on the ball, and I realized that I would not be able to wrench it loose from him. So before the refs forced everyone to get up from the pile (to see who had the ball), I started yelling loudly, "Browns' ball, Browns' ball," and continued tugging on the ball. The Brown player, thinking that one of his teammates wanted the glory of the fumble recovery, decided to let go and give me that distinction. You can imagine his surprise when he turned over and saw me holding the ball he had totally controlled seconds before. He didn't seem pleased when I winked at him.

There were a few times, more than I'd like to admit, where the opponent fooled me. Sometimes it was even before the game started. Once, Floyd Little, the great running back and Captain of the Denver Broncos, clearly said, "heads," when calling the coin toss. When the coin came up tails, Floyd said, "Great, it's tails, Denver's choice—we'll receive." The official, apparently not remembering that Floyd had called "heads," agreed with Floyd and gave them the ball. When I protested, Floyd just winked at me.

Of course, you aren't going to be a quality player just by occasionally confusing (or conning) your opponents. Only sound fundamentals and disciplined play will accomplish that. My point here is that a good player has to keep his mind attentive and focused on all aspects of the game.

CHAPTER FOUR

Football and Golf

Although we often refer to football as a game, it's really a serious contact sport. I won't insult our veterans by comparing it to war, but the violence is real, not like the bogus World Wrestling Federation. People had a fascination with accidents and tragedies long before the Roman gladiators were forced to do battle against each other. Modern football warriors aren't fighting for their lives, but with today's players being so much bigger and stronger, life-altering injuries certainly can and do occur.

I've always believed that there is a difference between a sport and a game. Games are activities like golf, croquet, ping-pong, pool, archery, and bowling—all of which require a certain level of athleticism to be any good, especially refined hand-eye coordination. I certainly don't mean to put these activities down, because they can be extremely difficult pursuits, but there is a difference between a sport and a game.

After all, Tiger Woods (despite playing probably the most difficult game ever devised) doesn't have to deal with someone knocking him down in the middle of his back swing or someone taking his golf club away from him. On the other hand, a golf competitor can't go back and knock down his opponent. Of course, I have read about Tiger striking the ball as he was sprinting down the fairway, without breaking stride. Now that is certainly athleticism.

But I wonder how Tiger would deal with getting sacked just as he's swinging his club—a quarterback's too-frequent experience. Perhaps that's why so many people admire quarterbacks.

One reason I admire quarterbacks is that they have to stand there and take a hit without being able to strike back or execute a move that would make their assailants miss. The other players can defend themselves by striking back at the team attacking them. Quarterbacks get too much credit when the team wins and too much criticism when the team loses. Neither is fair.

I can remember Buster Ramsey, my first defensive coach with the Steelers and a former NFL linebacker himself, telling me that I could ward off any blocker if I delivered a good enough shot to his head.

"Russell, you weigh 225 pounds and you're worrying about stopping a lineman who weighs 300 pounds. How much do you think that lineman's head weighs? Maybe 40 pounds? It's really a mismatch if you deliver all your 225 pounds of force squarely against his head," Buster said. Such tactics are, of course, no longer legal in the NFL.

But quarterbacks have to stand there, knowing they are about to be creamed, and still have the poise and the talent to deliver that ball downfield to exactly the right spot, just before getting nailed by some giant lineman. Maybe their great hand-eye coordination and their ability to deal with pressure is why most quarterbacks are normally pretty good golfers.

Let's talk about pressure. Does Tiger Woods really feel more pressure trying to sink a winning putt in a major tournament (like the Masters) than the average golfer feels trying to sink a putt and win $5 from his buddies? Maybe Tiger feels less pressure because he has worked on his game since he was two years old, often sinking 100 consecutive putts from six feet using only his right hand before quitting. I'd be there all night, or forever.

The duffer has not practiced and has no clue how to consistently make that six-footer. And he knows, unlike Tiger, that there is a much higher probability that he will miss. Tiger, on the other hand, is highly confident that his putt will go in, and therefore probably feels less pressure. Of course, the duffer has the built-in excuse of not having practiced and may feel less pressure than Tiger. The causes of pressure can be complicated.

However, ask Tiger to try and tackle Walter Payton in the open field, and he might understand fear, the same fear a professional football player has that he'll miss that six-footer. I bet that when Lynn Swann went deep in the Super Bowl, he felt less pressure than when trying to tee off in front of a large gallery at the Mario Lemeiux Tournament. Why? Because he'd spent his entire life learning the skills he needed to get to the Super Bowl, and he rarely practices his golf.

Granted, today's golfers are in much better shape, and it's sometimes exhausting to play thirty-six holes in the hot sun or walking a hilly, wet course, but it still falls short of a sport. It's a game I find to be an experience in ego reduction, having far too much SLOT in my game—that's Significant Lack of Talent.

Sports are events where the participants are required to run, jump, be strong, have agility and be in great shape—none of which are required by games. Games like golf and ping-pong may require greater hand-eye coordination than certain sports, but true sports require the participant to deal directly with the opposition, who is usually trying to stop you from doing what you want to do.

I'm not saying that one doesn't compete in games. Arnold Palmer was a great competitor, maybe the best ever, but he wasn't playing a sport. I think he was playing a game. An excruciatingly difficult game, but a game nonetheless.

But what about downhill skiing, gymnastics, fencing, ice skating—aren't those sports? They don't have an opponent trying to prevent you from succeeding; you are out there all alone. I'd categorize such activities as sports because they require strength and courage. Actually, who cares? Games or sports—why am I getting caught up in this semantic bullshit? The fact is that I'd rather watch the Masters than the Super Bowl, and therefore, I'm obviously very impressed by the athleticism of professional golfers.

Broadcaster Myron Cope once took the unpopular position that Arnold Palmer should not have been awarded the *Sports Illustrated* Athlete of the Year award. Myron was OK with Palmer receiving the title of Gamesman or Golfer of the Year, and I'm sure Myron would admit that no person ever did more for his game, or for that matter, his sport, than Arnold Palmer. On the other hand, it should also be mentioned that Myron has never broken 100 on the golf course!

Some people argue that individual games, like golf, are more difficult than team sports because you don't have anybody backing you up—you are out there all alone with no one to help. Well, believe me, despite having ten other teammates out there on the football field, you are essentially all by yourself. Joe Greene did not help Jack Ham and me defeat the tight ends or guards who were trying to block us. He had his own problems to worry about. Of course, it did feel pretty good when I got beat and one of my teammates made the play anyway.

Why then do golfers admit gagging during the Ryder Cup, complaining that there is so much more pressure because they have teammates (not to mention their country) depending on them? We, of course, hated to let our teammates down as well. Maybe it's easier to deal with your own defeat or poor play if it doesn't affect anyone else—such as your teammates or the entire city.

The Ryder Cup, or for that matter, any of the majors, are only single events, not like the Super Bowl or the World Series where your team's effort for the entire year is on the line. No other event waits for you to redeem yourself if you blow the big play. Hey, golfers, you can't have it both ways. Is it more difficult to play alone, or is it tougher to be part of a team, with teammates counting on you?

In fairness, I should say that golf seems to be entirely unique as compared to other games or sports. Golf is the only game in which "duffers" like myself routinely compare ourselves with the PGA pros. How? We try to score a par when, in fact, that is what the pro golfers shoot—they who have played since they were youngsters, had hundreds of lessons, watched themselves on video, practiced for years, and hit thousands of balls a day, often shoot par or only slightly better.

One year, playing in our own Celebrity Golf Tournament for the UPMC charities, I was teamed with Chuck Noll, who is a born teacher. On every hole, Chuck was giving me pointers on how to improve my swing, but I have to admit that I found it irritating because Chuck wasn't playing all that much better than me. Finally, after watching me slice another one out of bounds, Chuck just smiled at me.

"You know, Andy, everything we taught you is wrong for golf," Chuck said, shaking his head. I never could harness my lunge.

Aren't golfers like myself, who never practice, never see their "swing planes" on video, never hear a word from a coach, who complain when we don't shoot a par, being arrogant? I think the reason we have high expectations is that we can occasionally shoot a par, score a birdie now and then, and sometimes even bag an eagle. We should be deliriously happy when we score a bogey, not complaining about our shot that went into the woods. Even Tiger occasionally hits one in the sand trap, or in the woods, or in the water, and he's been practicing his entire life.

Golf also has to be the most embarrassing game ever invented. For example, when you hit a bad shot in tennis, it goes into the net or maybe onto the adjacent court. It doesn't go in the woods where you can't find it, or into a lake where you can't retrieve it. When you're skiing down a hill, no one says afterwards that you three-putted that hill, or that you double-bogeyed the slope, which, of course, is what you really did if anyone was comparing you with Franz Klammer.

Golf seems to be counter-intuitive. To hit the shot high, you must hit down on the ball. To hit it low, you hit up on the ball. To fade it to the right you swing left; to draw it left you swing right. In golf, less is more and more is less. A relaxed technique is everything. One of the things I liked about football was that when things were going bad, you could just try harder. You could even get mad. You could channel that anger, that energy, into exploding into the opponent. In golf, getting mad or trying harder will hurt your game.

Of course, you might say, "What would you know about pressure on the golf course, Russell? Unless you've been there, you've got no right to even have an opinion," and you'd be right. But I did have one experience that gave me some small glimmer of an understanding of how pressure works on a golf course, and I have to admit, I gagged big time.

In 1970, I was invited to play in the American Airlines Celebrity Golf Classic, a fifty-four-hole tournament held that year at the Wigwam Golf Club, outside of Phoenix. I had hardly played at all before that—never playing during the football season (too sore), and working too hard in the off season. When they asked me if I would like to play, I was slightly reluctant because I knew my game stank. I was a pitiful golfer and still am. When I reported that my handicap had to be north of thirty, they told me that the maximum handicap allowed was twenty-two (I'd have two shots on four holes and one on all the rest). I accepted the invitation anyway, figuring, at worst, it would be great fun to go to Arizona in January. After all, I reasoned, who will care if I don't play very well?

Arriving at the beautiful Wigwam course, I was informed that I would be playing with Bill Mazeroski, who won the tournament the previous two years. I also learned that we would be playing for $10,000 in prize money, which we could accept if we didn't mind losing our amateur status.

I hadn't met Bill Mazeroski, but I certainly knew who he was after watching my favorite Yankees go down because of his famous ninth-inning home run. It didn't surprise me that he would be a very good golfer, but I realized for the first time that he might care if I played badly, causing him to lose his share of the prize money, which in those days was a lot of money (certainly a lot more than the Steelers paid me to play a few games of football).

The night before the tournament, I saw Mazeroski sitting in the club bar. I walked up to him and introduced myself.

"Maz, I hate to disappoint you, but I'm a terrible golfer; they must have partnered me with you so that you were certain to lose. I hear you've owned this event."

"Don't worry about it. We'll just close the bar every night and have a real good time. We'll just do the best we can."

With that, he asked me what I wanted to drink, and surrounded by some athletes I really admired—guys like Ray Nitschke, Johnny Unitas, Johnny Bench and Ed Podolak—we stayed late and closed the bar.

The next morning I arrived only a few minutes before our tee time at the practice tee, slightly hung over, and was surprised to find Maz there already, sweating heavily and working on his game. I pulled out my driver and proceeded to hit five drives out of bounds over onto the heavily trafficked road to our right. Maz, watching me, just smiled and shook his head and then waved for me to follow him over to the first tee.

Arriving on the tee, I was surprised to find a large group of spectators mingling around the first tee, hoping to see a celebrity. I hated to disappoint them. I realized that I had never hit a golf ball with a crowd watching me. After Maz had hit one right down the middle, about 265 yards, I got ready to tee up the ball as the announcer introduced me to the crowd, giving some of my Steeler stats. I thought to myself that he should tell them to get back, out of the way.

I swung carefully, trying not to move my head and worrying about over-swinging, and nearly whiffed the ball, which rolled backwards, just off my right toe. As I stared down at the ball, I was truly shocked, disbelieving. I then started to re-tee the ball, expecting to take a Mulligan (a replay of the drive). As I reached for the ball, the tee master said, "You must hit it as it lies; you can't move it without assessing yourself a penalty stroke."

It occurred to me that even Arnold Palmer couldn't hit a shot like I had just hit if he tried to—it was really a trick shot. How could it possibly have gone backwards? So, with those negative thoughts in my head, I took out my three-wood and took an angry swing, with the ball coming off the heel of the club, diving right down into a flower garden to the left of the tee. I could hear people snickering as I walked into the flowers, trying to maintain some semblance of dignity. As I hunted for my ball, I realized that that moment could possibly be my most humiliating sports (excuse me, game) moment ever.

I figured it was a poise test, and as in football, I had to regain my concentration and not allow negative thoughts to enter my head. Positive imaging would be important. Six shots later, I had my first "snowman," an 8, but Maz seemed unconcerned, having parred the hole easily—the game was best ball of two. Walking to the second tee, Maz put his arm around my shoulder.

"Relax, partner. It's going to be a long day, and there'll be plenty of times when you help me."

I doubted it.

Four holes later, with my best score being a bogey, we came to a par 5, three under par. Maz, who had a handicap of ten, had parred two of the four holes and birdied one, a short par 3. Since Maz had strokes, we were three under. I hit a good drive, about 250 yards, almost in the fairway, a good second shot towards the hole, and was astounded when my nine-iron third shot somehow ended up about ten feet from the hole. I was even more amazed when my birdie putt fell into the hole. It was a natural birdie, for (since I had two strokes on that hole—thank God for handicaps!) a net two.

As we walked towards the next tee, a smiling Maz again put his arm around my shoulder.

"You know something, partner, that double eagle is going to piss a few people off big-time."

All of sudden, we were five under.

The rest of the day was a blur. I parred a few more holes, and Maz played great, always sinking the long putt when needed for net pars. We ended up tied for first that day, and no one was more amazed than me. That night we again closed the bar. Maz thought a few drinks might calm my nerves. He didn't want his partner to be too nervous the next day.

Two days later, late in the third round, I had a par on the last par 5, for a net eagle three. Maz played brilliantly for three rounds, shooting in the 70s, holding me up, but my occasional pars, for net birdies or eagles, had helped.

The Phoenix papers estimated that the crowd on the final day would be large (reported to be at least 6,500 people). I realized quickly that they weren't there to see Andy Russell (Andy who?) but were there to see Mickey Mantle, Willie Mays, Joe Namath, and all the other super celebrities in attendance.

As we approached the 54th and last tee, thankful that Maz had birdied the 17th, I heard an announcer on a very loud public address system tell the large crowd that the team of Mazeroski and Russell was only one shot back of the leaders. I knew immediately that one of us would have to net birdie the 18th hole, a tough 410-yard par 4. My heart sank as I realized that Maz didn't get a stroke on the 18th.

Maz put his arm around my shoulder but stared hard at me.

"Russell, I've carried your butt for three long days. You gotta par this hole for the net bird."

I looked into Maz's eyes, sort of expecting him to be kidding, but I could see that he wasn't. It was the ninth inning; the game was on the line. It was time to elevate my game, but I realized that I had no business being in this situation. I didn't play golf. I didn't practice golf. I had no skills to rely on, no lessons, no grooved swing plane, not a clue, and now I had to do it in front of a lot of people with a partner who would be very unhappy if I failed.

After Maz had hit one down the middle, about 250 yards, I walked towards the tee markers and realized people were lined up the whole way down the fairway, many of them pushing and jostling to see better, giving me a narrow funnel to hit through. I could see myself slicing a ball dead right, which I had done a number of times that day, and taking somebody's head off.

"Get back, I'm not a pro. This thing could go anywhere," I said.

The people closest to me reluctantly shuffled only a step or two backwards—brave souls.

At the same time I knew that I shouldn't be having negative images of what I was about to do. But it would have been irresponsible of me not to warn them. I could see Maz, off to the side, not wanting to watch, worrying that I would duff another one.

Just as I had collected myself, forced all negative thoughts out of my head, and taken a deep breath, imagining myself about to launch my best drive ever, a TV man ran up.

"Excuse me, but we need to put this microphone onto you for the TV coverage."

I stepped back, stunned, as he pinned a mic on my collar and adjusted it so that it was picking up the sound properly. I stood there, looking down the fairway with all those people staring back at me, probably wondering who the hell I was and why I was taking so much time. I again tried to focus on where I wanted the ball to go.

When I swung, it was truly an out-of-body experience as the ball flew right down the middle, about 265 yards. It felt like a miracle. It was certainly the best drive I had ever hit in my life, and I had done it under enormous pressure—at least in my head.

Walking down that fairway, I was amazed that I had hit such a good shot, but I still worried that there was some work left—knowing and hoping that there was still a possibility that Maz could somehow birdie the hole himself, even without a stroke. But I forced that thought out of my head and told myself I would have to par this hole for us to get into the playoff. When Maz hit his ball into the stands (there were stands holding hundreds of people all around the green) I knew it was up to me. Maz would have to chip it in from off the green for a birdie.

I had about 155 yards left to the hole and wasn't sure what to hit. My caddy was telling me to smooth a seven-iron, but I had no idea how to "smooth" anything. And since I was really pumped up, I thought I should probably hit the eight-iron. After much discussion, I motioned for Maz to come over to help me make the decision.

"Maz, what do you think? Should I hit the seven or the eight?"

"Hit the eight. If you hit that seven, as pumped up as you are, you'll be in the clubhouse."

He knew I was excited and into my linebacker persona, wanting to do what I had spent a lifetime learning, using all the strength in my body to hit people, not a tiny little ball. For a second I allowed myself to wish that I were back on the football field, on familiar terrain, with a running back in my sights, ready to deliver a blow and bring him down. Hitting a golf ball, feeling the way I was feeling, was not a good idea. It could go anywhere or nowhere.

Worrying about whether I had the right club, with my heart pounding as rapidly as it ever had in a football game (excuse me, sporting event), I took a careful swing but hit it thin. Miraculously, the ball rose up off the ground on a low trajectory, as though I'd intentionally punched a five-iron, and traveled up onto the green.

Arriving on the green, knowing Maz had not chipped in, I knew I had to get down in two putts from about thirty feet, slightly downhill, with a big left-to-right break. The first putt broke down, almost going in, before rolling three feet past the hole. It was a dead level putt, for a spot in the playoff and more money than I'd ever been paid to do any single thing.

I studied the putt from all directions, worrying that it had a small break to the left, maybe slightly uphill, or possibly against the grain, but the bottom line was that I was gagging, big-time. I was thinking about how disappointed Maz would be if I missed. I even thought about the caddies, who, of course, were hoping for a nice tip. I thought about what a jerk all those people, who had now gathered around the green, would think I was if I missed.

Knowing I should force those thoughts out of my head, I turned to Maz, who had his back to me, not able to watch.

"Maz, come look at this. What do you think?"

"It's dead straight. Hit the damn putt."

I stood over the ball gripping the putter tightly and realized that it felt like a heavy mallet. Finally, I took it back, with absolutely no sense of feel or touch, and pushed the club forward and the ball rolled directly into the hole. I was astounded and more jubilant than I had ever been in a football game. I had done something that I had no business doing, and I had been very lucky.

With that, the officials rushed Maz and me over to the scorer's tent. While reviewing our score, we were informed that we'd be in a playoff with Joe DiMaggio and Otto Graham, perhaps two of the most famous athletes participating in the event.

Feeling an enormous sense of relief, thinking that my job was over, I turned to Maz.

"It's up to you now, Maz. I got that par you wanted."

Maz just nodded his head, looking very serious.

Well, we went back to the 17th hole, a good par 4, a slight dogleg left, with a lake to the right and behind the hole. DiMaggio and Graham, both very good players, teed up first; both hit good drives right down the middle. Hitting next, I hit my drive dead right, over trees into the fairway to our right. Maz, playing his natural draw, hit a good drive, but it hooked slightly into the left rough, right behind a small palm tree.

I found my ball and hit an incredible shot, back over the trees lining the 17th towards the green, but at the last second it faded right and went into the lake bordering the green.

DiMaggio hit his ball on the green about 35 feet from the hole. Graham followed my lead by hitting his shot over the green into the water.

I walked over to Maz and looked at his shot. He needed to hook his ball around the little palm tree right in front of him, out towards the lake, and then draw it back onto the green. If the ball didn't draw, the tournament was over. I figured even a pro golfer would be challenged by the shot.

He calmly lined up his shot and hooked it right around that little palm tree, toward the lake, and it landed on the green about 15 feet above the hole, a truly fantastic shot under the circumstances. People were cheering and running up towards the green, and Max just walked down that fairway, smiling as if he owned the place.

But DiMaggio wasn't through. He stalked all around his long putt and then stroked it right into the hole, thirty-five feet away for a natural birdie. He didn't act surprised. In fact, he didn't show any sign of happiness and just walked slowly over towards the hole to retrieve his ball. Just before stooping down, he looked over at Maz and pointed his finger at him, as though he was saying, "Okay, kid, now it's your turn."

I walked behind Maz, who was reading his putt, a very nasty downhill slider, one that could easily get away from you and force a long putt back and possibly cause a three-putt. Maz, having a stroke on the hole (Joe didn't), now had to two-putt just to force the playoff to continue. Three putts and we lose. It was the kind of putt that would make most golfers' knees weak.

"What do you think, partner?" Maz said.

"Looks like you need to be careful going down. Could roll way past," I said.

"You know what I think?"

"No, what?"

"I think this tournament is over."

He then stood over the putt and drained it for the natural birdie, net eagle, and the win.

In the excitement, I realized that it wasn't by chance that Dimaggio had hit in fifty-six straight games (still the record), and it wasn't by chance that Maz had hit that World Series-winning homer in the ninth inning of the seventh game. These guys were sharks.

So to this day, that moment with Maz was the biggest moment I've ever had in golf, a moment that gave me some small appreciation for the pressure the pro golfers must feel.

After accepting my prize money, willing to give up my amateur status in a heartbeat, I returned home to Pittsburgh with the unique distinction of being the worst pro golfer in America.

CHAPTER FIVE

Coaching Tricks

What makes football so interesting is how it juxtaposes the violent aspect of the game, its aggressive physical side, with the complexity of the game. Football is truly the chess of major sports, a game where all twenty-two pieces are moving at the same time. Game plans, based today on computer printouts showing the previous three years or more of your opponent's strategies, tactics, and tendencies, are extraordinarily complex. Coaches create new formations, devise new plays, show multiple sets, and put players in motion before the ball is snapped—all strategies designed to make the opponent confused and hesitant.

Today's defenses should be too sophisticated to be fooled by double reverses, Statue of Liberty, or flea-flicker-type plays, but these plays are still called and are sometimes successful. Coaches try to confuse their counterparts, forcing them to have their defense check to a simplistic zone, allowing them to run those plays best designed to attack that formation, thus dictating the action.

Big games can be won or lost by coaches making the right or wrong moves. For example, our first Super Bowl against the Vikings was a game that was won by our coaches.

Steelers defensive tackle Joe Greene was having a MVP kind of year, having devised a new strategy where he would place himself in between the guard and the center, almost off sides, tilting his shoulders perpendicular to the line of scrimmage. This would allow him to penetrate upfield too quickly for the center to cut him off, thus requiring them to keep the guard in, not allowing him to pull.

However, in our week's practice in New Orleans prior to the game, our offense added a new play (a fake pitch to Franco with a handoff to Rocky) which they ran against our defense, completely fooling Joe every time. It was what they called a wham sucker play, where they pulled the guard wide, making it appear to be an outside play. They didn't even block Joe, who, they figured correctly, would follow the pulling guard, Gerry Mullins, down the line. Rocky scampered through Joe's vacant hole untouched, and it troubled some of us on defense. What if the Viking coaches tried the same play?

Well, the Viking coaches didn't try anything that clever, but true to the old school of their profession (in a Vince Lombardi fashion), they ran directly at our strength—right at Joe Greene. It was a mistake, and they only gained 17 rushing yards, their offense being no match for Joe Greene. Not once did they run a wham sucker, or anything like it, at Joe.

They also tried to roll Fran Tarkenton to his right, away from Joe, but they hadn't been able to pull the guard. L. C. Greenwood had a terrific game, frustrating Tarkenton by getting up in his face, pressuring him to release the ball early or just batting the ball down. If they had picked a defensive MVP of our first Super Bowl game, it would have undoubtedly been L. C., with Joe a close second.

Dwight White and I rarely saw Tarkenton, because he always rolled to his right. They did run a couple of counters our way, but we stopped them by penetrating upfield too quickly. Dwight, coming off a bad case of the flu, did a good job pressuring Tarkenton when he dropped straight back.

On offense, with Franco setting a Super Bowl rushing record and forcing the Viking defense to focus intently on him, that same wham sucker worked to perfection, with Rocky making key yardage in some of the game's most important fourth-quarter drives.

So it often comes down to which coaches have the best strategies and athletes smart enough to deal with those strategies. Chuck Noll, a brilliant football mind, was also somewhat of an old-school "play it straight, don't try and fool them" type of coach.

For example, when we played the Cowboys in Super Bowl X, Noll told us that Dallas would try to fool us by showing multiple sets and putting all kinds of people in motion. He told us the reason they did that was because they weren't confident they could just line up and go against us straight away. He said, "We aren't going to do anything different or change a lot of stuff. We're just going to line up in our basic 4-3 defense, essentially saying to them, 'Here we are—we aren't going to change what got us here; just see if you can beat us.' "

But that's not exactly what we did. Another thing Coach Noll believed in was to give a lot of authority to his assistant coaches, thus empowering them, but also holding them responsible for the results.

Our defensive coordinator in Super Bowl X was Bud Carson, a former head coach at Georgia Tech. Bud loved to try and confuse the offenses we played. He never wanted to allow the offensive coordinator on the other side of the field to know what we were going to do.

One year, we were scheduled to play a very good Bengal team in Cincinnati coached by the legendary offensive coordinator Bill Walsh. Bud worried all week how to stop their potent offense. Walsh was a genius at teaching quarterbacks, giving them clear sequences and always leaving them with a safety valve (an open receiver) in case they needed it. He had coached Dan Fouts at San Diego, and he was then coaching Kenny Anderson into having his best year ever, leading the league in completion percentage and virtually all other key quarterback stats. Later, Walsh would help Joe Montana become perhaps the best quarterback ever—except for Terry Bradshaw, of course.

Defenses always want to be in the formation best suited to stop the offense's most likely tendency (or best play, or most dangerous play) in every offensive set. Bud was no exception, but he was frustrated because the Bengal offense wouldn't hold still long enough for the players to audible the defense most effective against the set shown.

The problem was that Walsh would often show the defense four or five formations before Anderson would snap the ball. For example, they would come out of the huddle and set up in an I-formation (with the halfback behind the fullback). Then they would shift to a full formation (moving the halfback behind the tackle), then shift to a split formation (the fullback shifting behind the other tackle). They would then go in short motion to double wing, or perhaps go in motion the other direction, forming what we called a triple formation—three receivers on one side.

Each one of these sets had different tendencies, and we wanted to be in the most effective defense. But traditional theory had it that in order to minimize mistakes, the defense, lacking time to make a change, would just audible to a simple zone defense if any formation changed. Bud, of course, didn't want Walsh to know what we were going to do against his various offensive formations.

All week Bud and the other assistant defensive coaches (Woody Wodenhoefer and George Perles) agonized over how to deal with Cincy's offense. The defensive line didn't have to make many changes (staying true to Noll's position that we would line up in a four-three every time) but the other seven players (linebackers and defensive backs) were the ones forced to change pass defenses, if at all possible.

Finally, on Saturday, Bud told us his decision and gave us the audibles we would be playing the next day. We would change the defense every time the Bengals changed their formation, potentially putting us in five different defenses before the ball was snapped. I couldn't believe it—this was unheard-of. It was a first. In the past we had just checked to a simplistic zone pass defense and Walsh would run the plays most effective against that zone.

Ray Mansfield and I liked to take a cab over to the stadium early, to get our ankles taped without a crowd and review our responsibilities. I noticed that nearly all the guys on the defense were already there, most of them sitting on their bench, studying the automatic check sheet. We wanted to make sure that the Bengals didn't beat us because five guys were playing one defense and six were playing another. Mistakes like that will kill you.

Hours later, waiting in the tunnel for the defense to be introduced to the crowd, Bud frantically called all the linebackers and the defensive backs together. He explained that in the middle of the night, he had decided to change two or three of the automatics to ones he thought would be better.

As I ran onto the field, I shook my head. So much for the old theory that you repeat things so often that they become rote and you don't have to think—just react. Bud had taken the complexity of the game to a new level, but it was only the beginning. I wouldn't believe what he decided to do in second quarter.

During that first quarter, I could see Bud getting progressively more nervous. He didn't like that Walsh might be starting to understand what we were checking to. Once Walsh knew our audibles, Bud reasoned, he could then call plays that might hurt those defenses.

All defenses are vulnerable to certain plays. For example, if the coaches call a certain zone pass defense, requiring the weak-side linebacker to drop twelve yards deep to his hash mark, anticipating a crossing pattern by the tight end, it's not a great defense to be in if the offense runs a screen to the weak side. They'd be off and running. Sure, cornerback Mel Blount had theoretical responsibility for the weak-side short zone, but he'd be trying to prevent an inside release by the wide receiver and jamming him hard, trying to force him to the outside. Mel would have his back to the offense and wouldn't see the screen form until it was already there in full force— too late for Mel to beat the offensive lineman upfield. If, on the other hand, they called man-to-man coverage, I could easily make the play on a screen.

So in the second quarter, as we came off the field after our last series, Bud called us together and said, "Look, we can't be predictable. So we will rotate our checks every series. Use Saturday's checks this series and today's tunnel checks the following series. That ought to confuse them."

I thought to myself, "Right, Coach, but what about confusing us?" It was totally a unique concept. First, we were changing our defense (potentially as many as five times) every time the offense set up differently, all in a matter of a few seconds. Second, we would now change those checks, rotating them sequentially, every other series.

I doubt whether any team has executed such a complicated scheme prior to or since then. Many years later, my friend and former Steeler teammate Frank Atkinson invited me to a cocktail party at his home with Bill Walsh, then the Stanford coach following his amazing success at the 49ers. When I described what we had done, Walsh couldn't believe it. He realized that to do such a thing you would have to have a group of relatively intelligent athletes. I'm not talking physics here, but you'd have to have people who could remember all the cards in the deck and what had been played so far.

We had those types of guys on that defense. The other linebackers, Jack Ham and Jack Lambert, were both very smart and virtually never made mistakes. The safeties, Mike Wagner and Glen Edwards, were both savvy guys, as were the corners, J.T. Thomas and Mel Blount. The defensive linemen didn't have to worry about most of those changes.

That group had to remember that every time we came off the field we'd use another set of checks during the next series to adjust to the five or six sets that the Bengals would show us, with all those sets being shown on the same down before the ball had been snapped sometimes. It was also impossible for the middle linebacker to signal the changes because of the noise. Each player was responsible for knowing the automatics.

To do what Bud proposed was going against the philosophy of being in the best defense designed to stop the most likely tendency from that offensive formation. With us changing every series, Walsh wouldn't know what we were doing, but he might not care, choosing to attack what he perceived as any personnel weaknesses rather than a defensive set's weakness. Also, we would be forced to play defenses that might not be the best against the Bengals' tendencies.

In addition, it would not allow us the time to think about each formation's greatest tendency because we were too busy just trying to remember what defense to play. It also prevented us from recognizing more subtle keys, such as the opponent's positioning and body language.

Frankly, I think we had become too complex and that we would have been better off just attempting to predict Walsh's next play selection, call the best defense to stop that in the huddle, and execute it the old-fashioned way.

Against the undefeated Dolphins in the 1972 AFC championship game, the game following Franco's "Immaculate Reception," we used a defense called "Stack Over," and it hurt us so badly that we never used it again. I really believe that we had a better team than the Dolphins and that we should have won our first Super Bowl that year.

Terry Bradshaw had gone down to injury early in the game, and Terry Hanratty, who had not played all year, was forced to come in and move the team. Hanratty did a good job under the circumstances. Most importantly, he didn't make any big mistakes. Many people think we lost because of a fake punt that Miami executed effectively in the first half, but the score was still close at halftime.

Unfortunately, in the fourth quarter with the game on the line, we allowed them to run the ball down our throat, moving the sticks and taking time off the clock that our offense badly needed. The reason they moved the ball was that darn "Stack Over" defense, a defense that was first used by the Kansas City Chiefs against teams that had good outside running attacks. Granted, Miami had Mercury Morris as a wide threat, but in the crunch time, the Dolphins ran their strong fullback, Larry Csonka, right at us, up the middle.

The problem for us in the Stack Over was that it caused either Jack Ham or myself to be inside, lined up over a guard, an area referred to as the "bubble," a true mismatch in size and strength. Well, the Dolphins, seeing us in the Stack Over, began successfully running at the bubble late in the fourth quarter, eating up the clock, just barely moving the sticks and preventing our offense from staging a comeback.

Of course, Jack and I blamed ourselves for not being able to stop Csonka and not dealing better with the challenge of taking on a much larger guard, but I do think now, so many years later, that a major mistake in that loss to Miami was our sticking with the Stack Over. If we'd played our standard four-three, I think we would have won, but I guess we have to give the Dolphins some credit for taking advantage of our weakness. There were, of course, other factors that influenced that loss, but staying with the Stack Over was certainly a major contributor. The Dolphins won that game 21-17.

It was the last time we used the Stack Over, and we completely dominated the Dolphins' ground attack in future games in the seventies. After one Monday night game against them in Pittsburgh in 1976, I remember Don Shula being quoted as saying, "It's not much fun playing these Steelers. We can't even make a first down."

So against Dallas in Super Bowl X, executing a similar complicated strategy, we gave up the first touchdown, a crossing pattern to Drew Pearson, because a couple of guys missed the final check, the fifth one, before the ball was snapped. The reason this could happen might be because in a certain defense one might be responsible for denying the receiver an inside release, forcing him up and to the outside, rerouting him, so to speak. The problem with this is that to execute such a technique, one had to line up pretty much with their back to the backfield triangle, and if they moved one last time you wouldn't see it, because you definitely didn't want to be caught peeking back just as the ball was snapped, thus reacting late to the receiver's initial move.

In a big game, with a lot of noise, like Super Bowl X, you can't rely on calls from your teammates because you can't hear them. So every player is responsible for seeing and knowing the correct change. Clearly it became a little too complicated.

Sometimes the opponent could fool the coaches with comments in the paper or in interviews and we might design something special to take away their reported strategy.

Perhaps my career-worst game was against the Oakland Raiders in our 1976 AFC championship matchup. We had arguably our best team in '76, even though we didn't make it to the big dance. Terry Bradshaw was hurt for most of that year (after the Cleveland Browns' Turkey Jones had slammed him upside down, nearly breaking his neck) but the offense did well, with Mike Kruzak filling in ably for Terry and with both Rocky and Franco running for over 1,000 yards and keeping turnovers to a minimum.

The '76 defense was also on a roll, giving up only 28 points in the final nine games, with five shutouts—a truly astounding record. But you can't have shutouts if your offense is fumbling the ball or throwing interceptions for touchdowns. We were playing a very good Oakland team, a team that had beat us in our first game that year by throwing for a lot of yardage in the second half after trying unsuccessfully to run the ball in the first half.

Our '76 defense had played horribly in the first five games as the team won one and lost four. Most of the media, and the fans, believed that since we had won two Super Bowls in a row, that we were over-confident, cocky, busy checking our bank accounts (hardly), and too busy talking with our agents about promotional deals. The reverse was in fact the case.

We had worked harder that year than in any training camp, wanting to win three Super Bowls in a row, something no team had ever done. What went wrong? How could a team that good lose four out of its first five games?

When we analyzed the films of those losses, which incidentally were all against very good teams (Oakland, Minnesota, New England and Cleveland), our defense dominated the opponent on over 95 percent of the plays. The problem was that we gave up the big play for touchdowns on the other five percent, and this had nothing to do with a lack of effort. In fact, the films clearly showed that on nearly every occasion, one of our players had failed to execute his assignment because he was busting his butt to make a heroic play or to help out a teammate, over-playing something (guessing), being too aggressive, or just trying too hard.

I had broken a couple of fingers in that first game against Oakland, and the injury had frustrated me all year. Having to play with a makeshift cast to prevent further injury made executing certain techniques extremely difficult.

The Raiders came out in the papers and admitted that in the previous two playoff games against us they had wasted precious time trying to run the ball against our defense. Bud Carson, our defensive coordinator, was concerned that they had been so successful in that second half of the opener, passing nearly every down to come back and beat us, and rightly so. He had decided that we would come out and play each down as a passing down.

"So, Coach, what if I line up inside shoulder and they run the sweep?" I asked. "I'm dead meat."

"Don't worry about it—that'd be on us."

Well, the Raiders came out running, and we were totally discombobulated, unable to prevent them from moving the sticks, denying our offense the snaps they needed. Jack Ham and I, lining up inside Dave Casper, their excellent tight end, trying to prevent an inside release, forcing him outside for our pass coverage, were getting killed when they ran the sweep.

Well, actually, Ham never got blocked, not even when he lined up inside, giving the tight end a huge advantage. But I was really struggling, because Oakland was one of the few teams whose tendency was to be left-handed, running to their left, our right, most of the time. Casper was having a field day against me, because I was forced to line up inside and play all pass. I know I'm making excuses, but after all these years, it still bugs me.

Our coaches didn't adjust the strategy until halftime, but then the Raiders came out passing. With the Raiders down near our goal line, with the momentum clearly going their way, I felt certain they were going to run a sweep to our side, and I decided to penetrate upfield through the pulling guards' hole, hoping to avoid the fullback's block.

As I penetrated, I noticed the fullback ignored me as I ran by him and then realized too late that they had just run a play action pass and my man was the fullback. Too late. I was dead, the Raiders scored, and we lost.

Don't get me wrong, the Raiders were a very good football team and clearly outplayed our defense. I hated to retire on that game, because it was by far the worst playoff game I had ever played, but I deserved it, because I again became impatient, played too aggressively, and let my desire to win get in front of my brain.

A lot of people think that we lost that game because both Franco and Rocky were hurt, that we were forced to create a brand-new one-back offense, one that the Raiders had scouted through our Allegheny Club window so that they knew every play we were going to run before we ran it (Ray Mansfield claimed that the Raider defense had actually correctly called out the plays before the snap), but our defense had no excuse, other than that the right linebacker, Russell, played like a dog.

The examples of coaching tricks or mistakes are truly the exception. We wouldn't have won four out of six Super Bowls if our coaches continually made mistakes. In fact, most of the time they put us into excellent position to make plays, going with our strengths. But it is my failures that I remember most, still gnawing on me, surprised and embarrassed that we allowed weaker teams to prevail. Those opportunities to win a world championship were few and far between, and those losses still, to this day, irritate me. I tend to not remember our successes as vividly as our few disappointments.

Football is the ultimate chess game, with 22 pieces all moving at once, some incorrectly. We had great coaches who allowed us a lot of input into strategy, so if things didn't work, we players must share the blame.

CHAPTER SIX

The Super Bowl

Going to our first Super Bowl following the 1974 season was an incredible high. To get into the game we beat a very good Raider team, which I believe was the most important victory in Steeler history. It was the first AFC championship, the first win to get us to the big dance—a game against the Vikings in New Orleans, Super Bowl IX.

Most analysts thought that the Vikings were the favorite since they'd been there before and knew the ropes, thinking that we would be intimidated by all the Super Bowl hoopla.

But when we analyzed the Vikings, knowing we had beaten them soundly in 1972, we figured we could beat them again. However, we were anything but cocky. We just believed that we could, if we played our best, beat a good Viking team. I arrived in New Orleans with an attitude of "We're thrilled to be here, and if we win, all the better." Ray Mansfield and I had played on so many bad teams in the '60s that we found it difficult to believe that we could win a division title, let alone a Super Bowl. It was just hard for us to adjust our thinking and realize just how good our young superstars really were.

Having played in a number of bowl games (the Orange Bowl, the Bluebonnet Bowl, and the Pro Bowl), I had seen the hoopla and media and corporate attention, but I really couldn't imagine what it would be like at a Super Bowl.

Our first night in New Orleans, Coach Noll told us to go out and "get the city out of our system." It's interesting to note that the Vikings were held to a strict curfew the entire week, hidden far away in a hotel out near the airport and far from Bourbon Street. The Steelers would experience that great city and still get the job done when it counted. Of course, by Wednesday we were begging for a bed check.

That first night, Ray Mansfield and I tried to eat one oyster per year of our lives but only made it to a dozen, downing them with a few beers. It was a fun evening, and we enjoyed Bourbon Street to its fullest. When I finally hit the wall, I knew I needed to get back to the hotel.

The press was guessing that the Steelers were going to be harassed and potentially intimidated by the press, something the Vikings were used to. Ray and I arrived at the mandatory press expo in a ballroom of our hotel, each player getting his own table so he could be interviewed by various reporters from around the country. Ray and I sat at the same table and began to recount our journey from being so terrible in the '60s to the current superb team. Pretty soon I noticed that many of the reporters had moved to our table, probably because that was where most of the laughter was coming from. Winning is serious business. Losing because of horrible ineptitude can be funny. Ray was holding court—telling war stories and revealing past humiliations—and the press was eating it up.

"Are you fellas feeling intimidated by all this pregame hoopla?" one reporter asked.

"It just scares the piss out of me. You guys are so rough," Ray said.

"Seriously?" another asked.

"Well, actually I'm a little more concerned with Alan Page than worrying about you fellas," Ray said. "Hey, you want to hear about how bad it was in the '60s?"

"How bad was it?" one asked.

"It was so bad that when our defense would go out onto the field, the coach would say, 'Try and block the extra point,' and when our offense would go onto the field he'd tell us 'For God's sake, recover the fumble!'" Ray said.

"Actually, our offense was so bad that when they ran onto the field, we defensive guys would yell, 'See if you can hold them!' " I said.

Ray and I continued like that for nearly a half hour without any questions being asked.

When it came time for the press session to be over, they began gathering their notes and getting up to leave.

"Where are you going? Sit down, we've got a lot more stories to tell," Ray said.

So much for being intimidated by the press.

After the photo session, Ray and I sat next to each other on the bus back to the hotel.

"So, Ray, can we really beat the Vikings?"

"Absolutely."

"I wish we had bed check tonight. I'm exhausted."

"Don't worry so much. Coach knows what he's doing."

The next night, we returned to Bourbon Street, stopping at numerous watering holes. We ran into a lot of our teammates, but didn't see a single Viking. Were they taking the game more seriously than us? Would it matter?

The atmosphere of a Super Bowl was nothing I was familiar with. We weren't there to have fun. We were on a mission to win our first Super Bowl and felt the need to resist any distractions. But those distractions were everywhere, even the locker room.

After the first practice, I was approached by a representative of Puma Shoes, who asked if I would be willing to wear a new pair of Pumas in the game. He offered me free jogging shoes if I would try their new shoe. All of my teammates were getting similar offers. I told the rep that I would not wear any shoe other than the one I had worn all year, the shoe that had gotten me there, Adidas.

Later that night I met a guy in a bar who also seemed to be enjoying the party atmosphere.

"Would you wear our Riddell shoes?" he opened.

"No way, I'm sticking with my Adidas," I said

"You can have this nice watch if you'll wear our shoes," he said.

"Can't do it—got to use the shoes I've worn all year."

In the end, the guy gave me the watch anyway, and the next day Puma had upped their offer to a free hi-fi system. It was getting out of control.

The following day, the Adidas rep promised a free television set if I'd continue to wear their shoe instead of any other in the game.

That week we had excellent practices, each player understanding the importance of being intensely involved in the game plan, eliminating mistakes, executing quality techniques, and giving our all to get ready. The only concern I had was that we might be ready to play the game on Wednesday, with our energy declining by Sunday.

In the end, wearing my Adidas in pregame warmup, on a wet and cold Tulane Stadium artificial surface, I found it difficult to not slip and slide. When we returned to the locker room, Tony Parisi, our equipment manager, had a new Canadian shoe ready for us that had many small cleats—

ideal for wet, slippery days. I switched immediately, hoping they could improve the traction. Obviously, winning that championship ring was far more important than being loyal to Adidas or even getting a free TV.

Of course, you don't win Super Bowls by successfully dealing with the media or by making equipment changes. Big games are won by great athletes making big plays.

The images I have of that first Super Bowl win are still vivid in my mind: Jack Lambert getting hurt early and being replaced by Ed Bradley, who filled in for Jack exceptionally well; Pine Edwards making a huge hit on a Viking receiver near our end zone and Mel Blount intercepting the deflection; our guys tackling Fran Tarkenton in the end zone for a safety; Joe Greene blocking the extra point; L. C. Greenwood continually getting upfield and knocking Tarkenton's passes down; Dwight White coming out of the hospital to play well despite a bad case of flu; Franco breaking the Super Bowl rushing record against a very good Viking defense; Rocky making big yardage when it really counted; Larry Brown catching one of Terry's bullets for a key touchdown with the sound ricocheting off his shoulder pads; getting hurt myself late in the third quarter and being replaced by Loren Toews, who did a great job; and, finally, Ray Mansfield and a few others carrying Coach Noll off of the field on their shoulders.

There are too many important moments in that game to try and recapture them all in one paragraph. In fact, every play was critical, and even those plays that appeared to the fans as totally unremarkable were the result of a number of players executing their techniques and assignments at the highest level.

Being injured was only a big deal to me. It happened on a play where I had correctly anticipated the play to make—what I thought would be an easy tackle—only to almost miss the Viking fullback, Chuck Foreman, when he made an unbelievably quick cut back inside. Completely faked out, I was only able to swing my left knee at him, trying to chop him down with my leg.

This awkward maneuver worked, because Foreman went down in the backfield, fumbling the ball, and Joe Greene recovered. The officials made an incorrect call and gave the ball back to the Vikings. It would have been a huge play, giving us the ball in Viking territory. Unfortunately, Foreman's knee struck the middle of my thigh so hard that the blow bruised the bone and nerve and my leg went numb, the classic "charley horse."

I got up and played the next play but realized the best I could do was limp around, way below full speed. I hated to come out of the game. I had waited my entire career to get into a Super Bowl, but I knew that I had to fight letting pride get in the way of my brain.

Okay. I have to admit it. I am not a particularly humble person. I am a proud man, perhaps a little headstrong, someone who believes in himself and who hates to make mistakes and fail.

"Humble is overrated," I once told my ex-wife, Nancy.

"How would you know?" was her quick reply.

Having a healthy ego, being confident, isn't the same thing as being obnoxiously conceited or egocentric or arrogant, all of which are bad. I suspect all of those Steelers back in the '70s had healthy egos, but we knew that it was important to appreciate other people and their contributions.

With that said, I always found the game very humbling. Watching Jack Ham's superb play humbled me; watching Lynn Swan's incredible athleticism humbled me; all my teammates' and our opponents' play often humbled me—but I am still proud of what I was able to contribute to the team effort.

One thing I am proud of in my football career is that I forced myself to play hurt. I played with a broken big toe, a bad heel bruise, badly sprained ankle ligaments, a torn calf muscle, partially torn cartilage in my knee, torn hamstrings, bruised thighs, torn groin muscles, hip pointers, bruised ribs, a bruised lung, torn stomach muscles, bad lower back, bruised sternum, partially torn rotator cuff, hyper-extended and hyper-flexed elbows, broken thumbs, broken fingers, sprained wrists, sore neck, multiple abrasions, and at least ten concussions.

Some people would say that playing with those injuries was downright stupid. To me it was a badge of honor, demonstrating commitment, effort and a willingness to sacrifice my body for my teammates. Most of them felt the same way.

Playing hurt was not unusual in those days. Ray Mansfield played with broken ribs and a broken neck; Jack Ham played with a bad ankle; Mike Wagner played with a neck fracture; Jack Lambert played with turf toe. Everyone played hurt, and most players who played more than a few years dealt with similar physical problems.

I never missed a game in my entire career—high school, college, military or pro, over twenty years of football. But frankly, I must admit, that record is slightly bogus. There was a time where I cheated and put myself in for an extra point, my only play in the game, just to keep my "never missing a game" record in tact. It was my last year; we were playing in New York against the Giants. We had a big lead and had just scored again. I figured I could sneak in without anyone noticing or caring.

Despite a torn groin muscle that I shouldn't have risked reinjuring, I entered the game and replaced the out back on the extra-point team. At the snap, unwilling to really push off with that leg, I inserted myself in front of a Giant player who ran right over me, almost blocking the extra point with the back of my head. The coaches enjoyed running that play over and over again, showing my complete annihilation, with the whole team enjoying my ineptitude. Hey, I didn't care. It kept my streak alive.

People are always talking about someone's pain threshold. I don't believe people feel pain differently. If you gave a high-pain-threshold person and a low-pain-threshold person the exact same injury, I believe they would feel it the same way. The difference between the two is attitude. I always figured that injuries could be avoided with three things: being in very good shape, knowing what play the opponent is running and who is responsible for blocking me, and having a lot of good luck. Not necessarily in that order, of course.

I should mention that the injuries mentioned above were the good ones. I was hugely fortunate to not have the devastating career-ending injury, such as a broken leg, a destroyed knee, or a massive concussion. Believe me, we all worried about the total blowout in which there would be absolutely no possibility of playing hurt, just a trip to the hospital and the operating room.

But my injury in the first Super Bowl was bad, and I knew instantly that I could not play even at half-speed. This was no time for my ego to take over. I could have hurt the team by staying in the game and potentially give up the big play. So I waved over to the sideline for Loren Toews to come in. He was a gifted athlete and a smart, tough player. It was the right thing to do, because Loren made some big plays in the fourth quarter with the game on the line.

After the game the locker room was surprisingly subdued. We were all quietly congratulating each other, but there was no champagne over anyone's head or wild and crazy over-exuberance, as some might expect. I felt quietly sublime, somehow more complete, thrilled to be a part of such a great team that had finally reached the top of the mountain. We were world champions, at least for a year, and no one could take that away from us.

Arriving later that night at the Steelers' private party in a big New Orleans hotel ballroom, I was impressed by the number of security people checking to make sure that no uninvited guests got in. But as soon as my wife and I got our first glasses of victory bubbly, we were approached by one of the country's most famous uninvited guests, "Jerry the Gate Crasher." I had seen Jerry at many private sports parties—at the Pro Bowl, at the American Airlines Golf Classic, at the NFL alumni parties and at many others. It never occurred to me that Jerry could get into our private Steeler post-Super Bowl party, but there he was.

"Hi, folks, great game!" he said.

"Thanks, Jerry," I said. "I don't want to be rude, but how the hell did you get in here?"

"No challenge—just came through the kitchen. Only cost me a few bucks," Jerry said.

The party was fun but couldn't possibly live up to the highlight of the day, finally winning the ultimate trophy in the game. We were all tired and feeling very peaceful, basking in the glory of being part of such a successful effort. We reflected on the amazing journey, the ups and downs of the year, the big wins and the losses. We also met some of the family members of our teammates. I remember limping around the dance floor with one of Ray Mansfield's sisters, who, of course, was extremely proud of her brother's accomplishments. Ray was clearly one of the leaders of our very underrated offensive line.

The next day, hung over from too much celebration, those of us going to the Pro Bowl got on the plane to Miami, while the rest of the team went back to Pittsburgh for a first-ever Victory Parade, something we all hated to miss.

That first night, with my leg stiffening up and aching, I decided to go for a long walk. Unlike many of today's players, who seem more interested in being selected to the Pro Bowl but not in actually playing in the game, I wanted to play. To me, a Pro Bowl selection was one of the finest individual honors that an NFL player could receive, and playing the game seemed important.

Why? Because the players and coaches chose the Pro Bowl, not the press, who tend to only recognize big plays. Players and coaches watch game films intensely and see who consistently executes his assignments, especially noting those players who they have to make special accommodation for—like a double team.

Of course, the system isn't perfect, and even coaches and players could have their favorites. The old rule was that you had to have two good years in a row before you'd get selected—to sort of prove you were for real. Probably my best year, at least big-play wise, was 1967, but I was not selected until the next year. Today the system involves the fans, which I think is a mistake—they typically know even less than the press.

I limped around all week, but finally my leg came around and I was able to play. We were taught that the best way to avoid injury was to go full speed—playing safe in any game, particularly the Pro Bowl, with so many talented players, could be dangerous. Coach Noll would often tell us, "There is only one way to coast—downhill." Also, giving less than your best would be disrespectful to the game.

The following year we would return to the Super Bowl, this time in Miami's Orange Bowl against the Dallas Cowboys. Lynn Swann would make two of the most amazing catches I have ever seen—one where he somehow kept his feet in bounds despite his body being out, and the other, the famous catch where he bobbles it as he is falling down. The Cowboys shut our vaunted running game down, but our passing game buried Dallas. Terry Bradshaw would throw a TD pass a nanosecond before he was hit, sustaining a concussion bad enough to keep him out of the Pro Bowl. Our defense played well, stifling Dallas for the most part, with Mike Wagner and Glen Edwards making key interceptions late in the game.

It was hard for me to imagine, two Super Bowl victories in a row, after all those years of humiliating incompetence. Ray Mansfield, Sam Davis, Bobby Walden, Rocky Bleier and myself were the only players from the pre-Noll era to make that long journey from total failure to the top of the world.

CHAPTER SEVEN

Super Teams

After winning that Super Bowl, a number of us were invited to Hawaii to participate in the "Super Teams" competition, a made-for-television event in which the Super Bowl teams competed against each other in various events (swimming, running, obstacle course, volleyball, war canoe race, bicycle race, and tug-of-war). The winners would go on to compete in the finals against the winner of the two World Series teams.

We lost that "Super Teams" competition, beaten by the Vikings in the final event, a grueling seventeen minute tug-of-war which left us lying on the beach gasping for air, angry at losing and feeling slightly humiliated. We all knew it shouldn't have come down to the last event, since we had won the track race by over 100 yards but had been disqualified.

Franco, surprising the Vikings with his pure speed, had taken his time getting off the track after handing the baton to Rocky, who was far ahead of his Viking competitor. Despite being completely out of the race, the Vikings argued successfully that Franco had impeded their runner's forward progress, and we were disqualified. It was a bogus ruling, but it stood. Had we won that race, the tug-of-war would have been meaningless. Ray Mansfield and I, acting as team captains, should have argued more aggressively with the event officials. Our reluctance cost us all a lot of money and some injured pride. Later the Vikings experienced the final indignity by losing the tug-of-war and the championship to the baseball team.

The following year, we boarded a charter flight in Pittsburgh already occupied by the Boston Red Sox. We stopped to pick up the Reds in Cincinnati and the Cowboys in Dallas, and we were in a very festive mood. However, when Pete Rose cockily walked down the aisle assuring the football players that the Reds were about to "kick our butts," everything changed. He stirred our competitive juices, and this trip instantly went from a lark to a serious, personal challenge. We didn't want to lose again, especially not to baseball players. I also made a mental note that we would not be beaten by being out-negotiated if any disputes arose.

Sure enough, the very first event was controversial. It was the swimming relay race, which we had barely won. Lee Roy Jordan, the Dallas middle linebacker and captain, filed a protest, claiming that our swimmers dove into the pool before their teammates had touched the wall.

While walking to the TV trailer to watch the instant replays, I was concerned that Lee Roy might be correct. Just prior to the race, a Hawaiian spectator came up to me and introduced himself as a local high school swimming coach and a huge Steeler fan. He offered a tip that could help us win. He said that the next swimmer should dive in when the person in the water was one stroke away from touching the wall, because by the time his feet actually left the platform, his teammate would have completed that last stroke and touched the wall. Most beginners, like us, would wait until the swimmer actually touched the wall before diving in.

Realizing that this tip could save us precious seconds, I relayed the information to each swimmer on the Steeler team. After all, we wanted our shot at "Mr. Hustle," Pete Rose. As it turned out, we were incredibly even with the Cowboys during the race. Lee Roy noticed that despite his guys approaching the wall with our swimmers, we consistently got an edge with our dives. He naturally concluded that we cheated.

As I sat down with Lee Roy and the official to watch the race, I worried that the Hawaiian was really a Cowboys fan who may have intentionally misled me. Fortunately, the replays clearly showed our feet still on the platform (just barely) as our teammates' hands touched the wall.

Our next key event was the track relay race. No one wanted to run the 440-yard part of the race (the last leg), but I was convinced that Lynn Swann was our best track runner. The previous year, Mel Blount had run the 440 well, and Swann had run the 220. Swann seemed the superior track racer because of his fluid grace and relaxed running motion and therefore was less likely to bind up in the stretch if the race was close. Swann wanted nothing to do with the 440, but I finally harassed him into it. Swann received the baton almost even with the Cowboy runner, Cliff Harris, for the final leg of the relay. Unfortunately, Harris proceeded to run a miraculous 49-second 440, beating Swann easily. Of course, Lynn set the all-time record in the obstacle course, enabling us to win that event.

We went on to narrowly defeat the Cowboys and advance to the final against Pete Rose and his Reds, who had prevailed against Boston.

The last day, we found ourselves needing to win two of the final three events: volleyball, war canoe and tug-of-war. Since the baseball players were so much lighter, we doubted we could beat them in the war canoe race, as their canoe would ride higher in the water, skimming along the surface. Our boat had nearly sunk the year before with Fats Holmes and Ray Mansfield rowing in the rear. One of the native Hawaiians had said we performed amazingly well for a submarine.

It was important that we win the volleyball, where we had a significant height advantage, leaving the championship to the tug-of-war, where we should have a strength advantage.

Well, we lost the volleyball because of bonehead mistakes. We all played too aggressively, making lots of impressive smashes but inadvertently hitting the net with our follow-through, thus losing the point. The Reds, recognizing early that we were going to make lots of unforced errors, went into a cautious defensive posture and won easily. I thought we were dead in the water because of our weight problem in the war canoe.

Despite putting all our lighter guys in the race, we were still going to be much heavier than the Reds' team. The race, held in a small lagoon, required each boat to make four laps around two buoys, positioned about one hundred yards apart. We realized it was crucial that we have someone call out the stroke so that we would be synchronized. Being the captain, I got stuck with the job. We all pledged to pull as hard as we could for the four laps, regardless of how far we got behind; maybe the baseball players would swing too wide on one of the turns. Despite everyone's enthusiastic, "we can do this" attitude, I really didn't believe we could win.

As the starting gun went off, I began to shout the call for each stroke, yelling encouragement in between. Immediately the Reds shot out in front, first by half a boat, then a full boat, and soon by two boat lengths. We were getting waxed. By the time we completed the second lap, I was nearing exhaustion from the hard stroking and just hoping I could hang on for another two laps. My fatigue made my stroke call barely audible, and we were getting out of synch since the guys in front couldn't hear me.

Just then, Franco jumped in and saved us. His energy and strength, far surpassing mine, enabled him to call the stroke signal loudly and precisely at the right moment. Immediately our canoe surged forward and began to gain on the Reds, who had widened their lead to about two and a half boat lengths.

Franco urged us forward, "Come on! We can do this! *Pull!* We aren't going to lose! *Pull!* They're getting tired! *Pull!* They're not as strong as we are! *Pull!* We're gaining on them! *Pull!* We can do it!" I looked up and noticed that we had closed some more of the gap.

As we went into the last turn around the last buoy for the straightaway to the finish, the Reds' steerer made a mistake and their boat veered out too far. At the same moment, Rocky, our steerer, made his best turn yet and we came out of the turn dead even. With 100 yards to the finish, we pulled with everything we had left, which wasn't a whole lot in my case.

Franco's voice rose above all the noise from the crowd and the shouts of panic from the Reds. "*Pull!* I want all you got! *Pull!* Don't quit now! *Pull! Pull! Pull!*"

Our boat moved slightly ahead, and we held them off for the win. Bending over, feeling nauseous and trying to get my breath back, I knew I had made the right decision in announcing my retirement earlier that year. It was time—as Franco did that day—for my younger, stronger teammates to step up and lead this team in whatever challenges it had to face in coming years.

After lunch we lined up on the beach, surrounded by a huge crowd, for the final, championship-deciding event, the tug-of-war. The rules allowed as many men as we wanted on the rope as long as the combined weight did not exceed 1,500 pounds. We knew that the previous year the Vikings had lost because they chose their strongest—but heaviest—athletes and were only able to have six men against eight. Clearly, eight sets of legs and arms will beat six, regardless of disparate levels of strength. By again using our lightest athletes, we were barely able to man a team of seven. In fact, we had to take off our sweat suits initially, because we were a collective 1,502 pounds. The Reds, apparently unaware of the importance of having an extra man and wanting to use Johnny Bench as their anchor, also chose to go with seven men, but with less total weight—1,480 pounds.

There in the front was Mr. Antagonist himself, Pete Rose. He was grinning cockily across at Franco, who positioned himself in our front. When the flag was dropped to start the contest, we kept our feet in the sand. The Reds slipped onto their backsides, and we pulled them across into the mud in a record seven seconds. I will never forget the look of disbelief on Pete Rose's face as he was pulled headfirst into the pile of mud separating the two teams. Victory, even in a made-for-television event, is always sweet.

CHAPTER EIGHT

Paria Canyon

A few years after I retired, a group of us took a journey down Utah's Paria Canyon, wading thigh-deep in water and mud for forty miles, ignoring blisters and sore, aching legs. Top off the physical challenge by sleeping on the ground and eating freeze-dried food for three nights, and you might appreciate our discomfort. Why, you might ask, would we voluntarily choose to do something that was so unpleasant, so hard, when most of our friends think "roughing it" means staying at a Marriott? Wilderness challenges reminded us of something Chuck Noll used to say: "Nothing worthwhile is easy." Difficulty often brings out our best.

It was the mid-'80s, and Ray Mansfield and I were still trying to replace football, a challenge that dominated our lives for more than twenty-five years. After retiring from the Steelers in 1976, we were still finding it difficult to find a substitute for the game.

We didn't want to admit that we were getting older, that we had lost more than a step or two, or that old injuries and declining strength might make difficult physical challenges almost undoable—all of which were true. For most of our lives we had been required to get in shape for the football season, and we figured that we still needed to set goals that would force us to work out.

The Paria is one of Utah's many rugged but stunningly beautiful canyons. It drains down into the Grand Canyon, intersecting the Colorado

River at Lee's Ferry, not far down from the Glen Canyon Dam at Lake Powell. It can be entered either through the Upper Paria or the more difficult Buckskin Gulch, a gnarly twelve-mile crack canyon, where the walls pinch in to only a few feet wide. The canyon is so narrow that it's sometimes difficult to squeeze your backpack through the space. Naturally we chose the Buckskin.

Our group consisted of two dear friends, veterans of many of our Grand Canyon hikes, Jack Musgrave and Sam Zacharias; Jerry Prado, a good friend and former business partner; Rick Mueller, a young buck lawyer from Jack's firm; and two young men from the *Pittsburgh Press* (there to do a story for the Sunday supplement), writer Bill Utterback and photographer Randy Olson.

When I learned that the *Press* wanted to do a story (the obvious theme of which was to be two old washed-up jocks trying to replace football), I called them and warned the editor that it would be extremely difficult hiking and that they shouldn't send anyone out of shape. He assured me that they would send a young and strong twosome.

I had known Jack "Musky" Musgrave since 1959, our freshman year at the University of Missouri. Jack had made All-St. Louis and All-State as a high school football player and had been recruited aggressively by Dan Devine, the University of Missouri's head coach. We have been pals ever since. Jack is now the managing partner of one of St. Louis's largest law firms.

Sam Zacharias, the other veteran hiker, my partner since 1969, helped me keep my fledgling business alive while I was still playing with the Steelers. Sam has a very successful insurance business, is the president of the Pitt University Alumni, helps lots of charities and still has found time to drive our offshore business. Unlike Jack, Sam was a nonathlete who had never tested himself physically until Ray and I retired and pushed him to join us on various wilderness tests. Sam is mentally tough and always unrelenting in pursuit of his goals, but he was still learning that those same attributes would help him persevere in the wilds.

Jerry Prado, who ran our investment bank's (Russell, Rea & Zappala-RR&Z) LBO fund, was a CPA and the CFO of G. C. Murphy when Ames Department Stores acquired Murphy. RR&Z was lucky enough to hire him, and he did a spectacular job running our first private equity fund. Jerry left us to help solve some of Westinghouse Credit problems, and he made a name for himself as a turnaround guru, eventually starting his own fund. We remained good friends, and I urged him to participate in his first wilderness adventure despite some serious reluctance on his part.

The other newcomers on our team, Rick Mueller, Randy Olsen and Bill Utterback, were unknowns. How would they react to the misery, the pain, and the fatigue? Some people never learn that they have the toughness to keep going, to gut it out when they are hurting. However, they were all significantly younger—young is good.

Having spent the night in a motel on the rim of the canyon, we left our van at the Lee's Ferry takeout (on the bottom of the Grand Canyon), hopefully our finishing point in four days. There we met our shuttle driver, Fred, at 6:00 a.m. and drove through Page, Arizona, across the Glen Canyon Dam and up into Utah. It would take us about an hour to get to the trailhead.

I sat in the front seat, staring at the rugged Utah countryside, noticing buttes, mesas, gulches, side canyons and other difficult terrain.

"So, Fred, you ever hike the Paria?" I asked.

"No way, just occasionally shuttle folks like yourselves. Sure there ain't no rain coming?" he said.

"The weather looks good for the next week," Musky said.

"Can't say I'm thrilled that our lives depend on some weatherman," Sam said.

"Only job in the world where you get paid to be wrong most of the time," Ray said.

"How many people choose the Buckskin Gulch?" I asked.

"I've only been out to the Buckskin once before. Most folks do the Paria Narrows—a lot easier," Fred said.

"Great, we sure don't want to do anything easy," Jerry deadpanned.

"Right, easy is bad," Ray agreed.

We turned off the paved highway onto a washboard gravel road with a vast, open vista of flat-top mesas, towering cliffs, and side canyons showing a kaleidoscope of rich colors—red and pink from the iron deposits, the yellow sandstones, the orange and green of the lichen, and a sky as blue as the finest turquoise that the Navahos sold in the dilapidated shops we passed on our way from Flagstaff to Page. The only vegetation was various types of cacti, tumbleweed and small scrub pines.

Around 7 a.m. the driver stopped the van in a barren but open area butting up against a small dry desert wash, maybe twenty-five to thirty feet across, with crumbling banks. In the distance, up the wash, we could see more mesas and the beginning of canyon walls.

"Well, fellas, this here's as far as I go. Can't drive up this here wash. This vehicle don't have no four-wheel drive," Fred told us.

"So where's the Gulch?" I asked.

"Walk up the wash and you'll see a small gap, 'bout a mile up on the right—the only spot where you can climb down into the gulch. Keep your eye out for it. Be easy to miss."

I noticed that the two *Press* youngsters, Olson and Utterback, were strapping on enormous backpacks, clearly weighing more than we had recommended. Randy, the photographer, had twenty pounds extra of camera gear. We wondered how they would deal with the challenges of one of our most demanding treks.

About a half-hour later, after hiking up an easy grade while staying in the dry creek bed, we found a small opening, maybe four feet wide, between a boulder and a rock wall. The opening dropped down about ten feet to the sand floor of a gully leading to another rock wall, where it curved right out of sight.

We took advantage of a large log, apparently put there by a hiking group, to help us climb down into the gulch. We quickly discovered that it's difficult to climb vertically with a fifty-pound backpack.

"This is it, guys. Let's go. We've got a lot of miles before we reach the campsite," I said.

"Relax. Don't want to hear you bitching all day about how slow we're going," Ray said.

We started off down the Buckskin, winding down the slot, trying to avoid the water and mud when possible. The sun was still low, and we felt a cool breeze. Within a quarter of a mile, the gulch had narrowed to about eight feet, and we realized that walking in the water and mud would be unavoidable.

An hour later, we stopped for a rest, waiting for the team to regroup. Ray threw his pack down and started walking back up the gulch to help the media guys, who were struggling to carry their eighty-pound packs.

"Hey, Ray, you're just helping because you want more ink in the article. Never helped me," Sam joked.

"It always pays to be nice to the press."

As always, Ray was looking out for the other people he thought might need help, cheering them on just as he had our teammates so many years ago. Within five minutes, Ray came around the corner, helping Bill and Randy with their gear.

"Guys, we need to pick up our pace, or we'll end up spending a very uncomfortable night on the gulch floor," I said.

"Don't worry about it. It'll be a starry night, and we'll be able to see just fine," Ray said.

Back on the march, sometimes in complete shade, others in the bright sunlight, with the temperature climbing, I imagined the stress of my Pittsburgh life leaving my body, floating up the towering canyon walls, up into the azure sky. Maybe Ray was right. What did it matter when we got there?

High above us, the sky was still dark blue with a few lacy white clouds floating by. The walls were reddish orange and smooth. There were no ledges or handholds to use to climb out if we had a sudden rain shower. There were also no side canyons emptying into the Buckskin, only small gullies high above.

At noon, we settled in for lunch on a rock shelf, sitting with our backs against the high wall, legs stretched out in front of us.

"Hey, this is tough slogging. Hard to pull your boots out of the mud, up through the water and maintain any momentum," Musky said.

"This mud literally sucks," Sam said.

"But the tougher the better, right, Old Ranger?" Musky asked, referring to Ray's Steeler nickname.

"You got that right."

"It just doesn't get any better than this," Jerry said.

After a quick lunch, I jumped up and pulled on my pack, hoping that everyone would notice that it was time to leave, but no one even glanced up at me.

"Gotta get movin', fellas, we still got a long way to go," I urged.

"We'll get there when we get there," Ray said.

I sometimes found myself lost in the rhythm of the motion, enjoying the anticipation of waiting to see what was around the next bend. We had planned on stopping for rest every hour, but since we were moving so slowly, I just kept pushing on. My legs were already feeling heavy, and I knew we'd all be whipped by nightfall.

Unlike other hikes we'd been on, where our view remained unchanged for hours on end, here we were entertained with new towering walls and narrowing passages every 20 yards or so. Every step was interesting, and I didn't focus on my fatigue as I had in other hikes.

By 5 p.m. we spotted a sandy dune to our left. It was the first place we had seen where one might be able to climb out of the gulch. We all scrambled up twenty feet to a sandy ledge large enough for our tents and quickly set up camp, cooking our dinners on our small gas stoves. Ray grilled some Spam for our pita bread, and I cooked some chicken soup. After a carb-loaded dinner, we sat with our backs against the rock wall, staring up at the rapidly darkening sky.

"This place is amazing," Ray said.

"This damn gulch kicked my butt," Sam said. "Hope it gets easier tomorrow. My legs are killing me."

"It won't. Enjoy the pain."

"It doesn't get any better than this," Jerry said.

Jack reached in his backpack and pulled out a fifth of his favorite Irish whiskey, Bushmills, and offered it around. Within a half an hour it was all gone, and guys started to drift off to their tents.

Now it was only Ray and me talking about our lives and reliving the good old days despite our fatigue, enjoying each other's companionship, good whiskey and old stories. Ray reached into his pack and pulled out a small flask.

"What you got there, Bud?"

"Some fine single-malt scotch. Thought you might like a nightcap."

"Why do we relish these tough hikes, almost enjoying the pain?" I wondered.

"We're just odd that way."

"Maybe we feel we aren't tough unless we prove ourselves in the wilds."

"You might be onto something there, Pards. Some sense that making your living with your brain isn't very studly," Ray said.

We sat there for quite a while without talking, staring up at the most brilliant, star-studded sky that we'd ever seen, neither caring that it was already past ten.

"I think our need to hurt ourselves has more to do with missing the game," Ray said.

"Are you telling me that you miss the pain of football?"

"I loved the challenge, and pain was part of it. It gave us contrast and made the good times even more meaningful," Ray said.

"Business is different. Takes a long time before a deal closes. In football we always had instant feedback. Game films don't lie."

"Right, selling insurance just doesn't get my juices going like going head-to-head with Butkus. Incidentally, I owned Butkus," Ray said.

"Why did Butkus look like he was All-World against us?"

"Believe me, I owned the guy."

"Why was football such a rush? Was it the fear of getting beat or getting hurt, the danger, or the high of making a big play with the game on the line?" I said.

"Personally, I liked kicking people's butts."

"I know one thing. We can't spend the rest of our lives living in the past, always recalling the good old days. We got to live in the here and now, and, as you so frequently remind me, enjoy the moment," I said.

"Hey, I'm bushed; let's hit the sack," Ray said, our soul-searching now complete.

The next morning we were up and back on the floor of the gulch early. Within a few hundred meters of the campsite, the gulch began to narrow to five or six feet.

Our group moved slowly through the deep mud and standing water, feeling achy from the previous day. The walls pinched further in. The chasm turned back and forth, snakelike, always giving us a new challenge every thirty feet or so: climbing over large boulders, struggling through thick, gooey mud, avoiding a deep pool of water, just trying to get our scraggly butts down the gulch.

We plodded along steadily, silent, wondering how much worse it could get. Within half a mile the walls had pinched in so tight that we had trouble fitting our backpacks between them. At one point, we had to take them off and turn them sideways to go through the eighteen-inch gap.

"I feel like I should whisper down here. It feels like a cathedral," Sam said.

"God built this church," Ray said.

For nearly a mile we struggled through a chasm no wider than three or four feet, watching the water rise up our thighs.

Rick, up ahead, shouted back to us, "It's tippy-toe time."

Soon the water was at my crotch. Jerry, Sam and Randy, being slightly shorter, were dealing with water up to their navels.

The bottom was mucky and slippery, but also slanted against the left wall, where the water was nearly chest-high. This made for tough slogging, but we pushed on, slowly making progress, saying very little. I often stared up towards the sliver of sky. There wasn't much light, since the early morning sun was barely able to penetrate down so deep.

"Damn, Russell, didn't know we were going spelunking," Jerry said.

"Maybe we should have brought headlamps," Sam said.

"If the water gets any deeper, we'll need a snorkel," Musky said.

"I was hoping it would be higher, up around our shoulders—make it a lot tougher," Ray said.

"You really are sick," Jerry said.

Sam, clearly struggling, said, "I had no idea that it would be this hard. I guess carrying a backpack around Mount Lebanon twice a week just doesn't cut it."

"You got that right," Ray said.

"It doesn't get any better than this."

Soon we came to the Buckskin Gulch's only potentially dangerous obstacle, a shelf that dropped twenty feet to the gulch floor. In the wet season it would be a waterfall, but the water was trapped in standing pools behind us. We searched for the way down, eventually finding a large rock slab that had broken off from the wall above on the left side.

Ray dug into his pack and found our only rope, a simple laundry rope, and sat there trying different methods of leverage—around his waist or over his shoulder. With no pitons, chocks or blocks to secure the rope and no place to brace his feet, it would be a dangerous belay.

Rick quickly found the indentations cut into the slab of rock, mentioned in our guidebook, which were supposed to help us down.

Deciding to lower all the packs with the rope and climb unfettered, Ray threw me the end of the rope, and I tied it around my chest, under my armpits.

As I inched out over the edge of the rock, more squared-off than rounded, searching for the first foothold, Ray braced himself in case I fell. My palms were sweaty, and I was feeling the exposure.

Ray let out lengths of the rope, and I found the first few cuts in the rock weren't very deep.

"Don't fall. I haven't done a twenty-foot swan dive since I was a kid," Ray said.

"I'm not going to fall," I said, despite feeling very insecure.

"Guys, this doesn't seem like a smart move," Sam said.

"When I get down, I can direct you where to put your feet. It'll be a lot easier," I said, as I strained to see the next foothold beneath me.

"Be careful, we don't need any accidents out here," Musky said.

"I'm not worried. I know the Old Ranger can hold me."

"Well, maybe, but who the hell is going to help me, after I've lowered all you assholes down?"

"Good question," Sam said, as he and Randy began searching for another way down.

Finally I reached a point about six feet above the sandy rock floor below me and jumped, landing comfortably.

Rick started to tie up next.

"Look, I'm not real thrilled about this, and I'm ready to go right now, so let me get this over with," Jerry said.

"You're not afraid of heights, are you? Rick asked.

"No, it's not heights or falling that bother me. It's that sudden stop at the bottom that I'm worried about."

Minutes later, with me helping Jerry find the footholds, he was down. But as Rick roped up, Randy discovered a small chute in the ledge to the right of our rock slab that looked as if one could slide down through it, and he asked if we could grab his feet and prevent him from falling as he slid down.

After much discussion, Sam, the first guinea pig, came slowly down through the crack with Jerry and me grabbing his feet and legs to help him the last eight feet or so. It was clearly the least threatening way to get down, but I worried that Ray might not fit through the narrow chute. Even if he could, would Jerry and I be able to catch him when he let go and allowed gravity to take control of his 280 pounds?

Minutes later, it was Ray's turn.

"Russell, this could be your most important tackle ever. Don't miss. Keep your eyes open," Ray said.

He exited the chute quickly, free-falling the last eight feet and knocking Jerry and me to our knees, but we were all down and there were no injuries.

Within a mile we reached the intersection of the Paria and soon were walking down a real river, the water flowing slowly down towards the Colorado River, with the walls being higher and wider. The Paria River was running clear but with little force, as the incline was only slight.

Since the river was often snug against one of the cliff walls on either side, we were forced to hike back and forth across the river, but we made good progress. We began searching for a clear spring to refresh our water supply. It was shown on the map as a mile before our first significant landmark, a narrow side canyon on the left and a cave on the right. Unfortunately, we missed the spring but found the cave, known as "The Hole." We stopped for a lunch and a good rest. We had run out of water by early morning, so we were forced to use our filters and treat the Paria water with iodine tablets.

"Did you see that deer poop in the shallow water back up the river?" Jerry asked.

"Don't worry about it. Deer shit just adds flavor," Ray said.

Sitting on the other side of the river with our backs to a major side canyon, I stared across at The Hole, wondering what mysteries it held.

After lunch, Ray and I walked across the river to explore the cave. Entering the hole, we realized that it wasn't a cave but just a large room caused by a deep indentation of the cliff base, against which huge sloping rocks and boulders leaned. It felt as though we had entered a private chapel, where a single beam of sunlight came through a small hole above, filtering off the rocks and reflecting reds, pinks, and purples.

Water was seeping down from a spring above, trickling quietly through moss, ending up in a small pool of water at our feet; on one side there were some tadpoles and frogs.

I could almost feel the presence of those Indians and pioneers who had first sought shelter here. It was quiet except for the melodious trickle of the water down through the moss and rocks.

"Wow, this place is spooky," Ray said.

"Try to imagine some of the stuff that's happened here," I said.

I stood there, reluctant to leave. I tried to absorb the spirituality of the cavern before returning to the other side, where we encouraged the others to visit The Hole.

The Paria Canyon provided us with a dramatically different landscape than the Buckskin Gulch. The walls were wider and higher, with fewer bends.

The Paria had abundant flora of a widely diverse nature: cacti, scrub oaks, pinion pines and an occasional cottonwood. We also saw tracks and droppings (deer, rabbits, and coyotes) along the sandy riverbanks, which sometimes rose six to seven feet above the water.

By midafternoon, after hours of hiking back and forth across the river, we found a spring near the mouth of another small side canyon. Filling our water bottles with pure, clean spring water was far better than drinking the iodine-treated stuff.

"Hey, guys, this almost tastes as good as a tall glass of vodka," I said.

"Better than a fine bordeaux," Musky said.

"A lot better than that iodine-poop-flavored stuff," Jerry said.

After filling the bottles, Ray and I climbed up the steep alluvial wash deposit that dropped into the Paria from the side canyon, our curiosity apparently outweighing our fatigue. After walking a few hundred yards up the small ravine, we decided to return, fearing that the rest of our group might want to depart.

Climbing back down the wall, we rejoined our teammates, who were still drinking their precious water.

"Why would you waste your energy going up that side canyon?" Bill asked.

"Those canyon walls are so beautiful. I wish I could paint it," Ray said.

"Right, Vincent Van Mansfield," Musky said.

"I was looking for a way out in case it rains," I said.

An hour later, Randy slipped and fell down the crumbling river embankment, spraining his ankle and bruising his shin.

"How bad is it? Can you keep going?" Sam asked.

"Hope the film didn't get wet," Ray said.

"After the past two days hearing about you guys 'playing hurt,' I thought I needed to try it—have my own stories," Randy said.

He got up and started limping down the bank.

"I'll help you carry that load if you need me to," Ray yelled after him.

"Sorry, no more photos of you, Mr. Mansfield."

Bill and Randy were going through a trial by fire and were doing just fine. Regardless of how tired or sore they were, they never complained, asked for special favors, or failed to keep up. They basically hung in there despite their pain. They were good guys, and we all liked them.

As the afternoon wore on, the energy of our team declined considerably. Rick was still charging ahead up in front, finding the way, sometimes getting so far ahead of us stragglers that we'd find him waiting for us and smoking a cigarette.

Finally, with aching muscles and very sore feet, we reached our campsite for the second night, a flat rock ledge sloping gently down towards the river, up against a 300-foot wall that was so steep it almost seemed to lean over us.

Soon the tents were up and dinner started. After cramming as many calories as our fatigue would allow, we again sat with our backs against the wall, legs stretched out, staring at the water moving down the river.

"Why are we doing this?" Bill said.

I figured that Bill probably needed some grist for the article he was supposed to write.

"To help us appreciate our comfy life back in the 'Burgh," Ray said.

"To lose about ten pounds," Musky said.

"Yes, but isn't it something about male bonding, the camaraderie, about working together as a team?" Bill asked.

"I'd hate to be on this team. We'd be late for the game," Rick said.

"The challenge of getting down this amazing canyon, the pain, the fatigue, this lousy food, and the weird companions, will bond us—definitely reminds me of training camp," Ray said.

"Hey Ray, any more of that good scotch left?" Rick asked, apparently having heard us talking about it through his tent wall the previous night.

"Nope, Russell drained the whole bottle last night," Ray said.

We talked like that for maybe an hour before Randy crawled into his tent and Bill soon followed. Before long everyone was gone except my old buddy, Ray, who at that moment pulled out his bottle of scotch and offered me a swig.

"Private stock, huh?"

"That youngster wouldn't appreciate this good stuff."

"So, same question tonight. Why do we do this, Big Mon?" I asked.

"Why do you have to analyze everything? I have absolutely no fucking idea why we do this. Maybe we're weird. We've got to be a little crazy to play the game all those years," Ray said.

We sat there another hour, sipping our scotch, looking up at the starry night sky, comfortable with each other's company without feeling the need to talk.

The next morning everyone was raring to go, forgetting for the moment the aching muscles and the thirteen miles we had to hike before reaching another campsite that was near the bottom of the river and only six miles from Lee's Ferry, where our car was parked. Civilization.

That night, our third, our campsite was located on a flat space near a wash coming out from another side canyon. We were a different group. People were starting to feel better, beginning to get stronger.

"Well, guys, it looks as though we've got it made," Sam said.

"Don't get cocky, partner. We've got a little work left," I said.

"Let's get an early start and hurry out tomorrow, because I need a smoke bad—and a Bud might taste real good," Rick said.

We all laughed and sat talking, observing first a dazzling "angel fire" sunset behind us and then a starry night that would have made even Van Gogh happy.

"Isn't this one of the most beautiful places you've ever seen?" Jack asked.

"Beauty is in the eye of the beholder," Sam said. "To some people this place would appear barren, ugly and totally inhospitable."

"It just doesn't get any better than this," Jerry reminded us.

"It's working so hard that makes this experience seem so special," I said.

"Right, hard is good," Ray said.

"I'd sure love a cigarette right now," Rick said.

We bantered back and forth like that for at least an hour until Randy got up and limped to his tent.

"Where you going, Bud? No one goes to bed until we see a shooting star," Ray said.

Minutes later we all saw a bright star fall down across the sky, and exhausted, we stumbled to our tents.

The next morning was slightly cloudy, and most of our team was in a hurry to eat breakfast and break camp. I recognized it as the "going to the barn" syndrome, as in horses hurrying back to the barn. Three and a half days of denial—no contact with our families, none of the stuff we took for granted: good meals, soft beds, motorized vehicles, telephones, newspapers, televisions, or computers. It was just too much for our teammates; they wanted out.

When we finally broke camp and hit the trail, Ray and I found ourselves in the rear. The canyon walls widened with every mile to nearly a quarter of a mile wide. Ray, Bill and I fell back even further from the group, walking slowly, enjoying our last day in this deserted valley.

After walking about two miles, purposely taking our time, even Bill couldn't stand our slow pace and took off to catch up with the others.

At one point we saw an abandoned farmhouse off to our right, the first building we had seen the entire trip. The structure had fallen down, and only a few logs remained, providing a good place for us to sit down and take a rest.

"You know, Raymondo, the truth is that I really don't want this hike to be over. I'm not ready for this experience to end," I said.

"Me either. I love this place," Ray said.

"Do you think there's something missing in our lives back home? I mean, why would we want to stay in this gnarly canyon rather than go back home?" I asked.

"Maybe it's because we miss the challenge of football so much that we just can't deal with a normal life," Ray said. "Use to make our living as a sort of warrior and we need to do difficult physical stuff—otherwise we feel unfulfilled."

"I don't feel much like a warrior. My back is killing me."

Two miles further we stumbled into Lee's Ferry and were met by our happy teammates. We shook hands all around and all drank a cold beer.

Driving through the desert towards Flagstaff we were quiet for a while, as though savoring our trip and it's challenges.

"I'm glad that's over. The Paria really kicked my butt," Sam said.

"There were times I wasn't sure that I would make it," Randy said.

"Trust me, guys, you're going to remember this trip very fondly—in a month or two," Ray said.

I knew Ray was right. Every time we had done a hard trek or climb, our fellow hikers had complained, but a few months later they all wanted to do it again.

I realized that there is definitely something extremely rewarding about being on a difficult journey, appreciating the wilderness and getting back in touch with our instincts, using muscles and skills like route finding, problem solving, climbing and hiking, skills that are long forgotten in our "civilized" push-button lives. In a way, it's like getting in touch with our ancestors, who had worked so hard with their hands and their bodies and made such huge personal sacrifices to forge this great country.

As we sat down for a big Mexican meal in Flagstaff, and our first order of margaritas arrived, we knew that Jerry had finally gotten it right when he repeated his favorite phrase.

"It just doesn't get any better than this."

Postscript: You might wonder about the derivation of my referring to Ray Mansfield as Raymondo. That moniker came from a song, "Abandoned Garden," written and sung by Michael Franks, about a very dear friend of his, "Antonio," who was a gifted musician. Ray loved music and would always sing his favorite country and western songs as we wandered through the canyons. Antonio also loved to plant flowers (one of Ray's favorite things to do), and he had died unexpectedly, as did Ray. In the song, Franks refers to his friend as "my inspiration, my hero, my friend." When I first heard the song, that phrase resonated through me. That tribute totally defined how I felt about my friend Ray. Antonio became Raymondo.

One night, a month before Ray died hiking in the Grand Canyon, I asked Ray and his friend Judy to join Cindy and me in the living room of our home up in Mt. Washington, overlooking our great city, Pittsburgh, and listen to that song. When Franks finished the refrain, "my inspiration, my hero, my friend," I pointed at Ray and said, "That, Ray, is exactly how I feel about you."

He stared at me as though he was surprised but then smiled, and I knew that he understood how much I appreciated our friendship. I can't tell you now how meaningful that moment was to me. Perhaps I had some vague premonition that Ray's health was not what it should be. When we were still playing the game, living hard, he'd often say that he'd be lucky to live into his fifties. Ray had been taught to play hurt, and he might have ignored chest pains. We were taught, in my generation, to hide our feelings, to ignore our emotions, but this was one time that I went the other way. Now I feel so fortunate that I was able to tell my friend how I felt about him prior to his death.

You might note that I also referred to Ray as "Big Mon," a reference to a Cajun colloquialism, meaning a large, sweet man but one quite capable of being violent, handling problems with his strength and toughness. Since we won our first Super Bowl in New Orleans, a city we both enjoyed exploring, and because Ray was a strong, tough guy, capable of being both violent (i.e. football) and gentle (as he helped the photographer, Randy) I feel that referring to Ray as "Big Mon" is quite appropriate.

CHAPTER NINE

The Media Hype

Many of my former Steelers teammates are currently very involved in media activities, having fun and making a good living as well. Terry Bradshaw, taking his country bumpkin shtick to a new level, is laughing all the way to the bank as he analyzes pro football for Fox Sports, when he's not making his absolutely hilarious TV ads. Rocky Bleier makes a very good living giving motivational (and humorous) speeches all over the country. Lynn Swann, in addition to his entrepreneurial endeavors, works in television, commentating on college games. Franco Harris, Joe Greene and L. C. Greenwood have all been asked to promote various products and have thriving vocations of their own.

I can certainly understand the attraction to the business, because I too spent some time doing TV interviews, giving speeches, doing ads and making personal appearances at various establishments.

Ray and I started giving speeches all over Pittsburgh, at every imaginable kind of event, from Boy Scout dinners to Veterans of Foreign Wars evenings, generally for no fee or maybe just a free dinner, and we were thrilled. Benson Lincoln-Mercury supplied me with a Town Car for making a few appearances and helping with their ads. I loved freebies, and so did Ray.

Dan McCann, the Iron City Man, hired us to visit Iron City's best customers (bars, distributors, and corporate outings) on most Monday afternoons after games. It meant driving all over western Pennsylvania (typically after stopping by the stadium early Monday morning for treatments for various injuries) on my one day off.

Actually, since I had my own business at the time, Russell Investments, I never had a day off. If I wasn't giving a speech about the Steelers at some bar in Greensburg, I would have been pitching a prospective investor at some office or watering hole downtown. Hey, I'm not complaining. Life was good, and we had been trained to work hard and not complain.

One year, Franco Harris and I were asked to write a weekly report about the previous week's game and what we believed should or could happen the following week. Those reports were then distributed to fans who had signed up to receive them. As someone who grew up wanting to be a writer, it wasn't a bad gig. I would dictate the report on my way home from work on Mondays. Tuesdays my secretary would type it up and send it to the publisher. It was probably the forerunner of what is now known as the Steeler Digest.

Ray and I viewed this self-promotion as part of our education. We needed to learn how to speak in front of large groups, knowing that one's ability to communicate is clearly a big advantage in business. We also figured it wouldn't hurt our off-season business if the folks in Pittsburgh remembered who we were.

Another year, Joe Greene and I were asked if we would agree to being featured in a major billboard advertisement sponsored by PNC, the up-and-coming bank. Having already done Mellon ads, I thought it might appear somewhat disloyal of me to accept, despite the attractive financial benefit. Joe also declined, feeling that the monetary offer wasn't sufficient enough for the two of us to be on billboards all over Pittsburgh. In the end, we said no and Coach Noll said yes, despite the fact that he rarely did promotions. He did it just for his friend Tom O'Brien, PNC's chairman.

Dealing with the media was always a challenge. After one game in the '70s, long after we'd established ourselves as a very competitive team, a reporter I didn't recognize approached me. The locker room was bedlam, with noise from players yelling across the room and other interviews going on simultaneously.

"Is it true that a number of your teammates are taking drugs?" he said.

I stared at the reporter, trying to determine whether this was a serious question or one stated for humor, just to break the ice. He seemed genuine, as though he thought we might have a serious problem.

Having been taught by my mother that a nonreply is the same as a lie, that if I hold back the truth, it is the same as a lie, I decided to answer his question.

"No, I believe today's players take much better care of themselves than those in the past. Their bodies are their shrines, and they wouldn't think of polluting them."

"What did the players in the past take?" he said.

"Well, back in the '60s, guys were into amphetamines—uppers," I admitted.

"Did they help?"

This smelled like trouble. I knew that by answering his question, I'd be vulnerable to criticism for taking a pill. But I also knew that those pills were potentially dangerous, and in fact, they made you think you played well when the opposite was true. I had never really worried about it because I had only taken one "diet pill" per week.

I had heard that some high school athletes were using them, willing to try anything to get better. So I decided to step up, be accountable and take the risk. After all, we no longer took them, and if my quote stopped one young player from making that mistake, it would be worth it.

"No, they do not help. In fact, they give you the illusion of playing well," I said.

"How do you know?"

"I know. You think you played a great game, but the films show you stunk," I said.

"Did you ever take them?"

"Yes."

"Where did you get them?"

"Oh, they'd be around the locker room. They were available. But when Chuck Noll got here, he put an immediate stop to that. We went cold turkey," I said.

"What did that feel like?"

"Scary. But I became a much better player. High school and college athletes out there should not take amphetamines in the mistaken belief that they'll help them play better. They do not work, period."

As the reporter was busy writing notes, I moved away and started talking with one who wanted to talk about the game, not drugs. But deep inside, I felt as though I had just made a serious mistake. What if that reporter misquoted me and I got in trouble with the team? What if the interview damaged my reputation in the community?

The following Saturday morning, I opened the paper, and the lead article on the front page of the sports section had a headline that made my stomach sink.

"Russell—Ex-Pill Popper Goes Straight."

I read the article with great trepidation and discovered that if you read the entire thing, it was pretty accurate. The problem was that the headline and the first couple of paragraphs, all that most people read, essentially called me a former pill user. Worse, the article was syndicated nationwide. I would forever be labeled a drug user for taking a diet pill once a week, and I was devastated.

Arriving at the stadium later that morning for our short pregame practice, I saw Chuck Noll walking over towards me with a sad smile on his face. He stopped next to me and put his hand on my shoulder, shaking his head.

"I told you to be careful with the press."

"It was important to answer that question truthfully."

"Well, you're going to keep getting burned. They just love controversy."

With that, Chuck walked away, still smiling but shaking his head.

It was a painful lesson, but one thing I've learned from experience is that I hardly ever learn from experience. I just kept talking with the press, trusting them to report what I said accurately. *The Pittsburgh Press* was very supportive about that article, assuring Pittsburghers that I wasn't a bad guy and had honestly attempted to do a good thing.

During the super '70s, some of the guys kidded Ray and me about getting "more ink" than our play deserved. It probably had something to do with our being the oldest players on the team, giving us a broader perspective, being able to contrast the current with the former. Lynn Swann and Jack Lambert went to the Super Bowl in their rookie year. What did they know of the suffering, the humiliation, the embarrassment of playing on those sixties teams that lost so many games? How could they truly appreciate where they were and how many years it took to get there?

When we played in the Monday Night Football games, I would often see Howard Cosell in the lobby of our hotel. He'd motion me over, hoping to get an insider's view on what our defensive plans were those evenings. Not wanting to give anything away to the opponents, I'd usually just tell him something fairly generic that the opponent would intuitively know, and he'd broadcast it as though he had a real scoop.

Playing away games on Sunday afternoons, I would sometimes get an early morning call in my room from John Brodie, former great 49er quarterback turned broadcaster, asking me questions about our strategies. I guess he figured since we'd played against each other that we had a relationship and he could get an insider's viewpoint. Again, as with Cosell, I gave him only enough to sound knowledgeable but without giving up any of our secrets.

Having done stuff like speak to IBM's top salesman in San Francisco and Miller Brewing's top distributors in Chicago, doing TV spokesman ads for Equibank (you're right, in the end, I wasn't loyal to either Iron City or Mellon) and working one year as a color commentator for NFL games on NBC, I understood the attraction to the business.

During my career I found the process of being interviewed on television relatively easy; after all, it's not difficult to respond to someone else's questions, particularly if you know a lot more about the subject than the questioner or the listener. But there was the pressure of never knowing what they'd ask you or what might happen.

In the fall of 1973, Pete Gent, a former Dallas Cowboy, came out with his new book, *North Dallas Forty*. I finished reading it in a few days, and thought that it was very good at describing what it felt like to play in the NFL. But I also thought Gent had gone a little over the top in basically saying that most pro players were drug users and many were homosexuals.

The very next week, I got a call from Myron Cope asking if Ray and I would be willing to come on his show and debate Gent on some of those issues.

I eagerly awaited Myron's show, even going back to reread some of the more outrageous chapters. Ray and I invited our friend, writer Roy Blount Jr., to join us, and we met Pete only minutes before the show. He seemed like a really good guy. Myron got right down to business.

"So, Pete, we want to talk tonight about your new book. It's more than a little controversial, what with all your stories about drug use and homosexuality among the Cowboys. Was it really that extreme?" Myron asked bluntly.

"Myron, we had a wild bunch down there in Dallas. We worked hard and partied just as hard. It was a blast!" Pete said.

The interview lasted about fifteen minutes, and we found Gent a fun-loving and interesting fellow who readily admitted that he had exaggerated some of his positions to make the book more interesting (after all, it was fiction). Ray and I particularly ridiculed his position that everyone was taking drugs.

"I know of no Steeler that is taking drugs of any kind, recreational or for athletic stimulus. Our guys like a good drink now and then, but drugs, absolutely not," Ray said. I echoed Ray's denial.

After the show, Roy, Pete, Ray and I were invited to a friend's apartment overlooking the city. Blount was in the process of writing his book, *About Three Bricks Shy of a Load*, a reference to our inability to close the deal at playoff time. Arriving at the apartment, the host asked Ray and me if we would like a sample of his "Acapulco Gold," which to us naïve ones sounded like a fine expensive tequila, a drink we occasionally liked to sip.

"Sure, we'll take a couple of shots of that," Ray said.

Pete got up and went to the bathroom, and our host disappeared into the kitchen to mix our drinks (so we thought). Moments later, he reappeared carrying a tray of tiny little cigarettes.

Never having tried marijuana, Ray and I figured, "What the heck, one won't hurt us." It never occurred to us that Roy Blount, whom we knew was writing a book and had witnessed our interview with Gent, might just write this scene as a classic example of how hypocritical athletes can be sometimes.

Meanwhile, Gent finally came out of the bathroom and was acting very strangely. We figured he was enjoying some strange hallucinogenic mushroom that put him on another planet. As we attempted to enjoy our Acapulco Gold—neither of us being smokers (we didn't even know how to inhale)—we listened to an enlightened Mr. Gent.

"Have you dudes ever thought about how bizarre life can be? Like, you know, man, you reach a point in your life, let's call it point B, a place that you always thought you'd want to be in, but when you get there you realize that it's really point C, a point in space entirely different than what you had imagined, and when you look back on the place you once were, let's call it point A, it's not anything like what you thought about it when you were there, more like point D. Hey, dudes, isn't life a gas?" Pete rambled.

It seemed brilliant to me, and I wondered if it wasn't the marijuana affecting me. Roy Blount, being the good guy that he is, never wrote about that moment, and reader, I'm sure you'll understand that this piece would never have made it to print had Pete not given his authorization. This was one time I wasn't burned by the media and perhaps should have been. I only had marijuana twice more and never did like it. Anyway, smoking marijuana is illegal, and I don't believe in breaking the law.

Despite clearly being challenged by the broadcasting business, I viewed it only as a temporary way to wean myself from the game. I believed that I needed to distance myself from the game and spend most of my time working in my real businesses, RR&Z and Russell Investments, and only thought of the broadcasting experience as a way of coming down from the high of playing football.

I actually rejected a number of TV advertising opportunities, believing that I needed to focus full time on the investment banking business. How could an investor take me seriously if he would see me huckstering some nonfinancial product on TV that night?

Frankly, I never got comfortable with the role of a color commentator. My first experience was to broadcast a Steelers exhibition game, only days after Ray and I had completed a sixty-three-hour nonstop gut-testing canoe race in Canada. I was exhausted and not even marginally prepared for the broadcast, having exactly zero practice behind the mic. But since I was working with Sam Nover, I felt that it would be relatively easy to discuss what was happening on the field and leave the play-by-play to Nover.

By halftime I had discovered that I wasn't nearly as good as I had anticipated. The process left little time for me to make any meaningful comments with regard to what was going on, and admittedly, I frequently found myself speechless, with nothing of value to say or else not wanting to be critical or controversial.

Feeling very out of sorts, I was tapped on the shoulder by the producer, who informed me that in ten seconds I would be doing a live, unrehearsed, sixty-second impromptu advertisement for the program's sponsor, one of Pittsburgh's largest grocery chains.

I sat there, still numb from days of nonstop canoeing, staring at the camera, when a red light came on and the producer pointed his finger at me. I stumbled along, telling the audience about what had happened in the first half (thus demonstrating to them that this was a live ad), but when it came time for me to identify the sponsor, the only true purpose of the ad in the first place, I couldn't remember the name of the grocery chain.

I was supposed to mention the sponsor and then tell the audience what a wonderful company it was, and I was mortified that I couldn't remember its name, so I continued to improvise, stuttering away about how Franco had gained five yards a carry and how Terry was eight for ten, all on live television, with the producer rotating his finger, indicating that time was running out and urging me to complete the ad, hoping desperately that the grocery chain's name would come to me.

Finally, thinking that sixty seconds is a long time, the name of the grocery chain, Giant Eagle, finally popped into my concussion-depressed brain. I was able to tell the viewers what a wonderful company it was and how nice they were to sponsor this exciting (actually it had been quite boring) game.

Afterwards, I sat there, stunned, realizing that I had just made a complete ass of myself, and realizing that, at best, I would have appeared confused and uncomfortable.

Having already contracted with NBC to do NFL games as a color commentator, I decided that I would have to buckle down and study, to learn more about the opponents and their game plans. Struggling to find the time to accurately describe the game, to say something meaningful in short sound bites, I began preparing little gems of twenty-second thoughts that I might fit in at an appropriate time. It was a very frustrating experience.

After a particularly awkward, too-complicated broadcast of a Buffalo Bills game, I was asked to present myself at NBC's headquarters in New York with a number of other analysts, including Merlin Olsen, someone I had always admired as a player and as a gentlemen. After spending a day with the "experts" telling us how to do it and what to say, I remember telling Merlin in the hallway that I felt very uncomfortable with these broadcasts, because there just wasn't enough time to say anything meaningful, to educate the listener.

"You're making it too complicated, Andy. Just give them what they want," Merlin said.

A few weeks later, worrying about my poor performances, I traveled out to Denver for a Broncos/Chargers game a day early to spend some time with the players and coaches to see if I could distill the key aspects of their game plans into ten-to-twenty-second sound bites. After speaking with the players about what they were expecting and getting the coaches' insights, I felt ready to give my best broadcast and redeem myself.

My broadcast partner was Charlie Jones, an old pro with whom I had already had the privilege of working. But at one point, when one of the team's kickers was about to set an all-time record for consecutive successful field goals, I was surprised that Charlie didn't mention it to the audience. When Charlie paused, right before the snap, I jumped in with the information that this would be a record if the kicker made the field goal. He missed.

When we went to a commercial shortly thereafter, Charlie seemed miffed and told me, "Don't you offer statistical information like that. That's my job."

I was surprised, and it seemed to me that the viewer should be made aware of this record before the kick, not afterwards.

Still feeling confident from having done so much research, I finished the broadcast by making a number of perfect calls. For example, I correctly predicted to the audience at least four or five times what play the Broncos would run and why, and told them what the Charger defenders should do if they properly anticipated the play.

Afterwards, I felt elated. I felt I had finally executed a very good broadcast, correctly anticipating plays, suggesting what defenses would best stop such plays and giving the listener an insider's view of how to understand

and counter an opponent's game plan. I felt like I had finally earned my pay.

But as I passed the NBC production team, our producer stopped me. "Russell, you've got to lighten up. This isn't a religion," he said.

"You didn't like what I said?"

"Too damn complicated. Make it more fun."

I was shocked that he was disappointed with what I thought was quality stuff. Here I correctly predicted what would occur, and when it did happen, it felt almost as good as if I'd been on the field making the plays. Rushing to the airport in the NBC-supplied limo, I sulked, thinking that it was unfair to have been criticized for quality work.

The next week, I was given a Steelers game for the first time, the final away game against the San Diego Chargers, the team I had studied so hard the previous week. Confident that I couldn't possibly screw this one up, I was pleased when Charlie invited me to his home in La Hoya to have a few drinks and talk about the previous week's game.

Charlie showed me the video of our previous performance in Denver, and I was stunned how bad I was. It was clear to me, finally, that there is no place in football broadcasting for meaningful comments. I had to agree that my efforts to educate the viewers were far too complicated and left fans confused. It's not that the viewer isn't intelligent enough to understand; it's just that there isn't enough time to explain it properly.

The next day, after getting in too late and having far too many cocktails, I arrived hung over at the Chargers stadium. I had not studied anything relative to this game. I figured I knew the Chargers from the previous week, and I clearly knew the Steelers, having played with them for so many years.

I sat there that day and honestly made no comments that would require anything more than having played the game at the high school level. I talked about how good the weather was, how pretty the Charger cheerleaders were, and said absolutely nothing of any value. When I walked out of the booth, feeling totally incompetent, the NBC team congratulated me for finally getting it. The producer thought I had done my best job to date. I was incredulous!

I was pretty sure that I didn't want to continue with such a frivolous business. Later that winter, I would be interviewed about my broadcasting experience, and always adept at putting my foot in my mouth, I explained my frustration with the lack of time for meaningful comments and NBC's preference for witty, pithy little sound bites. I received a copy of that interview in the mail from Charlie, so I knew that NBC had probably seen my negative comments.

I wondered later whether I even wanted to bother doing another year of broadcasting. Well, I didn't have to worry, because NBC decided for me, calling me in the off season and telling me that they would not be renewing my contract.

It was the first time (and the last) that I have ever been fired. It didn't feel good, but I had to admit that they were right. I really hadn't paid the price to be a quality broadcaster. Everything requires practice and I hadn't done a very good job. I was just too driven in my "day job" (selling real estate syndications, gas drilling programs and pursuing other financial service-related projects) during the week to be concerned with what I had viewed as a fun, transitional activity to help me put football behind me.

CHAPTER TEN

The Running Backs

A linebacker has to deal with working to stop both the opponent's running game and his passing game, in almost equal amounts. Offenses, at the time I played, were about fifty percent run and fifty percent pass.

But I've got to tell you, stopping the running game always seemed the most important aspect of defense to me. It never seemed as humiliating to be beaten by a long bomb as it was to be beaten by an offense that was taking the ball and ramming it down your throat, four or five yards at a time. The ultimate insult to a defense is to have your opponent dominate the line of scrimmage, control the clock, and move the sticks by running the ball.

For that reason, I believe the most exciting offensive athletes are the running backs, not the quarterback or the wide receivers. Quarterbacks don't block or tackle, and they seldom get hit. Wide receivers are far more engaged in the real game (blocking and tackling) than quarterbacks because they have to come across the middle and take their punishment, and they are expected to block on running plays.

Believe me, a running back draws a crowd in a hurry. There are eleven sharks hunting him, trying to take the best shot they can. It's remarkable that any of them can last a season without injury.

Of course, running backs rely heavily on their offensive line. Without these behemoths, they would have little chance. The old joke in the NFL is that if a criminal wanted to disappear and hide from the law, he'd become an offensive lineman and become totally invisible and anonymous. Offensive linemen work in obscurity, fighting to protect their charges (quarterbacks and running backs,) and we only notice them when they get a holding penalty or miss a block. Frankly, it is difficult for me to imagine a more difficult job than trying to stop Joe Greene from getting to the quarterback. It is a thankless job.

People often ask me who the best running back I ever played against was. I had the honor of watching Franco Harris every day, and he was a superbly gifted player, someone who worked very hard to be the best he could be. Franco may have been the best ever when you had to move the sticks with the game on the line.

I also played against many outstanding running backs—guys like Leroy Kelly, Larry Csonka, Ed Podolak, Floyd Little, Gale Sayers, O. J. Simpson, Walter Payton, Preston Pearson, and Steeler backs Dick Hoak and Rocky Bleier. There are just too many other greats to even mention, but the one that I was most in awe of was Jim Brown. Some of that may have been because I played against him when I was a green, impressionable rookie.

Jim Brown could do two critical things: he could run over you, and he could make you miss. Every time I thought he was going to run over me, he made me miss, and every time I thought he was going to make me miss, he ran over me. It wasn't fair. How did he know? Csonka could run over you but not make you miss. O. J. could make you miss but not run over you. Franco was also one of the few who could do both.

What follows in italics is a piece I wrote in 1966. I had just returned from being in the army for two years after my rookie season, and I wanted to write about the challenge of tackling Jim Brown. It starts with the introduction of the Cleveland Browns' offense, during a Saturday night game, when the Steelers were leading the lead in rushing defense and the Browns were leading the league in rushing offense. I was an impressionable first year player, scared to death and about to start against the best running back ever. It would be an amazing night.

I'll never forget standing on the sideline waiting for Jim Brown to be announced. The starting offensive lineups were being introduced, and the stadium lights were off. A spotlight followed each player as he ran through the goal posts to the middle of the field, where he'd wait until the rest of the starting eleven were introduced. They'd then jog en masse over to the bench and the rest of their teammates.

The fans had booed the eleven Steelers without malice or enthusiasm. They probably felt it was their duty to extend a little token harassment to the visiting team. Then the 87,000 people greeted each Brown with a loud but short ovation, like a thunderclap that is over almost before you are aware it's begun. It was obvious they were waiting for Jim Brown, their superstar, whom the announcer had cleverly kept for last.

"And at fullback, number..." and that was all you heard. The noise was deafening. It was as though some great power had been released. I thought surely they could not sustain that fantastic volume for very long, but its intensity seemed to increase as Brown swung through the goal posts and moved with an awesome fluidity towards his waiting teammates.

Surely Jim Brown had never moved with such power and grace before. I had the distinct impression that if he chose to accelerate, he would rise smoothly into the air. I stood there spellbound. This effortless, almost liquid flow was, in a sense, rhythmical, like a clock pendulum, and had a definite hypnotic effect on me.

When Brown slowed to a walk, he became less graceful, which I think is the reverse of what most of us experience. He walked as though his feet were sore or like a person walks on gravel when barefoot.

Looking out at Brown from the sidelines, I felt I knew him. During the week's preparation, Coach Parker continually reminded us that if we could stop Brown, the game was ours. We watched film after film, concentrating almost entirely on Brown, practically ignoring his teammates. We studied all of Brown's running plays over the last three years; we knew how they were blocked, their probabilities or tendencies, and all his keys. For example, we knew that Brown sometimes would put his left hand down if he were going left, and vice versa.

By combining the keys with tendencies, we could predict with considerable accuracy where Brown would be going. After watching the first couple of films, it seemed to me that Brown made his yardage too easily, and I concluded that he simply had caught the defense on an off day. But after closer examination, I knew I was wrong. Brown had a fantastic ability to pick his holes. In many cases, the defense, having anticipated correctly, had closed up the designated hole, but Brown had veered inside or outside, sometimes picking his way through, sometimes bulling his way, but always making good yardage.

While watching the Dallas Cowboys-Browns film, we witnessed an amazing Jim Brown run. Buster Ramsey, our defensive coordinator, immediately flicked off the projector, and we sat there for what seemed like a long moment in the dark, totally silent. In the dim light I could see the faces of the other players, all looking a little stunned, frowning in disbelief.

Ramsey, sitting there like some great fat Buddha, was smiling sadly, as one might when remembering an unfortunate but humorous incident in the past. The spell, which lasted only a few seconds, was broken when John Reger, the defensive captain, said in an emotionless, flat, soft voice, "Run it again, Buster."

The projector light flashed back on, the play was reversed, and we watched it a second time.

It was a play we were to see many more times that week, both on screen and in our mind's eye. Brown took the ball and moved off tackle. As he went through the line, both the defensive tackle and the defensive end reached out and grabbed him and hung on for the ride, so to speak. Two or three yards past the line of scrimmage, both the middle linebacker and the outside linebacker, who had pinched in from their original positions, hit Brown simultaneously from the side. Brown, who still had some momentum, had by this time made about five yards, where he was engulfed by no less than all four defensive backs.

Now I know the reader must be thinking, "Who is this guy kidding—eight men on the runner and he still doesn't go down? Impossible!" It does sound ridiculous, but it did happen. The entire mass of bodies (you couldn't even see Brown) began moving slowly downfield, with a couple of the Cowboys falling off the pile. It was at this point that Ramsey had first turned off the film. He wanted us to ask ourselves whether it was possible that Brown could have escaped from all eight men.

I'm sure you've guessed the result. Brown broke loose and ran seventy yards for the TD. Buster just sat there, letting that play run over and over again. After a few more times through, we noticed how one Dallas player had ducked his head, a couple of them had failed to wrap their arms, and the whole scene became almost humorous. It was a mass of kicking and flailing bodies, moving downfield, struggling to subdue an invisible force. I'm sure that most of those Dallas players were very unhappy with their effort on that play, but the fact that it happened was unnerving to all of us.

But that film footage, shown over and over during that week of preparation, may not have achieved its purpose. It seemed as though, instead of becoming tense and excited, we loosened up. The pressure was off, like we had been asked to do a job that no one could reasonably expect us to accomplish. It was as though we had been told to beat Jack Nicklaus in an important round of golf or to defeat Poncho Gonzales in a set of tennis or to prevent Oscar Robinson from scoring his thirty points. Surely the coaches couldn't actually expect us to stop Jim Brown.

Instead, some of the veteran players were joking, saying things like, "When you hit Brown—hang on and yell for help." Or, "Hit him below the ankles or forget it." Or even, "I've found Brown's weakness. What's that? He's a lousy after-dinner speaker."

There was none of the bravado—no inspirational, confidence-building remarks that one usually hears around the locker room. These comments indicated something more than just respect for Brown's abilities. It was, quite

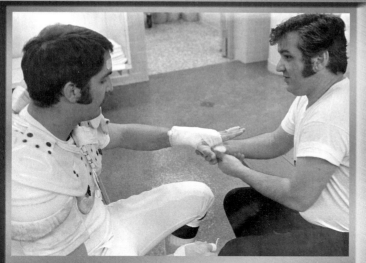

Trainer Tony Parisi tapes Andy up in the Steelers' locker room.

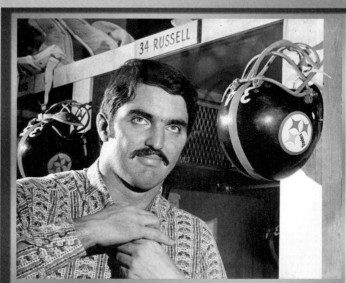

Andy poses in front of his Steeler locker.

334

Andy, Don McCafferty and "Mean" Joe Greene at the Pro Bowl.

While shooting a JC Penney ad, Andy and "Frenchy" Fuqua take a moment to crack up the camera crew.

What a life! Andy, Mike Wagner, and Ray Mansfield relax poolside in Singapore.

Andy, Chuck Puskar, and Ray pose in the woods.

Jim Clack, Ray, and Terry Bradshaw unwind beside a Hawaiian waterfall before the "Super Teams" competition.

Ray and Andy portage their canoe around a dam in Texas during the "toughest boat race in the world," the Texas Water Safari.

Andy relaxes after a tough day at the office.

The gang relaxes after a long day's hiking through Paria Canyon.
Clockwise: Jerry Prado, the author, Rick Mueller, Sam Zacharias,
Bill Utterbach, Randy Olson and Jack Musgrave.

photographed by Ray Mansfield.

Andy and three of his five
grandchildren. Jackie and
Molly Zemper, and
Carsten Russell.

A triumphant group takes a rest from climbing
Colorado's Princeton Mountain. From back to front,
and left to right: Dave Reavis, Andy, Ray Mansfield,
Frank Atkinson, "Moon" Mullins, and Rocky Bleier.

34

Andy and business partners Don Rea (left) and Jeff Kendall.

Andy climbing Capital Peak in 2001.

Andy and his "superior other," Cindy Ellis.

simply, honest awe, but the exaggerations were overdone. Even as a rookie, I thought the coaches had gone too far. I worried that by putting Brown on a pedestal and deprecating ourselves, we were protecting ourselves from humiliation in the eyes of our teammates, the all-important judges.

By setting Brown up as Superman, we, in a sense, had constructed a defensive mechanism. In other words, if one of us failed to stop Brown, a very real possibility, that person would not be judged harshly by his peers. By continually stressing and emphasizing Brown's awesome talent, we all, the coaches included, reinforced and substantiated our built-in excuse.

The blinding flash of the stadium lights being turned back on interrupted my meandering thoughts. The Browns had won the toss and elected to receive. I watched in sort of a daze as Lou Michaels lofted a deep high kick out of the end zone. Jogging onto the field, I still believed it would be possible for us to stop the Browns' running attack, despite Jim Brown's superman image.

You can see how excited I was to have the opportunity to test my ability against the great Jim Brown. On the first play, Ryan, the quarterback, faked to the halfback on the left side, deftly hiding the ball, handing off to Brown on the counter to the right. Brown made it easily through the large hole created by our too-alert linemen reacting to Ryan's initial hand fake and veered left outside.

For a second, it appeared as though he'd go all the way, but he was finally pushed out of bounds on the forty-five-yard line by Clendon Thomas, the left-side defensive safety. Rather than giving Brown a good shot, Thomas had very politely escorted him out of bounds without the slightest trace of malice or haste. It was as though Thomas and Brown had agreed to meet at that spot, to run side by side for a few yards, glance at each other disinterestedly, and then step out of bounds, almost hand in hand. It was such a dignified, matter-of-fact encounter that I wondered if this was going to be a pattern. Did players treat Jim Brown differently because he is so gifted, not wanting to make him angry?

I had the feeling that both of them had calmly sized up the situation, silently agreed that it was in fact untenable (that Clendon had too good an angle), and ended it like gentlemen. First play, and Brown had twenty five yards—what we had hoped to hold him to for the entire half.

The second play was a quick hitter up the middle. Somehow Brown got loose, veered to his left again and picked his way, in his easy relaxed gait, down to our five-yard line.

The situation pointed to the quick pitch to Brown to my left side. Brown had his right hand down. Lou Michaels, the defensive end playing next to me, muttered something like, "He's coming our way, Rook."

Lou was right. The play was the quick pitch. Michaels, reacting properly, cut off the pulling tackle, which meant there would be no blocker for me if I beat the crack-back from the out end. It was one of those classic tackling situations. I penetrated quickly and hit Brown on the seven-yard line. It was a perfectly executed tackle. I hit him with a rising blow, face in his numbers; I wrapped my arms and kept my legs driving.

But when I hit Brown, I felt like a man must feel who sees a fast-moving vehicle just before it hits him. There was a bright flash of light, and the next thing I knew I was lying on my back, holding onto Brown's right ankle. I was in the end zone

Brown was staring down at me, like one might look at a child who had tried to do something naughty and was caught in the act.

"Hey, Kid, let go of my ankle. It's over," he said.

I would be forced to watch that nontackle many times the following week, and I would see Brown literally run over me. But I had held on, slipping down his body, first down to his waist, then his knees, and finally hanging on to his ankle. Not only had I missed the tackle, I had been blown backwards more than seven yards.

It was a moment I'll never forget. I had done everything I had been taught, used all my athletic ability and still had been crushed. It was a new experience, coming head to head with someone just so much better.

After losing that game, I counted the number of times I had a good shot at Jim Brown that night. I attempted to tackle him ten times and made five tackles. Going in for the Tuesday film session, I seriously believed I'd be cut from the team. Parker chewed out the team for doing a horrendous job against Brown, but he picked me out as the only player who had done a *good* job against Brown. I thought he might be being facetious, but he wasn't—apparently, fifty percent against Brown was pretty good.

When we played the Browns in Pittsburgh, Coach Parker put a number 32 on one of the backup running backs, and we were not allowed to touch him the entire week. Parker told us that his strategy was to let Brown run free the entire game; he would eventually become so tired that he'd run out of gas, and we'd come back and win. It was by far the most ridiculous game plan I had ever heard of, but Parker stuck with it the entire week. We assumed he was kidding, trying to embarrass us into playing better.

Moments before the game, Parker said, "I want you to go out there and avoid Jim Brown. Tackling Brown could cause us injuries. Just avoid him until he gets too tired, and then we'll come back. In fact, the first guy to tackle Jim Brown will be fined."

We held Brown to seventy-five yards that day and won the game, tackling Brown in the end zone for a safety. The Browns had lined up on their own two-yard line and had pitched the ball back into the end zone to Brown. No self-respecting college coach would call that play, but the Steelers, anticipating the call, had called a blitz in the huddle. Bob Schmitz, our right outside linebacker, penetrated into the backfield and hit Brown just as he caught the ball.

But Brown didn't go down, and he began carrying Bob's 235 pounds towards the goal line. Other players hit Brown, trying to stop him, but he just kept moving slowly forward, trying to get out of the end zone. Finally the official blew the whistle, even though Brown was still on his feet, apparently not wanting to see Schmitz and our gang humiliated any further. Schmitz would receive the NFL's Defensive Player of the Week award for almost tackling Jim Brown in the end zone—the ultimate compliment to Brown. Football can be a strange game.

CHAPTER ELEVEN

The Huddle

The huddle is not nearly as important as it once was, at least in the tactical sense. Today's sophisticated offenses and defenses routinely change the play or the defense at the line of scrimmage once the opponent has shown their final set. We constantly see quarterbacks checking off to a new play that seldom works. Why? Because the defense hears the check, often knows their live color, changes to the defense best suited to react to that play, and often just plays the play. Consequently, the huddle has become almost anachronistic.

Jack Lambert, our middle linebacker, would call a defense in the huddle, typically signaled in from the sideline, but we'd seldom use that defense, and every player was responsible for knowing the checks. We'd change the defense automatically if the offense showed certain formations or went in motion to new formations, which most sophisticated offenses did almost every play.

Our offense, on the other hand, would only change plays when Terry Bradshaw called an audible, but the rest of the offensive players knew what Terry was supposed to call when he was presented with certain defensive sets. But if he didn't make the change, for whatever reason, they would not run a different play automatically.

Since I played defense, I can only relate stories about the defensive huddle, except to say that my pal Ray Mansfield told me that on rare occasions he called plays when Terry was either dinged or confused. Naturally, Ray called his favorite play—a running play up the middle. Like most offensive linemen, Ray subscribed to the theory that three things can happen when you throw a pass: a reception, an incompletion or an interception, and that two of the three are bad. Therefore, run the ball.

Of course, there is another aspect to the relevance of the huddle besides tactical communication. It is a place to analyze why you just failed to make the play, to receive encouragement from your brethren, to calm down and try to allow your brain to function. Often the huddle served as a refuge, a sanctuary, a place to recover from a big hit and a time to assess an injury.

Once in college when I was running the ball, a cheap-shot artist from Nebraska speared me in the head after I was down. We had been trained never to let your opponent know that he had hurt you and always run back to the huddle. Despite seeing a bright flash of light at the moment of impact, I remember struggling to stand upright. As I ran back to the huddle, the strangest thing happened. The ground kept jumping up and hitting me in the face. This weird sensation happened three times before I made it back to the huddle.

Despite being completely out of it, I was proud to just have reached the refuge of the huddle. Once there, my teammates, seeing my condition, called time out and got me over to the sidelines, where I was asked if I knew what position I played and whether I was male or female. Having answered those tough questions correctly, I was sent back into the game. So much for taking concussions seriously back in the '60s.

In the pros, I had a similar experience in Green Bay. I had thrown my head in front of a runner's knees, and he rang my bell, dead solid perfect, as they say. There was an explosion of light, but somehow I managed to stand up, stagger back over to the huddle, and even line up where I was supposed to be. But when the middle linebacker gave the defensive call, I had no clue. The defense sounded familiar, but I had absolutely no idea what to do.

I remember understanding that I was in a football game and that the defense called should alert me to my responsibility, but I didn't know what to do. I looked over at my counterpart on the left side, Jerry Hillebrand, whom I recognized, and asked Jerry my assignment. He looked at me sort of strangely and pointed at the running back nearest me.

"Cover the back."

This continued on each down until we made them punt, and we exited the field.

"Ralph, you better check Russell. He's out of it, acting real weird—probably got seriously dinged," Jerry told Ralph Berlin, our trainer, known as "The Plumber."

"Andy, what's your phone number?" Ralph asked.

"What's a phone number?" I said.

"How about your social security number?"

"I have no idea."

"Do you play defense or offense?" was the Plumber's last attempt.

"Defense."

"You're OK. Get back in there."

Fortunately, halftime occurred soon thereafter, and I was able to work with Jerry to relearn all the defenses. They came back slowly, and I was able to play the second half, but just barely. In those days, they didn't worry about concussions quite as much as they do today. They were viewed as an almost humorous injury.

When injured, you wanted to get into the huddle, because if you stayed outside where the fans could see you, it was viewed as "playing the crowd." We would often notice our defensive colleagues bent over in pain, but we wouldn't say anything, because we knew that each player could better judge his own pain than one of us.

You might have had a "stinger," a pinching of the nerves in your neck that would cause your arm to go numb and your fingers to tingle. You might need to reconfigure a dislocated finger. The huddle was the place where you shook those kinds of things off.

Other times, we'd witness a player with a different kind of pain, something far worse than physical pain—the pain of making a mistake that cost the team. Maybe you gave up a touchdown pass (the worst feeling for a defensive back or linebacker), or you missed a tackle that you should have made, resulting in a big play or even a touchdown for the opponent.

"Don't worry about it. We're still in this game," someone might say.

"You've made plays all year. No one's perfect," another might offer.

The huddle was also a place to get your breath back, to fight exhaustion and just pray that you would be ready for the next play. There were many times in my career when I was completely drained, fighting exhaustion rather than the opponent.

Once, while playing the Cowboys in Dallas on a very hot day in early fall, all of us were near exhaustion late in the game with the Cowboys' offense driving down the field. Joe Greene pointed down the field.

"We can't let them push us out of this shade into that sunlight. If they do, we're cooked," he said.

The Cowboys' stadium has a roof over all the seats but is open above the field, and that roof blocked the sun over half the field. Unfortunately, the Cowboys did make it into the sun, and we lost. All of us turned to butter in that final drive.

The Steeler defensive huddles were always quite lively. Joe Greene and Dwight White or Fats Holmes and L. C. Greenwood frequently debated some issue about how they should execute their respective positions. Joe, who is now a coach, liked to challenge all of us to play better and wasn't reluctant to make his point.

Take, for example, if Dwight and I were struggling to stop a certain play to our side, the rest of the team would be wondering what was going on. Why weren't we stopping them? Of course, Dwight and I were trying to figure it out also.

Once, on Monday night television, playing the Saints in New Orleans, Dwight and I were both executing our responsibilities exactly as we'd been instructed. The problem was that they continued to run the same play, a simple off-tackle run, and continued to make good yardage.

"Hey, Mad Dog, what's going on over there? You and the captain taking the night off?" Joe wanted to know.

"Just be minding your own business, Mr. Greene. We be doing just fine over here if we could just get some help from the inside," Dwight responded.

As soon as we came off the field, Dwight and I were in George Perles's face; both of us were convinced that we were doing exactly what we had been told to do and were asking what was wrong. Perles listened calmly and told us how to adjust, and we went back out and stopped that play cold.

Once we had an unusual problem. It was back in the early seventies when the defense called in the huddle had greater significance. You actually executed the defense called unless something really unusual happened. We had a middle linebacker named Henry Davis who had, unfortunately, lost most of his front teeth. Henry had a plate that he normally wore, but he had decided to take out it out for the first time.

The problem was that when Henry took his teeth out, it was very difficult to understand him. In fact, it was somewhat difficult to understand him any time because of his southern Louisiana, almost Cajun, dialect. If he got excited, it became almost impossible to translate his directives.

We were playing a big game in Green Bay, and Henry came into the huddle and called, "Blah, deBlah, deblah." I didn't understand a word he said. Some of the guys (maybe being Southerners themselves), apparently picking up the gist of it, broke the huddle, but we Northerners just stood there, not knowing what to do.

"Henry, could you repeat that, please?" I asked.

"Was wrong wis you? Ya got wax in your ears?" Henry replied, clearly trying to speak more distinctly but acting as though I had insulted him.

"No, seriously—what did you call?" I asked again.

By this time, the Packers had broken the huddle and were approaching the line of scrimmage, and still four of us didn't know what to do. Trust me, it's not good when half of the team is playing one defense and the other half is doing something entirely different. It usually means a touchdown for the opponent.

"Henry, what the hell did you call?" I asked again, urgently.

"Listen up, Mon, I can't be repeatin' maself alls the time," Henry said.

The other team had lined up, and their quarterback was calling his signals while staring at us, wondering why we hadn't lined up.

I could see that Henry was angry and he thought we were making fun of the way he spoke. In fact, we were just unable to understand his toothless communication. We had less of a problem during the week in practice when he kept his teeth in, and this was the first time he'd decided to play without them in a game.

"Play da faw-free, cova deux," he said.

It was an interesting problem, trying to interpret your toothless Cajun middle linebacker. Somehow we survived, but Henry was ordered to play with his teeth in for the remaining games.

Sometimes the opponent would be predominantly right-or left-handed, and always preferred to run one way or another because of certain perceived strengths or weaknesses. For example, the Raiders, who had All-Pros Gene Upshaw at guard and Art Shell at tackle on the left of the offensive line, always preferred to run to their left, or our defensive right.

In our big win over the Raiders in 1974, the game that got us into our first Super Bowl, the Raiders continued to run to their left, attacking Fats, Dwight, and myself. One could argue the case that not only did they believe their left side was superior to their right, but also that it was tougher to run against Joe, L. C., and Jack Ham than against our side. However, in this particular game they were having no success on either side.

I noticed Jack staring at me across the huddle, clearly making eye contact, seemingly trying to get my attention.

"Hey, Captain, how about letting me play your side? I'm getting bored over here," Jack said.

"Sorry, we be doing just fine over here, Hammer."

Of course, Ham would go on to make two critical interceptions in that game, the last one being perhaps the most important Steeler play ever, allowing us to go to our first Super Bowl.

When we played O. J. Simpson's Buffalo team one year, O. J. continually ran to his right, our defensive left, and Jack had all the action his side could handle.

Football is far more physically challenging than a spectator might imagine. You are required to exert maximum effort, and it can be totally exhausting—much like wrestling or boxing. The huddle is like the corner in a boxing match, a place to nurse your wounds and recover from your fatigue, to get your act together, to try and get ready for the next play when things aren't going well. It's easy to be a front-runner, perform when everything is going well, when the team is way ahead. It's a lot tougher to play when you're hurting, when the team is down and you've just screwed up big-time, letting your team down with the game on the line.

Hey, I've been there, done that, and I can still feel the pain, the humiliation of being beaten or making a critical mistake when your teammates are counting on you. In the huddle, your teammates could help a little, but in the end, we were all our own harshest critics.

CHAPTER TWELVE

Myron Cope

Early in my career, I met one of Pittsburgh's most uniquely fascinating characters, Myron Cope—a true original. At that time Myron made his living as a freelance writer, having worked some of the time for *Sports Illustrated* and the *Pittsburgh Post-Gazette*. Since I was interested in writing, Myron was a person I thought it would be fun to get to know better.

Having been encouraged to read books as a child by my English-teaching mother, I found that literature and writing courses were my favorites, despite my economics major.

One of the things I loved about training camp was that it afforded me a lot of time to read between practices and meetings. My off-season life was far more hectic and complicated, leaving little time to read. Normally, I would read five or six books each camp.

I probably found Myron far more interesting than did most of my teammates, but almost everyone liked his confidence, enthusiasm and unique perspectives.

Most players had a fairly aloof attitude about the press, barely giving them the time of day unless forced to cooperate. Conversely, most of us desired as much positive "pub" as we could get, so we had to be at least civil. The writers, of course, weren't always thrilled with the players, finding some of them arrogant, egotistical and boring, and in fairness, because of our bad play, they were often forced to be critical. Consequently, the relationship between players and the media tended to be somewhat strained.

Finding it interesting to read what the sportswriters wrote, wondering myself how I would try to make our latest humiliating loss interesting, I pursued a relationship with the beat writers, like Phil Musick and Pat Livingston, whom I thought did an excellent job of putting some human drama into their stories of the latest of many losses.

I also enjoyed chatting with the local broadcasters, guys like Sam Nover, Bob Prince and Dick Stockton. These guys were doing a difficult job, and I appreciated their talent and the effort they made not to discourage our fans any further than they already were and to try to put a positive spin on another humiliating defeat.

Because Myron wasn't writing for a local paper or broadcasting at that time, he wasn't someone most players came into contact with on a regular basis, unless, like Ray Mansfield and me, they frequented certain local watering holes where Myron also stopped occasionally on his way home.

I found Myron to be a very engaging character, one who enjoyed the same discussion topics Ray and I did, and we often found interesting his somewhat different perspectives on the game of football.

As a young man, Myron had grown up with the Steelers of the fifties, hanging out at Dante's in Brentwood, where he became friends with Bobby Layne, Ernie Stautner, Tom "the Bomb" Tracy, Myron Pottios, Lou Michaels, and all those other wonderful characters of the early Steelers teams.

One night at Dante's, Cope noticed immediately that a fellow he knew, a bartender everyone called "Lou the Greek" because he booked bets on the side, was getting smacked around by three guys down at the end of the bar. Thinking three against one wasn't fair, Myron charged into the fracas, yelling for his Steeler "pals" to join him.

Before Myron knew what had happened, he found himself knocked down and held there on the floor by a big guy who seemed to know how to handle himself in a fight. Myron struggled to get up, but his adversary easily held him down. Myron wondered why his Steeler buddies, still drinking down at the other end of the bar, weren't rushing over to help him.

All of a sudden, his foe picked Myron up off the floor and deposited him onto the top of the jukebox, which just then began playing "Popeye," a song Myron vehemently disliked, so he asked his adversary to put him on K-3, which was "I Left My Heart In San Francisco." Ignoring Myron's request, his attacker started slapping Myron in the face, back and forth, timing his strokes to the beat of the music.

Seconds later, Tom the Bomb finally stepped in between them, holding his fists up high, indicating he was ready to fight, and said, "Now, that's enough."

The fight was over. No one was apparently willing to set the "Bomb" off. It turned out that the three guys picking on Lou the Greek were all off-duty cops, apparently encouraging Lou to go into a new line of work.

Another time at Dante's, when Myron was attempting to demonstrate his punching technique and fancy footwork by hitting Bill Saul in his rock-hard stomach, he found himself hoisted up over Saul's shoulder and deposited outside on the sidewalk.

Myron has always reminded me of a Jack Russell terrier. He's small, feisty, clever, and he yaps a lot.

We spent many a night sitting at some bar into the wee hours, drinking our favorite brews, debating various sports issues. Often Myron and I would argue about the reasons for our Steeler failures. What irritated me the most was that he was often right, and I realized that I was just feeling defensive and making excuses.

Occasionally I'd ask him questions about writing techniques and what style he employed writing his books. He told me that he found writing hard labor, and that he considered the task of writing as "the most hateful work that God ever invented."

One off season, I tried to write a story about how difficult it had been to tackle Jim Brown. I'd discovered that it's a lot easier to tell stories verbally, using body language and expressions, than it is to write. After struggling with rewriting certain sentences too many times, I asked Myron to take a look at my first effort to put a football experience into writing. He said he'd take a look at it and get back to me with his comments.

I didn't really expect Myron to do much more than read it and give me a couple of casual comments about his reaction to the overall story.

Myron got back to me a few weeks later with a three-page letter critiquing my story, and he was his usual candid self. Some of his comments had to do with punctuation errors, others about structure, but the key, from my standpoint, was his reactions to parts of the writing. It was as complete a critique as any I had received from my college writing professor, Paul Doherty.

At one point, for example, after I had used what I had thought was a clever metaphor, Myron had written, "This figure of speech shows me no imagination. You probably used the first thing that came to mind."

Later, he commented that he thought a certain passage "showed a little laziness" and my "grammar is careless," but another paragraph was so well-written that he wished he'd written it himself.

At one point, Myron had accused me of being angry about some "tired issues." He wrote, "Indignation rarely makes for effective writing in sports, which after all is a fairly trivial field and perhaps not worthy of indignation."

Overall, I was pleased that Myron seemed to have enjoyed the story and had encouraged me to keep writing. I appreciated very much the time and effort he had taken to give me such a detailed critique.

Shortly after that analysis, Myron was asked to do a short morning radio bit, and I enjoyed listening to him rant, showing lots of "indignation," about some aspect of sports as I drove to work. He clearly had a gift for developing themes and identifying weaknesses, dissecting controversial issues, but he was still humorous and likeable at the same time.

The listeners, although slightly put off by his squeaky, somewhat irritating voice and his testy style, found listening to Myron irresistible. It wasn't long before he was asked to do an evening hour-long talk show, which became an instant success.

A few years later, in 1970, Myron became the color commentator for WTAE's Steeler coverage, partnering with Jack Fleming and entertaining Pittsburghers with his unique, somewhat eccentric but always enthusiastic style.

Myron would use words not normally associated with sports. For example, he might say that a player had dealt with his opponent "vigorously," or that a certain player would "eat your lunch." It wasn't unusual to hear Myron refer to some game as a "debacle," or that someone's style was "less than kosher." Whenever he would pause, he would use "Oom, hah" to give himself time to think of something clever to say.

He might say something like "That was a sweetie of a catch," or remark that a certain play was "luv-a-lee." I even heard him criticize a quarterback once by saying that he had thrown a "wobbly pass, like a shot quail, more like a whirlybird." His favorite seemed to be "yoi," "double yoi," and finally, even "triple yoi" and an occasional "zounds," reserved for the most exciting plays.

My relationship with Myron remained somewhat combative—both of us enjoying a good argument. We would often sit at dinner debating various issues, some of which neither one of us had a real understanding of. I would take the position that Myron knew absolutely nothing about sports, particularly football. Myron would defend his lack of knowledge, telling me, "Russell, it's not rocket science. Let's face facts, you guys just stink."

Myron says he once consulted Ernie Stautner, a Steeler defensive line Hall of Famer, with regard to the complexity of the game, probably hoping that Ernie would condone or overlook Myron's lack of knowledge.

"Ernie, I've been around football for a long time. I admit that I can't draw up the Xs & Os on a blackboard, but I can tell if a player can block, tackle, run, or pass," Myron said.

"Myron, that's all you need to know. Don't worry about that other stuff," Ernie said.

Of course, asking a defensive lineman about the complexities of the game is like asking a plumber about open-heart surgery.

I was always impressed by how much preparation Myron did for all his shows. For the Steelers games, he used file cards filled with background and current information about players and coaches, and on his talk show he used a notebook full of questions for his interviewee. Myron understood that success is in the details, and he worked very hard and paid the price for all his honors and achievements.

Sam Zacharias, my long-time business partner, got to know Myron so well that he sort of became Myron's unofficial business agent, advising him on financial issues such as investments and insurance needs and even helping him with suggestions on how to negotiate his radio contracts.

It just so happened that it wasn't long after his getting involved with Sam that I had my 30th birthday party at our home in Upper St. Clair. A number of my Steeler buddies and some of our good friends from the neighborhood and business were there. After too much celebration with the demon liquor, it was time to open the gifts, which were mostly gag gifts—stuff like Geritol, vitamin pills and canes.

At the end of the gift opening, Sam and Ray staggered in with a huge cardboard box. By their efforts I could tell that it was quite heavy, and it occurred to me just before opening it that it might even be a person.

As I tore off the large bow, the box moved, and I heard someone grumble, "Get me out of here." Looking down into the box, I was absolutely dumbfounded to find Myron staring up at me, looking irritated.

Myron said, "Kiss me, I'm yours." To this day, it's the most bizarre gift I've ever received.

Back in 1972, Myron came over to me in the locker room with a new promotional idea that he had been asked to create by WTAE, something about a "Terrible Towel." He wanted to know what I thought about giving all the fans these black and gold towels to wave at key moments during the game.

Despite knowing that the fans had played a hugely important role in our success during that great turnaround year, pushing us to play better with their enthusiasm, I didn't like the idea. Coach Noll had convinced us that emotion wasn't the key to winning games. He wanted us on an even keel that could be sustained during the entire game, not keyed up too much with the inevitable emotional downer. So I told Myron that it was a "terrible" idea.

"Myron, we aren't a gimmick team. We don't need our fans trying to get us up. You win with quality execution, proper techniques, and good game plans, not emotion. Forget the towels. Overly emotional players make mistakes."

Myron loves to kid me about that now, after his "Terrible Towel" has been such a huge success. He often recites a poem, sent to him by a fan, where as I trudge down the field with my teammates literally jogging past me, I am "smacked on my fanny by the Terrible Towel."

Myron and I have been roasting each other at various banquets for more than thirty years. I would tell people, after totally disparaging Myron, that I am actually a huge fan of his, so big, in fact, that I have a life-size photo of him. After a pause for effect, I would add, "in my wallet."

Myron would then rebut with some equally stupid joke about my lack of speed. After so many years of these shenanigans, worrying that nearly everyone in the audience would already know the stories, I told Myron we needed some new material.

"Russell, I've learned the hard way that when you've got something that works, use it. Don't go trying new stuff."

Apparently he had done a gig for a large corporate client two years in a row. The first year, he used all his favorite stories, all true but with a humorous spin, and they absolutely loved it, nearly falling out of their chairs with laughter. The company liked it so much that they asked Myron back the next year, and he felt the need to prepare all new material. Unfortunately, his second presentation wasn't as well received, and people told him afterwards that they had looked forward to hearing the same stories he had told the previous year.

Regardless of Myron's advice, I felt compelled to think of some new material about him. Of course, humor is always best if it's true. So I came up with the following at our last roast. I told the audience that Myron, who had just turned seventy years old, was looking pretty good for a guy who had had so much stress in his life. I then waited while the audience tried to figure out what could possibly could have caused Myron any stress—after all, how tough is it to be an announcer on the radio? I then said, "Can you imagine the amount of stress you'd have in your life if you made your living talking about something you know absolutely nothing about?"

Myron, bristling with the insult, then got up with some new material of his own. He said, "Russell is considered to be the thinking man's linebacker. A thinking man's linebacker. Isn't that an oxymoron?" The crowd seemed to like both of those new thoughts, so maybe we'd better work on getting some new material after all.

Myron was always looking for a scoop. One year, my pal Walt Bent organized a trip down to Orlando to see Arnold Palmer, who acted as the celebrity chairman of our annual golf tournament for children's charities. The idea was that we would have some photos taken with Arnie and then play his beautiful course, Bay Hill.

The night after our round of golf, we were invited for before-dinner cocktails up at Arnie's beautiful penthouse condo overlooking the golf course and a pond. Then we all left for dinner at his club, but at separate tables because Arnie had another engagement.

After dinner, I realized that I had left my wallet at Arnie's condo. Knowing that he was still entertaining his friends at the club but needing my wallet, I decided to go over to the condo and see if anyone was there.

Walt waited for me at the bottom of the steps. When I knocked on the main door, no one came. I tentatively tried the door, hoping it might be unlocked and I could run in and get my wallet.

But that door was locked, so I tried another door that opened into a storage room alongside Arnie's condo. I then went over to the window and was able to climb up onto the roof and then drop down onto Arnold's deck. Worrying that he might return from dinner and find me in his condo, I picked up my wallet, ran to the door, wrenched it open, and there was Arnie.

Fortunately, Walt, always the jokester, had already told Arnie that I was upstairs stealing his fine silver cutlery, but then he had mumbled something about looking for my wallet. I quickly explained the reason for my intrusion, showed Arnie my wallet and, just instinctively, opened my sport coat to jokingly show him that I wasn't hiding anything.

Arnie was a perfect gentleman, asking how I had gotten in, since the door was locked, and I explained about going over the roof. He laughed, gave me a pat on the back, and sent me on my way. As we drove away, I realized what a stupid thing I had done and hoped that Arnie wouldn't tell people about this crazy Steeler Russell.

Unfortunately, I mentioned the story to Sam Zacharias, who apparently told Myron as grist for his morning show. The following Monday, about to enter the Fort Pitt tunnel, I almost ran off the road when I heard him describe the incident, calling me "Russell, the Cat Burglar."

Myron always referred to his little "birdies," moles he had that were giving away insider Steeler information not meant for the media. I had just learned that one of those birdies was my partner, Sam.

Myron wove his unique personality into the Pittsburgh psyche. He would amaze us with his various antics. He once promised to swim across the Monongahela if the Oakland Raiders beat the Cincinnati Bengals (or the "Bungles," as Myron prefers to call them). The Raiders were the superior team, but Myron had assumed that they would not want to face the Steelers again in the playoffs and would purposefully lose to the Bengals, making Cincinnati the Division Champions and thus eliminating the Steelers from the picture. Myron had to swim the Mon, but he did it at night, televised by WTAE. Even when Myron lost, he seemed to win.

None of us ever had a clue that Myron was destined to become a Pittsburgh icon, but we should have. His combination of insightful observations and analysis—all delivered in his unique style of grouchy irreverence, slightly abrasive and wacky humor—captivated our town for more than thirty years.

Now, after all these years, I consider Myron a good friend. Sam, still his unofficial agent, and I try to have dinner with Myron as often as his busy schedule will allow, and we enjoy debating current Pittsburgh sports issues. We still rarely agree on anything, but as we are mellowing slightly in our old age, we are more respectful of each other.

Myron is a lot more than a feisty character with a squeaky voice. He is first and foremost a very good person and one who cares a lot about people and their problems. Myron has worked extraordinarily hard to get where he is, always doing his homework, honing his verbal skills. He has given back to the community in many charitable efforts and given all Pittsburghers many moments of pleasure. In short, Myron is a class act and we are lucky to have him in our city.

CHAPTER THIRTEEN

A Texas Safari

The current grabbed our canoe, and suddenly we were out of control. The boat lurched forward, gripped by a powerful force. Pulling hard, trying to escape from the rapids, straining in the dark to see what was ahead, I dreaded the outcome. We were in whitewater around midnight, in a river full of water moccasins, and I was afraid. If there were any more fallen trees in our way, we could easily capsize and be in danger of being pulled under the tree and pinned beneath the surface by the strong current.

Ray and I had decided to compete in something called the Texas Water Safari, billed (absurdly, we thought) as the "toughest boat race in the world." It was a 220-mile downstream race, involving two rivers, the San Marcos River and the Guadalupe, eventually ending up crossing a deepwater bay in the Gulf of Mexico.

The previous year, a top platoon of British Commandos competed but quit before the halfway mark. Ray and I just hoped to finish. The record time for the Texas Water Safari was just over thirty-six hours nonstop.

The race required the competitors to have a ground crew to replenish their water supply at various spots where roads intersected with the rivers. This crew was not allowed to replenish any food, equipment or manpower—only clean water. The only other rule was that the boats had to be propelled only by human muscle.

So upon arrival at San Antonio (the closest big city), we rented an RV camper and set out for San Marcos, Texas, with our crew: Ray's business partner Chuck Puskar, and Carl Behling, a young friend of ours.

We arrived in the early afternoon with plenty of time to rent a canoe, obtain our food at the local grocery and still make happy hour at the local beer joint. After a few beers and a good steak, we convinced ourselves that we could win.

The next morning, we found a small park that bordered the river, which was full of boats of all sizes and shapes. Contestants were fixing large spotlights and battery packs on the fronts of their boats, and we realized that all we had was a small flashlight. Our fellow competitors also had large caches of high-energy foods, and I noticed Ray looking unhappily at our measly grocery bag containing only a few granola bars and two cans of Spam.

Immediately spotted as Yankees, since Ray was wearing a Steeler sweatshirt, we were soon surrounded by some tough-looking classic redneck types.

"You fellas from Pittsburgh?" a young stud asked. "By the way, I hate the Steelers."

"Yes, we're from Pittsburgh, and damn proud of it," Ray told him. "If you hate the Steelers, you must hate losing, 'cause we kicked the shit out of your Oilers and your Cowboys."

With that, Ray showed the guy his Super Bowl X ring. I worried that we weren't exactly making any new friends.

An older guy with a twinkle in his eyes, sporting a full beard and a ponytail, stepped forward.

"Why you boys think you can finish this here race?" he asked.

"Well, we finished a canoe race in Canada that took us 63-plus hours," I said.

Apparently unimpressed, he said, "This ain't no canoe race—this here's an obstacle course."

"No way you Yankees can finish our bad-ass safari. It just be too gnarly for you dudes," said an ex-fullback type.

"What makes it so tough? I mean, it's all downstream." I said.

"Well, for one thing, it's going to be really hot."

"How hot?"

"Well over 100 degrees the next three days, and I figure you fellas ain't used to that kind of heat."

"Anything else?" Chuck said.

"Lots of rapids, and the water is runnin' higher then normal. It'll take all your strength to avoid running into stuff."

"What kinda stuff?" Ray asked.

"Gotta carry your canoe around dams, bridges and culverts, and worse, the spring rains have washed out a lot of the banks and big trees have fallen across the San Marcos."

"Does sound kind of tough," I said.

"You like snakes?" the older guy asked.

"Not especially; why?" Ray asked.

"Lotta water moccasins."

"Terrific," Ray said.

"No way you dudes can hack it. Too old and too fat," the young stud said.

Ray stood up, showing off his NFL bulk, and said, "You might have just put your crocodile mouth in front of your hummingbird ass."

"I don't mean no insult," the young man said quickly.

"To tell you the truth, Son, this race doesn't sound like a whole lot of fun to me. We're not in shape, don't have enough food, got the wrong kind of boat, no lights, and God only knows what other problems we'll run into," Ray conceded.

Moments later, it was time to put our boats in the water. There were more than a hundred boats, mostly kayaks, and Ray and I were near the back of the group. The starter ran through the rules and gave out maps to our ground crew. I could see the cocky young Texan up near the front, and I wondered if we could beat him. I noticed that Chuck had already opened a beer.

Moments later, the leaders were out of sight, and we were paddling along in the rear with those competitors who were just drifting along, waving at the spectators who lined the river's edge, but easily staying up with us, despite the fact that we were canoeing at nearly our maximum stroke.

It was already hot and humid, and we were barely moving. Within an hour, my arms ached and I felt a slight pain in my lower back. We soon were referring to our new boat as "The Barge."

"This is tough sloughing," I said.

"I forgot how much I hate Texas!" Ray said.

Already soaked with sweat, I said, "Feels like an outdoor sauna."

The time and miles passed too slowly. We were near dead last, out of sight of any other boats. Despite our agonizingly slow pace, we enjoyed the scenery, the river twisting through large willow and cottonwood trees, covered with hanging moss, leaning inward, towards the center of the river.

We were seldom in the sun, paddling instead in the shade, under tree limbs with thick leaves. Unfortunately, the trees' canopy seemed to hold the heat down along the river, and we felt as though we were paddling in a hothouse. The temperature was already well over 100, and it was stifling. I felt my strength beginning to ebb, and it wasn't even noon.

We passed through a number of small towns, most of which had small parks along the river's edge. By noon, after three hard hours of fighting the river, I wondered how we could possibly continue for eighty-plus hours. Maybe the kid was right about us Yankees; we were too old and too fat, and it was sure as hell too hot.

Slightly before noon, we canoed along a small park on our left, and I immediately noticed that the current was accelerating. Near the end of the park was a small group of people standing along the river's edge, drinking beer. As we approached them, we waved, smiling, and they gave us the thumbs-up sign.

"Make sure you fellas stay as far right as you can to avoid the rapids coming up," a bearded guy yelled, raising a Budweiser as though he was toasting us.

"Thanks for the advice," Ray shouted.

They waved for us to get further over to the right, which we did, but moments later we knew something was very wrong. I tried frantically to turn us towards the left bank, but we were trapped in a strong current pulling us even further to the right.

Seconds later, we flew around a bend, out of the trees, into a sunlit natural amphitheater, rimmed on both sides by hilly embankments and full of spectators, all apparently waiting to see dopes like us go over the dam. Over to our left we could see an unloading area, the portage take-out. Some of the crazy spectators were cheering, obviously hoping for us to crash and burn.

As we approached the lip, I tried to remain calm and turn the canoe to the left so that we would hit the edge broadside, but I couldn't turn it. Just as the bow and Ray were about to go right over the dam, we lurched to a sudden stop. I was stunned, wondering how it was possible that we could have stopped, and then I saw the reason. The top of the dam was a cement ledge lying just a foot below the surface, about thirty feet above the water below.

Ray's weight had caused us to run aground, and the stern immediately had began to drift around towards the right. Fearing that my end wouldn't be deep enough to get stuck, I shouted for Ray to jump out onto the ledge and hold the bow as I prepared to leap out in front of the stern onto the dam. Together we strained to keep the canoe from going down what we could then see was not a dam, but a forty-five-degree sluice.

Ray began pulling the canoe towards a cement brace running down the slope. We could hear the spectators booing their disappointment as they realized that we wouldn't crash. Ignoring the jeers, we concentrated on getting down, Ray pulling the canoe as I held it steady so it would remain centered.

At the bottom of the sluice, we got back into the canoe and pushed off down the river. Ray, always the hambone, stood up in the front of the canoe, and began unbuckling his shorts, clearly about to moon the crowd.

"Don't do it," I said.

"The bastards deserve it."

But then Ray just bowed from the waist and saluted them. The crowd roared with laughter and some even applauded. We were both pumping with the adrenaline that comes from a close encounter with any serious threat to one's safety.

"Can you imagine those jerks telling us get over to the right?" Ray asked.

"Maybe the word got out that two Steelers are in the race," I said. "They really do hate us."

The rest of the afternoon, however, saw our adrenaline quickly dissipate as we continued to canoe down the San Marcos. By around four we were still straining to control our canoe and dodge the numerous obstacles that seemed to pop up around every turn as the river snaked through the countryside.

We tried to avoid rocks and fallen trees that were directly in the current's main path, but occasionally we would bump into them. Sometimes, when the canoe hit the powerful eddies caused by the current, we'd find ourselves spun completely around, facing upstream.

Around midafternoon, we caught up with the some of the kayakers who had gone by us with so little effort. One young lady in a one-person kayak was moving along easily at our speed, as though it took no effort at all. I marveled at the ease with which she could avoid the current's force, but the reason was obvious. She barely weighed 100 pounds, and the kayak hardly penetrated the water's surface. We, on the other hand, had a 100-pound canoe with 520 pounds inside it (Ray's 285, my 215, and twenty pounds of water and gear), and our boat's gunnels were barely above the water's surface.

As we rounded a bend, a large tree was overhanging the right side. Just as the young lady passed beneath the tree, we heard an enormous crack as the roots holding it to the bank snapped in half and the tree crashed into the water only a few feet behind her, with the resulting wave almost swamping her kayak. Her scream ricocheted off the river's surface.

We paddled up to her, noting the fear in her eyes as she realized that she had just narrowly escaped death, totally by chance. If that tree had fallen seconds earlier, it would have crushed her and her boat. Of course, had it fallen ten seconds later, it would have crushed Ray and me.

Ray smiled at me, clearly relishing the danger, and said, "You know partner, this Texas Water Safari is turning out to be one hell of lot more exciting than I had bargained for, but we're getting entirely too old for this shit."

Soon we were alone again. By evening, the heat had taken its toll. We were exhausted. But with the sun low in the sky, the heat started to abate and it felt a bit cooler. There was even a slight breeze. Around 9 p.m. we passed under a bridge high above us. We were back into the rhythm of canoeing—the constant pull and the coordination of our strokes. Despite the pain in our backs, I realized that it had been a very good day.

"Let's stop and eat something. Been paddling for 12 hours straight and haven't taken a break. I need to re-energize with some food," Ray said.

It seemed like a good idea to me, so we pulled over just past the bridge. I dug into our pack to see what I could find, pulled out some granola bars, and flipped a couple to Ray.

"Don't we have anything more substantial? We need some protein, Boy!"

I looked through the bag and pulled out a can of Spam, but when I tried to open it, I realized that the little key used to peel back the top was missing.

"Sorry, Bud, we're out of luck. No key to open the damn thing."

"Give it to me."

Ray took it into his powerful hands and ripped it apart. He pulled the entire chunk out, tore it in half, and threw me my half, which I fumbled. He then gobbled his half in two bites.

I noticed Ray was looking hopeful that I wouldn't want to finish the whole piece. His look was so pitiful that I broke off a small chunk and tossed it back to him. We were animals, scrounging for food in some godforsaken place in Texas. The sun was going down, and we still had more than one hundred miles to go.

Just then we heard someone yell. We stood up and walked over to a spot where we could look up through the trees towards the bridge. There was Chuck, his enormous torso leaning way out over the bridge's railing, straining to see through the heavy foliage.

Chuck cupped his hands around his mouth and shouted, "Ray, are you there? Ray! Where are you?"

His voice echoed off the gorge's walls and off the river. I heard Chuck's concern, his anxiety that something bad had happened to his team. He sounded tired from worrying that his team had disappeared— imagining what might have happened and how best to determine where we were. He had, of course, witnessed our near-wipeout at the dam, which now seemed like days ago.

"Chuck," Ray shouted.

The name reverberated back and forth between the walls of the gorge. "Ray!"

"Chuck, can you hear me?"

"Yes, but what happened to you guys?" Chuck demanded.

"We're doing the best we can. The barge won't turn," Ray said.

"Watch out for a dam about twenty miles down. It's about thirty miles down to the next crossing. I'll be in a park on your right. Be sure to stop there and replenish your water."

"How about some cheeseburgers and a six-pack?" Ray shouted.

"Watch out for more rapids and fallen trees coming up."

As we got back in the canoe, with darkness quickly approaching, we felt a surge of energy. I figured it was the Spam.

"This is great. I can't imagine anything I'd rather do than canoe with a bad back, when I'm totally exhausted, shooting rapids in the dark, around fallen trees covered with snakes. Well, you've done it again, Partner. This is almost as much fun as going up against Butkus," Ray said.

Around midnight, after dodging rapids that yanked the canoe in directions we didn't want to go, avoiding rocks and fallen trees and caved in edges, we tried using our flashlight but found it useless. The light just bounced off the water, giving little help in identifying floating debris or other obstructions. We realized that the current could force us into a fallen tree, and we could easily be sucked underneath it.

Ray said, "Hey, Old-timer, I take that back. This is worse than Butkus. At least I could get out of his way!"

It was this moment that we had found ourselves coming around a bend, picking up speed and straining to see into the darkness. We were moving far too fast to avoid anything if it was there. Sure enough, in the middle of the river, only fifty feet away, was a huge fallen tree that spanned the banks. There was no way around it.

We hit the tree broadside. Ray, reacting quickly, pushed the canoe away from the tree, but his effort caused the upriver gunnel to sink beneath the waterline, and the canoe was gone in a flash. I found myself washed over the huge trunk and holding onto to the end of a large branch downriver, ten feet from the tree trunk.

Worried that Ray might have been sucked beneath the trunk, I yelled, "Ray, where are you?"

"I'm okay. This tree's not going anywhere without me. In fact, I'm becoming quite attached to this beauty."

Hearing a few plopping sounds, clearly snakes dropping into the water around us, I crawled up the branch and could see Ray with his arms and legs wrapped around the huge trunk, holding on for dear life.

My next effort was to find the canoe. If we were going to extricate ourselves from this setback, we would need the canoe to get down the river to where Chuck was waiting for us. As I got back up to the trunk, I could feel the canoe with my feet, wedged against some branches, three or four feet beneath the trunk. With my feet on the downriver gunnel (the canoe was lying parallel to the tree), I jumped up and down on it, hoping to free it from the tree's grasp, but it wouldn't budge.

"Hey, Ray, do you think you could stop making love to this hunk of wood long enough to help me get the barge out from underneath it?" I said.

"Partner, right now this tree and I are getting along just fine—don't interrupt," Ray said.

But Ray slid to the other side of the trunk, and we both began jumping up and down on the two sides of the canoe. Surprisingly, it came loose from the branches and rose to the surface. Almost totally submerged, it began drifting downriver.

We grabbed onto the sides of the canoe and soon found ourselves floating slowly down the rapids, in the moonlight, each paddling with a free hand. After a few minutes, I swam up to the bow and grabbed the rope in front and began swimming towards the shore, hoping to be able to pull us out of the river.

I could see in the dim light that the shoreline was extremely steep, maybe 50 degrees of muddy slope, ten feet or so to the top. I tried vainly to climb up, slipping and sliding, grasping out for something to hold on to but worrying about snakes waiting to strike in the darkness.

Finally, unable to grab anything substantial, I gave up, rolled down the bank and swam back out towards Ray, who was inexplicably pulling all our gear and food out of the canoe and tossing it aside. He was apparently hoping to make the canoe lighter and more navigable. By the time I got to the canoe it was still full of water but empty of our gear.

For nearly fifteen minutes we floated downstream, until the current finally slowed and we were able to make our way over to a sandy beach.

We sat with our backs against the canoe, completely exhausted, our food and water containers lost down the river into the darkness. The only thing left in the canoe was a spare paddle we had taped to the inside.

Ray sat with his back against the canoe and glanced up at a star filled night, unspoiled by city lights.

"You know, partner, I wouldn't mind a good cigar right now and maybe a cold beer. I mean, this isn't such a bad view. Actually, it's quite preferable to dodging tree trunks in the dark."

"Big Mon, I figure we're damn lucky that our barge is okay."

"Lets wait here until first daylight and then see if we can somehow meet up with Chuck."

"Sounds like a good plan to me."

We huddled together, leaning against the canoe, totally exhausted and sore from fifteen hours of paddling, and quickly dozed off.

Only moments later, it seemed, we both awoke to see the dawn barely beginning. We had slept soundly for a few hours and felt renewed, ready to take on the challenge of completing the trip, or at least the ten miles or so down to our crew. We were both very thirsty, but our water bottles were gone and we weren't ready to drink the muddy river water. We would discover a few days later that we had slept on a bed of poison ivy.

Back in the canoe, with me using the only paddle, we moved slowly down a comfortable current, winding our way through some swampy areas, where we found one of our missing paddles caught up against a tree stump. We were now confident that we could at least get down to where we hoped Chuck would be waiting, maybe another seven miles or so.

Two hours later, after having to portage around another large dam, we found ourselves again moving quickly in the current, rounding a big bend in very muddy water, and there was Chuck, waving to us to get over towards him, near a boat ramp that led into a park.

Chuck, seeing that we wouldn't make it to the shore without his help, ran down a steep, muddy ramp towards us, slipping and sliding all the way down, just barely staying upright, only to fall at the bottom of the ramp, sliding onto his knees onto a cement abutment at the water's edge. But Chuck, a true tough Pittsburgher, leaped to his feet, waded out into the strong current up to his waist, and grabbed the gunnel of our canoe just as we went barreling by.

We were soon up into the park and enjoying a box of donuts and coffee that Carl had made in the RV.

"Where the hell have you been? I've been up all night waiting, waiting in the shallow water, knowing the current was swift there, hoping to be able to grab the canoe. I was worried sick when you didn't show. What happened to you guys?" Chuck asked.

"Raymondo jumped to avoid a snake and sank our boat."

"Russell tried to ram through a three-foot-wide cottonwood trunk."

"Look, I don't want to sound like a quitter, but we're now so far behind it'd probably take us 48 hours more to finish," I said.

"Chuck, how far back would you estimate we are?" Ray asked.

"The leaders went by here nine hours ago, and they were still punching out 72 strokes a minute. Hell, they're at least a full day ahead of you."

"Maybe we should bag it," Ray said.

"You're not far from the wider Guadalupe River where there won't be any more serious rapids or trees to maneuver around. We can resupply you. We'll tell them that we broke one of their stupid rules, and you can just finish this damn thing. I don't care how long it takes us—just do it," Chuck said.

That sounded familiar—one of Chuck Noll's favorite sayings.

"We could try to keep going—see how far we can get in the next 24 hours, but I got to admit, guys, my back is killing me and I can't put any power into my stroke," Ray said.

"Look, the way I see it is that we've only got two options. One, gut it out and come in dead last, days behind those obnoxious Texans, or two, act like adults, ignore the devil ego and abort this mission. We've got nothing to prove. The only other decision is where to eat in San Antonio," I said.

"You know what I think?" Ray asked.

"No, what do you think?"

"I think a pitcher of margaritas sounds real good right now."

Later that night, sitting in San Antonio's best Mexican restaurant along the canal, sipping a salty margarita, I realized that I was pouting. I didn't like quitting. It was against our nature. We should have hung in there, played hurt and finished—no matter what. But Chuck Noll had always stressed that the secret to success is preparation, and we hadn't made the commitment. Our not having prepared properly was a clear path to failure.

"I know what you're thinking. You're pissed off that we didn't finish, aren't you?" Ray asked.

"Yep. We'll have to work harder next year, train for this, lift a lot of weights, maybe lose some weight ourselves, and bring a two-man kayak. They sit a lot higher in the water and are a lot easier to turn."

"I don't know, Andy. I was kinda gettin' attached to that old barge. Got to admit, though, that we're a little old for this kind of shit. There were nothing but kids out there."

"I know, but we could definitely do this thing—different boat, better preparation," and then, winking at Chuck, "and a better crew, we'd bag this race. No question in my mind."

But we never went back to do the Texas Water Safari. Maybe we were finally growing up and really felt we had nothing to prove. Maybe we were just getting older and smarter, but possibly those redneck Texans were right. We just aren't tough enough.

CHAPTER FOURTEEN

Training Camp

Most players feel ambivalent about training camp. On the one hand, you welcome the challenge of being part of a team effort to improve and possibly reach the Super Bowl. But on the other hand, you dread camp because it is so exhausting.

In the '60s and '70s players needed to have off-season jobs, because they didn't make enough money during the season to support their families during the off season. Unlike today's players, we had very little time to devote to physical conditioning.

Paul Martha and I met three or four times a week at the Mount Lebanon high school track at 6:00 a.m. and ran until 7:00 a.m. We'd then return to our homes for a quick shave and shower, take the trolley downtown to our jobs, work late, often missing dinner, and take the trolley home, hopefully just in time to put the kids to bed.

Training camps are never easy. The schedule is fairly intense. Up at 6:30 a.m., mandatory breakfast at 7:00; morning meeting at 9:00; taping at 10:00; practice from 10:30 to 12; mandatory lunch; rest until the 2:00 meeting; taping, practice, dinner and the evening meetings.

Those twice-a-day practices take place on the hottest days of summer; the three daily meetings are packed with learning new defenses or offenses and getting familiar with the new playbook that always seems to change every year. My only break from the effort would be an hour or two each evening spent "replenishing my bodily fluids" at a local pub, The 19th Hole, in Latrobe, close to St. Vincent's college, our home for those camps.

The best you feel is on the first day. From that day forward, for the rest of the season, players deal with injuries and aches and pains all over their bodies. It is a nasty game, but we all love it.

Training camp is not exactly a no-pressure work environment. It is one of the few workplaces in our society where your employer tells you every year that they've brought in four or five superstars specifically to take your job and then ask you to teach them to take your job. Following NFL tradition, we'd do it to help the young guys learn the intricacies of the game, even with the knowledge that those young players were acquired specifically to replace us.

"What you've done in the past means nothing. You will be evaluated every day on what you accomplish now. This is the last bastion of capitalism. Only the strongest and the best will survive," Coach Noll would say each year.

Of course, there were always a few old vets who resisted teaching the rookies, and in some cases, even went the other way, trying to confuse the potential job replacements. Bobby Walden, the punter, would work with promising high-draft choice punters and within a few weeks the new recruit would be shanking the ball, barely able to kick it twenty yards.

"Bobby, what are you telling these guys that gets them so screwed up?" I asked.

"Oh, just ask 'em stuff like whether they breathe in or breathe out, just as they are making contact with the ball, or get them to thinking 'bout the ball's rotation or where the strings oughta be. It's sort of like a golf lesson—takes a while to sort out what works and what doesn't, and you need months of practice. Fortunately for me these rooks don't have months, just a few weeks before they get the axe."

Sometimes it works the other way, and the rookie is so good that you learn from him. I was absolutely astounded at how good Jack Ham was the first day of training camp. He executed perfectly what I considered difficult drills. I would go on to learn a lot about playing linebacker from Jack. He was the best ever.

It is tradition for the veterans to haze the rookies, much like fraternity "hell week," but not nearly as intense, basically because the veterans see enough of the rookies on the field. The harassment that does take place is minimal, usually requiring the rook to get up at dinner and sing his college's fight song, or to accept the challenge of a drinking contest at the local pub. Fortunately, I was able to fool Bobby Layne and the other vets by pretending to chug beer from a can. They failed to notice that I had used the same can for multiple chugging contests.

At training camp, players tend to get a little wild. There's a feeling of being penned up in an institution that allows little contact with the real world. Many of us looked forward to the couple of hours each night when we could go off campus for a couple of brews before hurrying back in time for "bed check." Can you imagine being thirty-five years old and having a bed check?

My first year back from the army, we had our training camp at Rhode Island University, which wasn't far from the Atlantic coast beach. My room-mate that year was Bill Saul, a rough and tough classic middle linebacker.

I would soon learn that he was also a serious hell raiser who loved to party until the wee hours nearly every night. I actually think they roomed Bill with me in hopes that I might be able to discourage his wild side.

Frankly, I found training camp so exhausting that I couldn't even imagine having enough energy left to sneak out after the 11 p.m. curfew. But Saul managed to almost every night. He slept through most of the meetings but still played hard every day and never made a mistake on the field. I was amazed.

After a couple of weeks of this behavior, Bill Austin, our new coach, reminded the team that we had a strict curfew and that any player caught out would receive a heavy fine and suffer serious repercussions—like being cut from the team. He was sending a very clear message—screw up and you're gone.

That same night, after returning from two hours of partying at our favorite beach joint, Saul decided he just had to go back. When he heard one of the coaches coming down the hallway for bed check, he jumped into his bed with his clothes and shoes still on. I sat there reading a book and waved at the coach, who looked at Saul lying there with his tough guy face appearing almost angelic above the sheet that was tucked neatly beneath his chin.

"Yeah, right! Sound asleep, I'm sure," the coach said. His voice almost dripped with sarcasm as he closed the door.

Upon his departure, Saul jumped up, went over to his dresser and began applying liberal amounts of aftershave. Then he came back and sat down on the edge of his bed.

"You know, I think those assholes are gonna check one more time. I'd guess around midnight. We'll just have to wait them out," Saul said.

"What's this 'we,' Roomie? You're on your own, pal. By the way, it might be a bad night to sneak out."

"Austin's just trying to show us how tough he is."

I knew from previous evenings that it was hopeless. Saul would keep me up talking for another hour before he finally snuck back to the beach.

He stretched out on his bunk, placed his hands behind his head and stared up at the ceiling.

"I can't figure out why you do so much better than me in the 'Oklahoma drill'—hell, I'm bigger, stronger and tougher," Saul said.

"It's all about quickness and technique, Bill, not your strengths."

"I bet I could whip just about anybody in the NFL in a street fight."

"Football is not a street fight."

"Hell, I could kick the shit out of a lot of those offensive linemen if they'd just hold still."

"You've got to stop their initial charge and then release from them. You stand there pounding the lineman and the running back goes right by. You've got to work on separation, on disengagement."

I could almost hear him processing the words "disengagement" and "separation," questioning their meaning in relation to football. Bill was a smart guy but tended to let his machismo get in the way of his brain. He was old-school, definitely not a finesse player.

We talked like that, back and forth, for about an hour before we heard a coach's chair push back and the sound of someone coming down the hallway. I noticed that the coach didn't stop at any of the other rooms but came straight to ours. He poked his head in and saw both Bill and me pretending to be asleep—Bill still had his clothes on beneath the sheet.

The door shut, but I could hear the coach breathing as he stood there in the dark and I could smell alcohol and smoke. Finally he sighed and turned, opened the door and went out, apparently satisfied that we weren't faking it, and we heard him walk on back down the hall.

"Who was that?" I said.

"Who gives a shit?"

"Whoever it was smelled like booze and cigars."

"Love that smell."

Saul jumped up and went back over to his dresser and mirror and to again apply more aftershave and recomb his hair. He walked over to the door, opened it a couple inches and peered down the hallway, rubbing his hands together, as though he couldn't wait to get back to the beach.

"You know, I'm guessing those bozos are going to check one more time—about a half an hour from now," he said.

"Look, either go to sleep or get the hell out of here. I can't take this. You're killing me. I need my sleep."

"Poor baby."

Bill sat back down on his bed, checking his watch, ignoring my appeal for sanity.

"You know, I had a coach when I played for Baltimore that I just couldn't stand," Bill said. "The dummy just didn't respect my aggressiveness!"

"It's not about aggressiveness. There are lots of guys in the steel mills that could kick the shit out of both of us. Sometimes it's about patience, waiting that nanosecond to see what the opponent is going to do. It's also about executing good techniques."

"I don't want to hear about it."

We lay there on our beds, talking for another thirty minutes or so about the game that we both found so difficult. At around 12:30 a.m. Saul got back under the covers.

"They're gonna check one more time—I'd bet big money on it."

Seconds later the door opened and another coach looked in. Seeing us both in bed he said, "Good to see you boys where you're supposed to be; good night."

I recognized the voice—it was Torgey Torgeson, our defensive coordinator, a former player and a good guy.

The door closed, but Saul waited another fifteen minutes, clearly not trusting the coaches to go to bed. Finally, he got up and was ready to go.

As he walked out the door, he turned and said, "I'll be back by breakfast. Order me two eggs, over easy."

Saul walked down the darkened corridor, went down the back stairwell, and sauntered out the back door. He crossed through the main parking lot to an auxiliary lot behind the gym where he had hidden the beatup old Ford that he'd brought to camp. He jumped in behind the steering wheel, and putting the key in the ignition, looked forward to a night of mindless freedom, the elation of a good night out.

He smiled as the engine started. No one, especially those hard-ass coaches, was going to tell him what he could not do.

Just then a strong hand gripped his shoulder and he heard a triumphant voice say, "Gotcha, big boy. That'll be five hundred bucks."

It was the head coach, Bill Austin, who waited in Saul's back seat until 1:00 a.m., making sure that he didn't sneak out. If Saul hadn't been the starting middle linebacker, he would have undoubtedly been cut and held up as an example for the other party boys.

We spent the next week practicing at a university facility in Salem, Oregon, waiting to play an upcoming preseason game against the Vikings in Portland.

In those days the NFL played in smaller venues. I kind of liked those times, because they took us to places we wouldn't ordinarily get to. Towns like Nashville, Baton Rouge, Norfolk, Toronto, Canton and Portland were interesting places and the fans were certainly enthusiastic.

Our room was on the top floor of an old dormitory building, and it was only moments after the coaches had conducted their bed check. Paul Martha, the team's No. 1 draft choice in 1964 and Saul's best buddy, had just joined us, the two of them having apparently made preparations to sneak out, only one night after being caught by Austin

The only stairwell ran down outside our room, emptying out on the bottom floor across from the coach's office where they were playing cards with the door open. Anyone going down the stairs would be easily spotted.

"I know the officials are sometimes blind, but the coaches aren't. How are you going to get by them?" I asked.

"We're going down the fire escape," Saul pointed at our room's window, outside of which we had noticed a large tube running three stories down to the parking lot.

"Are you sure that's a fire escape? Looks more like a laundry or garbage chute to me."

"Whatever, we're going down," Paul said.

"Dumb idea. Did you check out what's at the bottom, the height above the alley? You could hurt yourselves. Forget about it," I warned.

"Roomie, you worry too much," Saul said, donning a clean shirt and dousing himself heavily with his favorite aftershave. "We're outta here."

Around midnight, the two of them climbed out the window into this narrow funnel that spiraled steeply down the side of the building. Saul went first and Paul followed right behind him.

Seconds later, I heard them crash at the bottom into something metallic; the sound echoed loudly up off the surrounding buildings. I waited, straining to hear something more and hoping they weren't hurt. Then I heard some major cussing and even giggling. Surely, I thought, the coaches would have heard the noise and rushed outside to determine the cause. I heard them get up and run down the alley. Apparently both were all right. I learned later that they had landed on top of a stack of garbage cans placed there for the summer.

They walked four or five blocks into the city where they entered what reportedly was the best after-hours bar in town. As they entered into a narrow bar area, with Paul leading the way, they noticed Coach Austin sitting on one of the stools halfway down the bar. Austin happened to glance in their direction, catching sight of Paul but only getting a glimpse of Saul's white shirt as he raced around the corner. Austin ran to the door, but Saul was gone and Paul refused to identify him.

The next day all the players knew the story, and after Austin fined Paul, he ranted in the morning meeting about the man "in the white shirt," promising us that he would find out his identity "by the afternoon practice." We figured he was more upset about being discovered in a trashy joint than about his rules being broken.

Under a very hot summer sun, the team prepared to go through its usual prepractice routine of stretching and heavy calisthenics. Austin gave his usual pep talk, focusing on our preparation for our exhibition game that weekend.

But then he glared at us as though we had all personally insulted him, and he acted as though he was afraid to speak lest his anger get the best of him. Austin stared down at his feet for a long time without saying anything. Finally he looked up, with an expression that revealed he had reached a decision.

"All right, I know by now you all know the identity of the man in the white shirt, Mr. Martha's buddy. I want to know who it was. Perhaps that person will be man enough to step forward right now and tell the truth. If he doesn't, you are all going to suffer."

We stood there, silent, some staring at their feet, some glancing over at Saul. Saul said nothing.

"OK, we are going to do your favorite drill, Ups and Downs, until someone tells me the identity of the man in the white shirt."

"Ups and Downs" is a drill requiring players to run in place until the coach yells, "Hit it," at which point the player falls flat on his chest and stomach, catching himself in a pushup position. When the coach yells "Up," the player jumps up and starts running in place again. The player breaks his fall with his hands and then must lie flat, with his stomach and thighs touching the ground momentarily. This drill is usually a short drill, and the player rarely hits the ground more than five or six times.

"The Green Bay Packer record for this drill is eighty-seven repetitions—that's right, eighty-seven times throwing yourself down on the ground and getting back up. Lombardi was real proud of that. Today, we'll stop when someone tells me who it was, or we will break the Packer record," Austin yelled. "It's your choice."

I couldn't believe my ears. Why would a coach reward a player who'd rat on a teammate? Maybe, I thought, he really doesn't want us to tell and wants to find out what we're made of to bond us together.

Well, we broke that Green Bay record, carrying out eighty-eight Ups and Downs. However, Coach Austin never learned that it was Saul. It was a humid ninety-five degrees, and some of the bigger guys threw up after 30 reps. After fifty, some guys weren't getting up fast enough to get back down and probably missed some reps. But the bulk of that squad, a team that would lose most of its games, pulled together that hot day, refused to tell on one of their teammates, and set the new record.

Back in the dorm that night, sore and exhausted, I said, "Bill, how could you not step up and tell him it was you. That drill damned near killed us!"

"Austin wanted to break that record. He thought it was good for team morale. Hell, I figured it would get some of our lard-ass linemen in shape and bond us. It's going to be a long season. Hey, you want to go out tonight? Martha begged off," Saul replied offhandedly.

Occasionally there would be fights during training camp, usually on the field but sometimes off the field after a night of drinking. Jobs were on the line, and the pressure to perform was constant. The frustration of making mistakes or getting beat was present, causing constant tension.

Years later, in 1976, my final season, we attempted to win our third Super Bowl in a row, something never done before or since. We were driven to win that third bowl and were equipped with players willing to devote time and effort to the commitment. We often stayed out after practice to help teammates work on techniques or spent extra time in the weight room. This team was on a mission, and it was not going to be denied.

Joe Greene wanted to have a team party to celebrate the last practice of that preseason to bond the team even closer. He received Chuck Noll's permission to have a party and purchased a keg of beer and snacks for everyone. We met out in front of the dorm, after showering, giving us an hour or so before our mandatory dinner.

It was a fun event, and we all talked about the upcoming season and what it would mean to us to win three in a row. Joe complained that a few of our teammates apparently decided not to come and instead went directly to dinner.

After the short party we all walked over to the dinner hall feeling pretty good about our chances of winning another Super Bowl. We had worked harder than ever before, and the team had grown closer than ever.

When we entered the dining hall we saw five or six of our teammates who had apparently decided to boycott the party. Walking to our table, we passed the players who hadn't attended. I wasn't angry with them; maybe they hadn't even been told about it.

But Joe was hot, and when he passed the table he leaned over to speak with the closest guy, sitting at the end of the table. It was Jimmy Allen, a defensive back and a real tough young man who had played at UCLA.

"So why didn't you dudes join us at the team party?

"Didn't hear nothin' about no party, man."

Joe reached down and took one of Jimmy's shrimp. He ate it in one bite and said, "We had a beer party. You should have been there."

"Don't you be eatin' my food."

Joe reached down and tipped Jimmy's plate, full of red cocktail sauce, onto his lap. Before any of us could react, Allen jumped up and slapped the plate across the side of Joe's head, breaking the plate and nearly severing the lobe off Joe's left ear. I could see it hanging there by just a thread of skin. Jimmy then proceeded to hit Joe with two or three solid punches before Joe could even react.

But when Joe countered, he did so with such an unbelievable fury and force, backing Jimmy up across the room, that we were all stunned before finally jumping into the fray and stopping the two men. It took four of us to hold Joe back, while Gordie Gravelle, an offensive tackle, restrained Jimmy. Astounded that anyone would pick a fight with Joe Greene, I watched Jimmy straining to get free.

Seconds later, the fight was over, and we rushed Joe to the infirmary so that his earlobe could be sewed back up. He had tried to have a party to celebrate our truly unique team, a group of guys who really respected each other, but it had ended up in an ugly fight. Even good families have an occasional scrap.

Later that night Joe, feeling bad about the fight, would go to Jimmy's room and apologize to him for his over-reaction.

But fights and bad boy behavior only provided the players with an occasional, almost humorous, distraction from the relentless effort to improve as a team, to build good habits and techniques, and to learn the fundamentals of the game that gave us the ability to become a championship team. Training camp was hard work, but it was well worth the effort.

CHAPTER FIFTEEN

The Locker Room

People sometimes ask what it was like in the Steeler locker room. How did we get along? Were we close personal friends? Did we occasionally get into any fights there? How did guys react to the pressure?

I suspect it isn't that different from how people treat each other in their own workplace if their business is successful. It is always important for fellow workers to support each other, to pull together, and when appropriate, to give advice.

I have always maintained that Chuck Noll's greatest legacy is that he taught us how to be a family, a team that helped each other and appreciated each other's efforts, even in failure. We were a very cohesive group of players. There were no office politics. There were no petty jealousies. There were no cliques. It was a great culture.

Don't get me wrong—we weren't perfect. Can you imagine a room full of alpha males who are highly competitive by nature, extremely aggressive, and who take any failure very personally? Just returning from a meeting room where you were forced to watch every little mistake you had made was a challenge. There was definitely a certain amount of tension in the room.

Once after a big loss, when everyone's nerves were a little frayed, Jackie Hart, our equipment man, took it upon himself to enforce a rule prohibiting anyone from entering the locker room until after Coach Noll spoke with the team.

In this case Art Rooney, one of the founder's sons and a superb Steeler scout, wanted to come in with a small group of his friends, but Jackie rather rudely told them to get out. Before we knew what had happened, they were fighting. Art threw Jackie on top of a waist-level cooler in the middle of the locker room before a number of the players broke up their spat. We all watched in amazement when the chief came in and made the two apologize to each other as though he was scolding a couple of his kids. Well, Art was his son, and he always treated Jackie as though he was part of the family.

During the week, we followed a tight schedule. Everyone arrived on "Noll Time," at least fifteen minutes early (usually around 8 a.m.) or expected a heavy fine. When we weren't in meetings, we sat around and talked. Some of us, perhaps to break the tension, started playing a game where we would throw a Frisbee across the locker room into an open metal grocery cart used to collect used towels. The competition was always friendly, and most of the guys seemed to lose interest quickly. When the contests came down to the last two, they often involved Frenchy Fuqua and me. We loved to compete and there were, of course, always a few bucks on the line. Frenchy just loved taking my money.

One of the most important places in the locker room was the training room. Football is a tough game, and you nurse injuries constantly throughout the year. Ralph Berlin, nicknamed "The Plumber" because of his ability to put us back together, was a former player at Iowa State. A bad knee cut short his career and caused him to get involved in physical therapy.

Ralph, a former marine, would berate us continuously for having the nerve to come into his domain complaining about our injuries. He called us sissies, wusses, malingerers and worse. But Ralph could take it as well as he could dish it out. His training room was always a place with a great deal of laughter. This was one of Ralph's gifts to us, because normally one would expect it to be a very miserable place filled with injured players depressed over not playing. But Ralph spared no one, even accusing Fats Holmes of being a sissy if he complained of a sprained ankle. Ralph just loved to harass his players, all the while hiding his true affection for us.

Ralph's tough-guy style was offset by Bob Milie, his assistant, who, unlike Ralph, acted as though he really cared about our injuries and was always there to help us through them.

Another equally important part of the locker room was the equipment room. Tony Parisi, a former hockey player, ran a buttoned-down equipment room. In addition to supplying us with any and all equipment we might need, he knew a lot about training and taping, and would give shoulder and back massages, and tape our hands.

Tony was so important to the team's success that he was allowed to have his own business outside of the Steelers. Of course, his new business fit with his responsibilities as our equipment manager. Knowledgeable about athletic equipment and shoes, Tony started a sports shoe store in Washington Mall, and it was quite successful.

Tony's equipment room housed the only locker room telephone, and it would irritate Tony when people would call. With Sam Zacharias and I trying to run our syndication business during the season, Tony was often irritated with me as I ran back and forth to the phone, interrupting his card games with Jack Lambert.

After practice during the '70s, there would usually be a number of the local media in the locker room, talking quietly with a number of players about injuries or their thoughts on an upcoming game. Of course, players weren't always thrilled by what had been written or said regarding their play. Once Fats was angry over a comment made by Phil Musick, a sportswriter for the *Pittsburgh Press*. He went over to Phil, grabbed him under the armpits and suspended him in the air for minutes as he quietly explained to Phil that his comments were unacceptable. It was a bizarre scene.

Sometimes the tension would get to people, and they'd play practical jokes. Terry Hanratty was always putting small cups of water in Jack Lambert's shoulder pads. The pads were stored on the top shelf of each locker, and when Jack would pull down his pads, he'd get soaked.

On another occasion, Joe Greene and some of his pals decided to teach rookie Lynn Swann a lesson. They taped a naked Lynn into one of the grocery carts used for dirty towels and pushed him outside into the hallway. Fortunately, one of the coaches soon found Lynn and freed him.

In a purely practical sense, the most important things that went on in the locker room happened immediately before the game and, even more importantly, at halftime.

Most of us arrived early on game day, wanting to get our ankles taped without waiting in line, putting on knee-length stockings and getting into the always tight-fitting pants. When I complained about the tightness to Tony, he claimed that tight pants prevented leg injuries during hits.

The locker room prior to games was always quiet, like a tomb. Players, sitting on small stools, ritually don their gear—taping their socks up, putting pads in their pants, taping sponge pads on various parts of their bodies, and tightening the underarm strap on their shoulder pads. Generally, no one would talk about the game, but instead flip through the pages of the game program with little interest, or review the game plan, mumbling occasionally to those nearby.

No one gave an appearance of being particularly nervous or tense. Instead everyone seemed sort of somnambulistic, yawning frequently as they got dressed.

It really shouldn't take more than ten minutes to put on a football uniform, but many of us would take anywhere from a half-hour to an hour. Preparing for a game is a semiserious ritual, one that few players will rush.

Just prior to going out to start the game, we all recited the Lord's Prayer, and then I would always add my own little private prayer that no one would be injured.

I found it interesting when fans would tell me after a game that we looked awfully sluggish in the first half, but that we came out in the second half and totally dominated. Their assumption would always be that Coach Noll must have given us a super pep talk and that we came out fired up.

The truth is much different. That is generally not what happened. When we got to the locker room at halftime, the first thing we did was to take care of any injuries. We'd do anything—get a new tape job or have a shot of cortisone and a pain killer.

In those days, injuries weren't X-rayed until after the game. Of course, many players refused to get X-rayed and played with broken bones. In college, Ray Mansfield played with a broken neck, never getting it X-rayed until many years later. I broke my big toe, told the Steeler coaches that it was fine, and played the final few games with it broken. Those were different times, and I think the players in those days thought differently about playing injured. In the early years of the game (the '40s, '50s and '60s) it was a badge of honor to play hurt, a way to show toughness and commitment. Today's players, risking multimillion-dollar careers, seem to think differently about injuries.

After attending to our injuries, we met with our individual position coaches and discussed problems we were having against the opponent. We would then quickly move to a meeting involving the entire defense, in which the coaches drew up every play that the opponent ran in the first half and focused on the plays that had failed. It rarely had anything to do with a player's lack of effort.

In fact, sometimes you made bad plays because you were trying too hard. For example, once while trying to stop the Bills from making a first down (on third and short) deep in our territory, Glen Edwards, the team's toughest player pound for pound, got too aggressive when he tried to fill the off-tackle gap that the play was designed to attack. Jack Ham, executing his assignment perfectly, had closed the off tackle, forcing O. J. Simpson to veer outside. If Glen had scraped off to the outside, as we were supposed to do, he would have had an easy tackle for no gain. Instead, O. J. went over eighty yards for a touchdown. Glen was guilty of trying too hard.

After dissecting what went wrong, the coaches would calmly make changes and put in new automatic checks to the different offensive sets that the opponent was showing us. After breaking that down, they would tell us to keep the communication going, because surely there would be more changes to make between the third and fourth quarter.

We then came together for a short, unemotional speech. Coach Noll would typically tell us to not only execute our techniques, but to believe in them—be disciplined, maintain our concentration, and play with maximum "intensity." Probably the most emotional thing he might say would be, "Go out and do what ever it takes."

Typically, the opponent who had been having some success in the first half would come out and do the same things. In the second half, we would often totally dominate those plays that hurt us in the first half, because we no longer made the same mistakes we did earlier. It had nothing to do with getting fired up or trying harder.

The locker room really did feel like family. The team allowed us to bring our children to the Saturday morning practices. These practices were normally short (around forty-five minutes), involving only special teams and an overview of some defensive or offensive changes—spit-polishing the next day's game plan.

During practice, our kids would run around on the sidelines, throw passes, try to kick the ball, shag balls for our kickers, etc. My son, Andy Keith, fondly remembers riding around on the back of Terry Hanratty's huge Saint Bernard. My daughter, Amy, enjoyed running around on the stadium turf. After practice the boys were allowed into the locker room where they received a "red-cream soda" while the girls enjoyed cartoons on the TV in the media room.

I remember watching my son playing with Joe Greene's and Bobby Walden's sons, as the players sat on their locker stools, watching the boys tackle each other and applauding their success.

I always felt that my son had an advantage in his own football career, as he learned the game almost subliminally by watching professional players block and tackle as he grew up. Eventually, he started for the Dartmouth

College football team. Amy went on to a successful soccer career at Fox Chapel High School, where her team won the WPIAL championship her senior year.

Of course, the locker room was either a place of great joy or great sorrow depending on the huge swing of emotion from wins or losses. Granted, it's just a game, but the pain of defeat always seemed greater than the joy of winning.

After all these years I have to admit that I miss the locker room, the horsing around, the fun we had, the camaraderie, and those meaningful friendships that can only be forged through facing adversity and pressure together. The locker room was indeed a special place.

CHAPTER SIXTEEN

The Mountains

Needing to replace the game, Ray and I were still seeking out challenges, but since we were more than a little burned out physically, we needed something that would not require practice or super conditioning but still give us that euphoric fatigue that we experienced after hard-fought games.

In June of 1980, we decided to try mountain climbing. We traveled to Colorado, hoping to climb four of the State's fifty-four fourteen thousand-foot mountains in one day. The record for all fifty-four is now 11 days, and even a dog has climbed them, so how tough could it be? For two out-of-shape ex-jocks, Ray and I discovered it could be very difficult.

The four mountains—Mount Democrat, Mount Lincoln, Cameron Peak and Mount Bross—are located near Breckinridge, and all four are considered easy climbs. (Cameron is no longer counted as part of the fifty-four because despite being over fourteen thousand feet high; the saddle between it and Lincoln is not low enough.)

We got up early and drove up a steep four-wheel drive jeep trail in our rented Lincoln Town Car (talk about rubes). At one point it was so steep Ray had to get out and push the car. When he got back in the car he was gasping harder than I had ever heard him coming off the football field. We somehow got that car up to the high trailhead and next to a small lake.

We climbed those four mountains that day. We did everything wrong. We went way too fast (usually slower-moving climbers do better than the impatient), hurried over loose rock, risking a turned ankle or sprained knee, ran down a steep scree field, got too hot and then too cold and didn't bring nearly enough water.

We were caught in a blizzard so strong that it forced us to hunker down in our bivvy sacks and wait out the storm. Later marble-sized hail rained down. But we did it, and it felt really good. Certainly not a Super Bowl feeling, but good just the same.

Later that summer, my business partner, Sam Zacharias, and I went out to Mount Rainier in Washington and attended a one-day climbing school (which basically taught us how to put on crampons, use ice axes for self-arrest, learn a high-altitude breathing technique and a stepping technique called the lock-step).

It was all fairly intuitive stuff, no true athleticism required, but necessary to learn if you want to climb Rainier, all snow and ice (glaciated).

The next day we left the 5000-foot trailhead with a group of about sixteen climbers and four guides. Our goal was to reach the Muir Hut (10,000 feet) where we'd spend the night. Exhausted, we arrived in the early afternoon. I worried that the next day's summit climb might seriously exhaust us. Our guides had pushed all of us to climb faster than we wanted to, explaining that they needed to determine who was fit enough to make the summit.

The next morning at 1:30 a.m., we started off with four rope teams of three or four rookies, each with a guide leading the way. I was the last guy on the last team and I felt my competitive juices start to rise. I just don't like being in the back of the line, and I never have. Sam was in the rope team just in front of mine.

I soon learned that mountain climbing is not a competitive sport but that it does require patience, determination, concentration, good decision-making, and a high level of conditioning and teamwork.

We headed off across a broad glaciated valley where we had been warned there might be deep cracks. If the guide yelled "I'm falling," you were supposed to immediately drop onto all fours and dig your ice axe and the front points of your crampons into the ice.

We climbed slowly across the large basin towards a rock rib we could see outlined dimly by the light of the moon. In front of me I could see the headlamps of the three groups winding their way up the slope. My rope was attached to those of two teenagers and the guide. It was quiet, except for the chink of our crampons against the ice and the audible rhythms of our breathing. We were lost in our own thoughts. Time went by slowly. I worried that my business partners back home would think I was taking too much time off for frivolous pursuits, and they'd be right.

"I'm falling," I heard the guide yell.

I hit the snow hard, dug in, and faced away from the guide, expecting to feel a jolt as the guide's full weight hit the rope as he fell into a crevice. I kicked the front points of my crampons into the ice and dug the ice axe hard into the glacier, but I felt no tug on the rope. I glanced back towards where the guide had fallen and could see that my two teenage partners had not heeded the command. They just stood there looking around, wondering what had happened. The guide, who had dropped to his knees, explained that his command had been a test to remind us to pay attention and have our ice axes ready. He then reprimanded the kids for not doing what they'd been taught the day before.

I got up thinking that it's probably not a good idea to be roped to people who don't know what they're doing, and my level of comfort with my new team fell significantly. What if somebody slipped higher up and those two just stood there, not reacting to the command and the danger? The thought was not a confidence builder.

Within a half-hour, we had traversed the ice field and ascended a rock rib on a barely discernible, narrow ledge. The climbing was steep, and our pace slowed, listening to our crampons chinking against the rock. Within minutes, we were forced to stop, as the group in front of us was blocking the narrow path.

We waited, enjoying what we thought would be a short break.

"Now, what seems to be the problem, Sam?" I heard the guide ask up ahead.

"I can't breathe."

Our guide suggested that we carefully move past them on the narrow ledge as the other team sat there. We passed the group, and as I glanced to my right I saw my buddy, Sam, sitting there, looking totally exhausted, breathing hard. As I climbed past him, I patted him on the shoulder but moved quickly by, figuring the guides would know how to handle the situation.

Coming up off the rock rib, we entered a small snow bowl and found the two advanced groups waiting for us, apparently taking the first break. We were informed that we would wait for the last group and then make a decision as to who would be going forward.

After about fifteen minutes, Sam's group finally appeared, straggling up the slope. We were all ready to go, having grown cold waiting. Moments later Sam slumped down next to me.

"I just couldn't get my breath. This altitude is killing me!"

Just then the lead guide, Peter, said, "If any of you feel even slightly tired at this point, I would strongly advise you to turn around right now and go back. Because of impending bad weather we will be moving very fast from here on and we will take no breaks. Normally we'd take two or three more rests before attempting the summit. Any of you that don't feel up to it should go back with the guide right now."

I think if I hadn't played all those years of football that I might have opted to quit. Sam, having no such athletic ego to deal with, decided immediately to go back with six or seven others to the Muir Hut.

We reached the summit hours later, shortly after I had nearly convinced myself to quit. The fatigue I experienced angered me, and I was doubly irritated that my teenage ropemates had no problem making the ascent. Afterwards, I learned that they had been climbing nearby for the past twenty days and were well acclimated to the altitude.

We stayed on the summit only a short time, just long enough to rehydrate and eat an energy bar before the approach of an impending storm.

We quickly descended towards the trailhead starting position. Within a half-hour, the storm passed, the sun came out, and the heat of the previous day returned.

Two hours later, we climbed down the steep rock spur that overlooked Cadaver Gulch, a place where a number of climbers had died the previous year. We saw huge ice towers rising at least five stories tall. Though they stood there, they appeared unstable in the heat, and ice crumbled at their bases. As we descended the steep rock rib, I couldn't take my eyes off the massive chunks of ice and continually worried that one might fall as we crossed underneath.

Stunned, I looked on as at that very moment, one of the towers fell and crashed right where we would have been in twenty minutes. Our guide stopped, shook his head as though dumbstruck, and hesitated before starting down.

"Does that happen often?" I asked.

"Never seen one fall before, and I've climbed the mountain over 200 times," he said.

"Should we wait till the second tower goes?" I asked.

"We can't stay up here," he said.

When we reached the bottom of the ridge, still protected from an avalanche by a rock spur, we peered up at the remaining tower, again noticing the ice at the base crumbling—the heat of the past two days was taking effect. It seemed to me that it was definitely going to collapse. I glanced across the slope where the other tower had exploded and could see huge blocks of ice blocking the trail. The guide, exuding little confidence, decided we should unrope and run across the exposed area one at a time.

"Russell, you go last," he said.

I stood there watching as the three of them ran across the slope, running between the blocks of ice, and it occurred to me that it really wasn't necessary to sprint. By running you might actually increase the likelihood of being crushed under a falling ice pack. I figured the chance that the remaining ice tower would crash while I was crossing the expanse of approximately seventy-five yards was very low, but it did feel a little like playing Russian roulette. I walked across.

Exhausted, I arrived back at the Muir Hut, where Sam was waiting, and he eagerly asked about the climb. He was feeling so fresh that he second-guessed himself, thinking he should have climbed it. But mountain climbing isn't about summiting—it's about the challenge, and Sam had been there. He eventually came to respect his judgment to retreat.

Rainier piqued my interest in mountain climbing. I later scaled Mt. Kenya and Mt. Kilimanjaro with my kids and Sam. In fact, my athletic daughter Amy reached the summit of Kilimanjaro before the rest of us, who struggled with the lack of oxygen at 19,000 feet.

My kids also climbed three of Colorado's fourteen thousand-foot peaks–Castle Peak near Aspen, Wilson Peak and Sneffels near Telluride. However, they never seemed to find it as exhilarating as I did. They told me that they "enjoyed" the experience, but I could tell that they weren't in any hurry to do it again. I guess we're all lucky when we find an activity that is an exquisite neurosis.

Ray enjoyed coming with me but often ventured only half way up. One time he just drove me up to the trailhead, where he sat by a bubbling brook and read a good book with his favorite six-pack until I finished six hours later.

Upon my return, Ray said, "Partner, that was my favorite climb so far."

After many years of climbing, Ray and I decided to organize a Steeler climb of Mount Yale. I assumed everyone would want to be a part of the first-ever Steeler climb, financed in part by the Rooneys, who always encourage us old guys to stay together. But when I asked L. C. Greenwood and Mel Blount if they'd like to join us, they looked at me as though I'd lost my mind.

"Why would anybody climb a mountain? What's the purpose? I don't get it," L. C. said.

"It'll be fun, L. C., trust me," I said. "It's a great workout, beautiful scenery and almost as challenging as trying to tackle Tarkenton on a scramble."

"No way I'm going anywhere near any mountain," Mel returned. "It sounds like a real dumb idea, even for you, Captain."

Finally, after many calls and discussions, Mike Wagner, Gerry "Moon" Mullins, Dave Reavis, John Banazak and Frank Atkinson decided to join Ray and me on the climb. I also recruited some of my business teammates, Jeff Kendall and Jim Cronin, and my old college buddy, Jim Card, who promised to be our base camp manager. My ex-brother-in-law, Bill Comfort, an ultramarathon athlete, also joined us.

We used a friend's huge home on the Beaver Creek Golf Course as our home base and arrived there two days before the climb. The morning of the climb, I got up at 4 a.m. and shouted into all the rooms that we needed to get up and get going.

"Damn, Russell, you sound like my marine drill sergeant," Banazak complained.

As we drove up the Cottonwood Pass Road towards the trailhead, I worried that we might miss the turnoff, as it is frequently more difficult to find the starting point than the guidebooks indicate. If we missed the turn, I knew I was in for some serious harassment.

"Come on, Andy, if you can't even find the trailhead, how're you ever going to find the summit?" Atkinson said.

"Sometimes the old-timer can't find his ass with both hands," Wagner added.

"Remember the gear you might need: compass, sunglasses, suntan lotion, parka, rain suit, pile pullover, gloves and ski hat. It might snow up there," I said.

"Hey, you old worry wart, it's 60 degrees," Ray said.

As the guys fumbled around in their packs to ensure that they had everything, I realized that I'd forgotten the Xerox pages of the route that I had intended to give to everyone.

"When we come out of the woods we'll emerge into an open bowl, and you will see two mountains to your right," I said. "Mount Yale is the taller one to the left. Climb up to the saddle between the two mountains and then turn left and proceed up the ridge to the summit," I said.

"Damn, Russell, don't you have any topos?" Banazak asked.

"It's probably a good idea to team up with a buddy whose traveling at your pace," I said. "Take care of each other. Take your time, go your own speed and turn around if the weather gets bad."

Some of the guys were horsing around, barely listening, and probably assumed that we'd all climb together. However, I knew that all climbers ascend at different speeds, and that since it wasn't a dangerous mountain, there was no need to stay together.

As we headed up through the woods, winding back and forth, crossing a creek numerous times, the group separated almost immediately. Mike Wagner, a conditioning freak, and Bill Comfort, just back from the Boston Marathon, moved out way too fast—at least for the rest of us.

Meanwhile, guys in the back fell behind quickly. Being competitive in nature, I hung in there with the two stronger horses but found myself sucking wind, big-time.

They finally stopped when we came out of the treeline into the open bowl where we could see Mount Yale and the saddle. It looked exactly as I had imagined.

We looked down where the trail came out of the forest, expecting to see at least some of our teammates, but no one appeared.

"Let's go. I'm freezing," Mike said, five minutes into the break.

With that he jumped up, threw on his pack, and headed up the mountain with Comfort right behind him. I hesitated while trying to decide whether to wait for the rest of the group but then charged after them.

Within a half-hour, we found ourselves scrambling up a steep ravine full of loose scree. Following a faint trail, marked by a lot of footprints, we headed directly for the summit. It was tough slogging, as we would take a step up only to slip a half a step back. It appeared to be a logical and direct route to follow, but something seemed wrong. Fifteen minutes later, it occurred to my oxygen-deprived brain that we were off track.

"Hey, guys, we should be heading up more to our right, towards the saddle," I said.

"This is more direct," Mike said. "Look at all these footprints."

"We should climb up out of this ravine, cross over to the saddle, and then head up the ridge," I said.

"You go your way; we'll go ours. The shortest distance between two points is a straight line," said Mike, always the independent thinker.

So I climbed up out of the ravine and onto a path with much more secure footing before heading up towards the low point between the two mountains. I soon was on a path that appeared more heavily used and felt comfortable I had made the right decision.

A half-hour later I reached the saddle and took a short break, wondering how Mike and Bill were faring in the ravine, as their path appeared to be getting steeper. Once on the solid rock ridge, the ascent went quickly and I moved towards the summit with little difficulty.

Hearing a shout, I looked down the ridge and saw Mike and Bill climbing out of the ravine, about 100 yards back down the slope. Ten minutes later I peered down again and saw them drawing closer but still not near enough for us to meet and reach the summit together. Minutes later, I climbed up onto a small summit.

Sitting on top of Mount Yale was very serene. The weather was beautiful; bright sunshine, no clouds and clear view of the Sawatch mountain range, where I could see many of the fourteen thousand-footers we had already climbed.

When Bill and Mike arrived, still appearing very fit, we all drank from our water bottles, ate something and enjoyed the view. Mike informed us that we had scaled the mountain in three hours, breaking the four-hours mark we had anticipated. We pointed out various points of interest and wondered how our teammates were doing.

After less than a half-hour passed, we decided to begin our descent, and Bill and Mike again led off. I followed them down, feeling very mellow and proud that we had been successful.

Ten minutes later, however, something appeared wrong. We seemed to be heading down the same ridge we came up, but I suddenly realized it wasn't.

"Hey, guys, we're going down the wrong way," I said.

"No, this looks like the same way we came up," Mike said.

"Do you remember passing any lakes on way up? I asked.

Mike stopped and stared down the mountain, as though he was trying hard to remember those lakes, unbelieving that he was wrong.

"I definitely got hit in the head too many times," Mike said.

Then without saying another word, he turned and started back to our right, traversing a steep rock field. When descending from the top of a mountain, a misstep of only two or three feet can consequently mean a misdirection of ninety degrees, a margin of error large enough to cast the climber down dangerously steep ravines. In bad weather, when visibility is close to zero, this can be a serious problem, and that is why I asked everyone to bring a compass.

An hour later we arrived back at the treeline where we'd taken our first break. Sitting there waiting for us was Ray.

"Hey, Partner, what's going on?" I asked.

"I'm tired; forgot how hard these are. Figure I'll head down to join Jimbo and see how the base camp is doing," Ray said.

"Where is everybody?" I asked.

"Well, the group split up, but they're all up there, somewhere," Ray said, pointing up the mountain.

After a short break, Mike, Bill and Ray headed down, but I felt responsible, since the climb had been my idea. I waited for the rest of the group to reach the treeline. I had no idea that it would take another three hours to get everyone off the mountain.

As each twosome returned, appearing fairly exhausted, they recounted different stories about getting hung up on this rock, or taking the wrong route near the top, or whatever.

When the group of Jeff Kendall, Dave Reavis, Moon Mullins and John Banazak arrived, the guys spun their own story. They had, like us, chosen to follow a route up the steep gully and struggled to exit out of it near the top. They were excited that they had all reached the summit except for Banazak, who was struggling with a bad back. He had been in such pain that near the top he laid down, and staring up at the sky, began talking to his deceased father.

Finally, the last group, Atkinson and Cronin, showed up, admitting that they too had started down the wrong way. I felt relieved that everyone was off the steep part of the mountain, that there had been no injuries and they all seemed pleased that they had reached the top. At 4:30 p.m. we arrived back down at the base camp.

"Damn, Cronin, I didn't know you dudes were going to make it a two-day climb," Ray said.

"At least we got to the top, Mr. Mansfield," Cronin said.

"What did you guys do? Crawl up there on your knees?" Mike said.

"We tried to go slowly and appreciate the flora and the fauna, something you undoubtedly neglected to do," Frank said.

That night we stopped in Leadville's great hamburger joint, Buffalo Bob's, where we charged the dinner to Dan Rooney.

"You'd think, Captain, that you'd pick a fancier place than this if the Steelers are paying," Moon said.

"Right, it's not like we made any money playing the game," Mike said.

"Hey, it doesn't have to be expensive to be good," I said.

"Rooney knows your Scottish nature. Only reason he agreed to pay," Ray said.

We arrived at the big house, exhausted and happy, feeling as we always felt after a big game—bonded once again. We had done something difficult, kept our cool, made enough good decisions to succeed and felt the harmony of a job well done. Granted, Chuck Noll would not have approved of our teamwork.

I realize that peak bagging is a dumb idea—too much about the devil ego (there it is again). We should enjoy the challenge and the beauty of the mountain. The summit shouldn't really be all that important, but it does help me to set a goal, forcing me to work out regularly to achieve it.

But the joy is in the doing, not reaching the summit; the journey is the destination.

My significant other, Cindy Ellis, has been a great companion on many of these climbs, enjoying the physical challenge and appreciating the beauty of the mountains. We have done a number of "Couples Climbs" where we have invited other friends, and everyone seemed to enjoy the effort.

Cindy, my true soulmate, a great lady, will sometimes reach the summit, but on other occasions will climb very close to the summit only to become concerned about the "exposure" and will stop, pull out a book, appreciate the beautiful scenery and wait for me to complete the climb. She doesn't need to reach the summit to enjoy the effort. I'm not quite there yet. I met a climbing guide in Colorado who refuses to stand on the summit, preferring to stop a few yards before, in a conscious effort to not be a peak bagger.

Sometimes we meet people in their eighties climbing up the steep slopes, trying to complete the Grand Slam (climbing all fifty-four). We always praise them for still setting goals and pursuing them despite the toughness of the challenge so late in life.

This past year we climbed our first thirteen thousand-footer, Palmyra Peak in Telluride, and enjoyed it every bit as much as a fourteen thousand-footer. There are over six hundred thirteen thousand-footers in Colorado, and if my beat-up old body (lots of aches and pains from football) holds up, I want to be climbing those 13ers with my friends and family well into my eighties. God willing, of course.

CHAPTER SEVENTEEN

A Paris Boondoggle

J oe Greene and I were once asked to join an NFL All-Star team on a trip to Paris where we would play in an "exhibition" game as a fundraiser for the American Hospital. The group consisted of my fellow team union reps, as well as some legitimate superstars like Joe, Bob Hayes, the former Olympic hundred-meter sprint champion, and Merlin Olsen, the great Rams defensive lineman.

I was thrilled to be asked to participate in the one-week, all-expense-paid trip to Paris, where the American expatriate community would host us. Frankly, I considered it somewhat of a boondoggle—a real lark and ultrafrivolous but hard to turn down.

As you might expect, professional athletes receive invitations to all-expense-paid trips to some wonderful and interesting places. During my career, Ray and I, along with our able pal, Sam Zacharias, who acted as our unofficial agent/manager, flew around the world five times, financed by various NFL promotions.

We were the guests of Aramco in Saudi Arabia; invited to a cocktail party at the U.S. Embassy in Kuwait, guests of *Touchdown Magazine* and the Sony Corporation in Japan; hosted by Westinghouse executives in Korea; asked to deliver speeches at the American Clubs in Hong Kong, Singapore and Tokyo; held sports clinics for the children of oil company executives in Singapore; spoke to customers of the Mellon Bank in London; entertained the U.S. military in Vietnam (me), Korea (Ray), and the

Mediterranean (both of us); assisted Coca-Cola to combat hunger in America with the "Taste of the NFL" event at every Super Bowl; and participated in golf tournaments all over the United States.

But this Paris trip seemed to be exceptionally sweet—after all, who wouldn't enjoy a free week in Paris? And it was scheduled for April, a great time to visit France. My wife at the time, Nancy, took all of two seconds to confirm that it was a trip she wanted to go on.

Since Nancy and I lived in Germany for two years and were familiar with Europe, we took our friend Bill Curry, an All-Pro center for the Colts there and rented a car to tour our favorite spots—the "Schloss" Castle in Heidelberg, the Casino in Baden-Baden, the Romantische Strasse, a highway to Rothenburg, my all-time favorite German city, and Nuremberg, where I had been stationed. We had a fabulous time meandering around for a few days before flying from Munich to meet our new team.

After arriving at the new Meridian Hotel, we received an invitation to a cocktail party at which all the couples were to be introduced. Everyone showed up on time except Dante Pastorini of the Houston Oilers.

Dante, a confirmed bachelor and a great player, made the grand entrance, showing up late with a knockout babe from Houston, a topless dancer who was barely in her twenties. Dante introduced his sweetheart to all the players and their wives. The guys couldn't help but stare at this luscious female as the wives pulled us to the other side of the room.

As Dante made the rounds, his lady friend only made eye contact with the men, as her hands rested on her gorgeous hips. Of course, all the wives were very polite, but you can only imagine the conversations aired in the ladies' room.

The next morning we had our first meeting with hospital officials and some of the big brass from the expat community who organized the event. We were surprised when they informed us that the game would be broadcast on national TV, after an important rugby game between the top German and French teams. They had already arranged for our uniforms and pads to be sent over and we would be expected to play "live," a full-speed game.

This news shocked us all. Professional football players do not play live football games unless they are paid to do so. The reason pro teams, unlike colleges, never scrimmage is that every time they do, people get hurt, often seriously. We had come over expecting to play at most a flag football game, and they wanted us to go live. Their plan simply would be impossible to carry out, as our NFL contracts wouldn't allow it.

After much debate the sponsors agreed to allow us to stage a game, or rather, to fake it. With a week already crammed full of activities, they couldn't send us home and therefore had no other option.

We offered to write a script full of big plays you might see in a real game. We'd deliver long touchdown passes and runs. We'd have devastating hits, sacks and interceptions; in essence it became a precursor to the XFL. We told the organizers that we'd put it together later in the week, but in the meantime we wanted to take advantage of all the parties and games they had planned for us.

Despite the misunderstanding regarding the game, the expat community went all out to ensure our trip was enjoyable. On the social side, we attended a series of sumptuous cocktail parties: one on the top of the Eiffel tower, another at a famous author's apartment that overlooked the Seine, and another in a fabulous Isle d'Saint Louis apartment.

One night we had dinner with John Wilbur, who then played for the Redskins and claimed to be a wine connoisseur. John bought me a bottle of 1941 (my birth year) Bordeaux. It was spectacularly tasty except for the two inches of sediment on the bottom of the bottle. This wine tasting was followed up by a great party at the U.S. Embassy where we met President Kennedy's sister, Pat, and Robert Kennedy's wife, Ethel, and the ambassador, the brother of a former IBM chairman. During the day we hobnobbed with our new friends over cordials at the Ritz bar, and I realized that despite trying to resist the lure of the good life and all that corrupting stuff that accompanies it, I enjoyed rubbing shoulders with the rich and famous.

After the parties, which always took longer than scheduled, we were free to dine wherever we wanted. We followed the advice of the locals and dined at great places from a list of superb restaurants, all of which had quiet elegance, great food, outstanding ambiance and relatively reasonable prices.

As to athletic challenges, they kept us busy. We teed it up at the finest Paris golf course along with French touring pros and then played a game of flag football in the park, crushing the expats, defeating them by 48 points. We couldn't help but notice that Dante, who apparently was too busy with his new friend, failed to show for any of these events.

Not to be embarrassed by the football game, the locals, who were all super-talented and competitive guys that worked for U.S. worldwide conglomerates, challenged us to a game of softball, a game few of us had played since high school. The expats, selecting an all-star team from their local league, thought they had finally found the sport that would allow them to recapture some of their lost dignity. Surely, we couldn't beat them, having not played the game since we were kids.

A makeshift baseball diamond in a beautiful wooded Paris park played host to our scrimmage, with a small stand containing the ex-pats' wives and kids, thirsting for vengeance. Things weren't looking too optimistic for the good guys. Trying to be gracious (not easy for us), we let them bat first.

After a rousing game riddled with laughs, stumbles and blunders on our part, it came down to the final inning. Facing a three-run deficit, our team had two outs, but the bases were loaded. Feeling sort of embarrassed about the way we had beat up on these very nice people, I felt comfortable with the fact that we were only one out from losing.

But as everyone waited for us to designate a final batter, an irritating noise distracted us, and everyone turned to glare at the source. Behind the backstop, a black limo pulled up with its horn blaring. As the rear door opened, a bottle of champagne fell to the ground, shattering on the cement. Next emerged two attractive legs of a clearly beautiful woman, none other than the Grande Dame herself, Dante's new pal.

Finally, out tripped Dante himself, obviously influenced by too much bubbly.

As Dante ambled over to our bench, the thought came to me that allowing Dante to take the last at-bat would be the most gentlemanly thing for us to do, since we really had to let our hosts win something. It would be a classic gesture of good will, but also one that would help us save face.

So Dante staggered up to bat and tripped over home plate, nearly falling down. "This is not going to be pretty," I thought. He took a couple of mighty practice swings and settled in, hiccupping loudly as he waited for the first pitch. When it arrived, he missed it by at least a foot, swinging below the ball and way too early for the slow, high-arched pitch. His next swing was nearly as bad, and he missed the ball high by a good six inches, this time swinging far too late. Two strikes and no balls; the game was nearly over.

At that moment we all heard a young child in the stands say, "Daddy's team is going to win, Mommy."

Dante was not a person familiar with failure. I watched him pull himself together, shake off his alcohol-induced buzz and focus on the task at hand. After all, Dante had gone to college on a baseball scholarship. The next pitch seemed to take forever, but Dante remained patient and timed his swing perfectly, blasting the ball high over the center fielder's head and 50 yards into the woods. The guy just stood there, stunned.

Dante jogged around the bases, high-fiving the opponents as he went by, and I noticed that even the expats appreciated the display of awesome talent they had just witnessed. The game was over, and we had won again.

The next day, a number of my fellow teammates were loitering around the hotel lobby. I approached them and asked what they were going to do that day. They delivered a disappointing answer. They had no idea what to do in Paris and were bored. The first thing that jumped in my mind was that they should see the Louvre, one of the most famous art museums in the world. I asked them if they'd been there, but they hadn't. In fact, they hadn't even heard of the renowned tourist destination.

As a teenager, I was forced to go through the Louvre for three days, stopping at each painting to listen to my sweet mother, Esther, read to me all about the painter and the painting's background. Frankly, it was a lot more than I wanted to know.

On a whim I asked, "So, do you guys want to go with me to the Louvre?"

"What's the Louvre?"

"One of the finest art museums in the world."

"No chance, Russell. There's no way I'm spending my vacation time in some museum, looking at art. Where's the nearest bar?" one said.

"Why don't we try and break the four-minute Louvre?" I said, remembering a classic Art Buchwald article in which he made fun of the "ugly American" tourists who rushed through the museum just to say they'd been there. Always appreciating a challenge to their athleticism, they agreed to join me.

I explained Buchwald's farcical rules. "You can race-walk but not break into a trot. You must stop at five of the most famous works of art, such as the *Mona Lisa* and the *Winged Victory*, and maybe we can actually break the four-minute Louvre. No one has ever done it. I think some Swedes set the best time ever, around four minutes, thirty-six seconds."

So we trekked to the museum, sporting jogging shoes and sweat clothes, paid our entrance fee, got a map showing the five most famous works of art and started walking as fast as we could.

At the *Mona Lisa*, Joe Greene paused and asked, "What did she just swallow?"

Four minutes and fifteen seconds later, we once again arrived at the front door, and my teammates began congratulating each other on breaking the current Louvre record. I was embarrassed, of course, by our insane competitiveness and failure to appreciate the world's best museum and its truly fine art. I worried that someone might have observed our irreverence, and I could almost hear my mother scolding me for failing to honor these world-famous artists. Maybe, I hoped, some sliver of respect for the quality of the art had penetrated into our thick skulls.

Later that evening while having a cocktail in the hotel bar, I noticed Joe Greene and his wife Agnes sitting in the corner. I walked over to them and sat down.

"So, Joe, what do you think? Isn't Paris a special place?"

"Can't stand this city, Captain."

"Why?"

"The people are rude. You can't get a cab. Everything is outrageously over-priced. The food is inedible—they got the crème d'this and the crème d'that—this city sucks."

"Don't candy-coat it; how do you really feel about Paris?"

"I'm ready to go home right now," Joe said.

"Look, why don't you and Agnes join us tonight? We're going to The Crazy Horse Saloon—supposed to be a fun place," I said.

After a meal in a restaurant across the street from our hotel with, admittedly, a strange sauce on tiny, unrecognizable pieces of meat, served after a long wait, by a surly waiter, in a hot, overcrowded, snobby place, we took a taxi over to the Crazy Horse. Joe offered to pay, but he complained when the driver told him the price and even climbed into the front seat to check the meter, not believing the rate could be so high.

Entering the Saloon, we were rudely asked to wait while the Maitre d' searched for our reservation. When he couldn't find it, I flashed a twenty-dollar U.S. bill, but that really seemed to really irritate him. Finally, after much hemming and hawing, I forced a bigger bribe of francs, and we were taken to our seats with just enough time to order a round of drinks before the show started.

The host seated the four of us in a tiny alcove, barely big enough for two people, let alone four. Joe—all six feet, four inches, and 298 pounds of him—was sitting on a tiny stool, with hardly enough room to hold one of his cheeks. The place was very hot, and sweat was literally rolling off Joe's face. He was clearly agitated. It took forever for our overpriced drinks to arrive, and the glass looked like a thimble in Joe's huge hands. Our grand evening was not going well.

A bunch of stunningly beautiful Swedish ladies pretending to be lesbians staged the show, dancing to weird music while they feigned stroking each other's vital parts. Despite finding the show weirdly erotic, I watched Joe, sitting on his miniature chair, balancing his drink on his huge lap, wearing a scowl that would have frightened Vince Lombardi. Before the act ended, Joe bolted towards the door, and the three of us reluctantly followed suit.

Joe hurried over to the closest taxi—a small Peugeot—opened the door and started to get in, waving for us to follow. But a strange thing happened. The taxi driver reached across the back seat and gestured with his open palm, pushing Joe back out of the car.

I heard the driver, who had quickly gotten out of the cab, ask Joe where he was going.

"Hotel Meridian," Joe said.

"How much you willing to pay?" the cabbie asked.

"Turn your meter on, man-whatever it is we'll pay it."

"No meter this time—how much you pay?" he asked again.

By then, Joe's temper flared—he was still irritated by the overpriced dinner and bizarre show. He was not someone to mess with, particularly if he felt insulted or the recipient of any behavior that could possibly be interpreted as racial prejudice.

"Look, Mr. Taxi Man, we'll pay whatever the meter says. Let's get going," Joe said, as he started to enter the cab once more. But the driver, apparently angry at Joe's refusal to bargain, yelled at him to stay out of his automobile, and he started to walk away towards the restaurant, as though searching for more reasonable customers.

Unknowingly, he was walking away from the wrong guy. Joe glared after him, seething with anger. He bent his knees and grabbed the underneath of the small car. As Joe grunted under the strain, the car slowly began to rise, and when Joe had it about eye level, clearly intending to turn it upside down on the pavement, he let it rest in that balanced position. With the slightest nudge, it would have toppled upside down.

"You might want to reconsider your attitude, Cabbie, or you're going to find your taxi belly up."

"Gendarmes, gendarmes!" The cabbie yelled at the top of his lungs.

People emptying out of the Crazy Horse after the show stared in shock at the sight before them, a huge man about to turn a taxi upside down.

I grabbed Joe's arm, pulled it down and said, "Joe, we've got to go, man. This could be trouble."

Joe stood back from the car, allowed it to crash down hard, and left it shaking violently on its axle, rocking back and forth. I pulled Joe away from the scene, and the four of us ran for the subway.

"Where are we going, Captain?

"Let's ride the subway back."

"I don't ride subways."

"We'll get back to the hotel sooner and a hell of a lot cheaper than those taxis, which, by the way, you are required to negotiate the fare after 11:00 p.m. Sorry, my fault, I forgot," I said.

Joe sat fuming in the crowded subway car, and I realized just how close that taxi had come to being turned upside down. It would have made quite a scene. My effort to show Joe a good time in Paris had totally backfired, and he just sat seething. I figured it was a good time to not talk.

The next day's itinerary boasted our first "fake" football game. Maybe, I hoped, the enthusiastic French fans and the expats will find it believable. Quarterback Jim Hart and I, with a lot of help from the group, had written a script, but we were less than confident that we would be able to pull it off.

When we arrived at the stadium, the roar of a packed house greeted our surprised ears. Thousands of people packed the stands to observe a big game between the top German rugby team and the top French rugby team. I was surprised that we weren't scheduled to go first, to give the rugby teams the top billing.

Once we got on the field, the significantly smaller rugby players were still competing, and we stood in the end zone for at least five minutes watching the game.

Armed with no equipment to protect themselves, the rugby players left the field with broken noses and bloodstains, while we stood there, dwarfing them in size, yet clothed in layers of padding and tip-toeing down the sidelines. None of us could help but feel slightly absurd. I glanced at Joe, and I could tell that he was uncomfortable with this format and that he suddenly wanted to go live. I realized that our game could turn ugly in a heartbeat.

Well, I have to admit that we went out there and made complete asses of ourselves. There is just no plausible way to fake the game of football. Like our coaches always told us, the best way to not get hurt is to go full speed. If you let up just for a second, lose your focus or intensity, you are inviting injury. It dawned on me for the first time that allowing someone to knock you down in an impressive fashion could be dangerously awkward. Maybe those WWF wrestlers who stage their matches are pretty decent athletes after all.

Our plan was to call the result of the next play and then wait until the offensive unit was up to the line of scrimmage. Then we would repeat in a whisper, back and forth, from the QB to the defense, the play that was to be run—to ensure that we were on the same page.

It was a very unusual scene. Jim Hart or Dante would arrive at the line of scrimmage and whisper over our defensive line, "Sweep right for 20 yards." Translated, this meant that the defensive players would allow themselves to be blocked yet someone would make the tackle 20 yards downfield. You can imagine how absurd it felt for us to fake that we were being blocked, to pretend that we were failures, to consciously allow an opponent to prevail. It was against the nature of the team, and I felt myself resist.

I could also see Joe Greene standing in the huddle hearing that he was about to be blocked by John Wilbur—a solid journeyman Redskin guard who was someone Joe couldn't even imagine blocking him (unless John tackled him), and then being forced to let the runner go by, without reaching out.

By the second quarter Joe was out of his mind, fuming exactly as he had with the taxi driver the previous night, and I just knew he wouldn't be able to stifle his competitiveness any longer.

The next play scheduled was supposed to be a deep touchdown pass to Bob Hayes, but Joe sacked Dante with his usual slam. Dante, despite knowledge that he was supposed to throw a TD on that play, took it good-naturedly and laughed it off.

"Joe, lighten up. Stay with the script," I said.

"This is killing me, Captain. I can't just let these dudes move the ball on down the field," Joe said.

"Look, let the guy block you. We need to show these fans how the offense can score and the only player they've ever heard of on our entire roster is Bob Hayes," I said.

So the next play, all of our defensive linemen, including Joe, granted amnesty and supplied Hart with the time to loft a perfect pass to Hayes, who was allowed to get behind one of our defensive backs. Unfortunately, Hayes dropped it. The guy really did have cement hands. The fans started whistling, a sound that we all initially thought was an indication of their approval but actually only signaled their disgust.

We tried it again on the next play, and Hayes dropped another pass, right in the numbers as he crossed the goal line. We were improvising now, because we hadn't imagined the possibility of one of the offensive guys screwing up without our help.

The following play, we threw a pitchout to Hayes and allowed him to evade all of us as we dove to make the tackle. As he scored, the fans appeared happy.

Truthfully, that "exhibition" proved to be a nightmarish humiliation for NFL Football. That game probably set the possibility of generating interest in American football in France back for ten years.

What did I learn from that experience? Never agree to fake anything, unless the audience understands that they are witnessing a farce.

CHAPTER EIGHTEEN

Tricks of the Trade

Football is a complicated sport that relies heavily on concocting plays that will confuse your opponents. Like all teams, we often implemented fake alignments, positioning ourselves to appear we were playing one defense when we were really playing another. I enjoyed these mind games, and sometimes I would attempt to mess with an opponent's mind even before the game began.

In the locker room prior to the 1973 Pro Bowl, I sat near Oakland's great receiver Fred Bilitnikoff, from Erie, Pennsylvania. Fred, slow by today's standards, was extremely successful because of his precise routes and incredibly good hands. He simply never dropped a pass.

I watched Fred spread enormous amounts of "stickum" onto his arms and jersey. Not unfamiliar with the stuff, I was still astounded at the huge amounts Fred applied all over his hands and arms, and even on his jersey and pants. You could apply it by either smearing or spraying. Fred did both.

Stickum is a thick, dark, gummy, glue-like substance that receivers routinely apply to their jerseys, arms and hands to help them catch the ball. Quarterbacks hate the stuff, fearing correctly that it might interfere with their ability to release the ball properly on their throws and often ask the officials for a clean ball after every reception.

Apparently, to test the adequacy of his application of this gooey substance, Fred stuck the underneath of his forearm on top of a football resting on the bench across from him and lifted his arm upwards. Amazingly, the ball stuck to his forearm without any assistance from his hands.

A year later, watching Oakland play the Miami Dolphins in their play-off game and knowing we'd be playing one of them in the AFC championship round, I recalled Fred's heavy use of the stuff when he caught a key touchdown pass in the endzone. Ken Stabler had been forced to throw the ball early, and it arrived before Fred expected it, barely allowing Fred time to get his arms up. The ball stuck to his right forearm for a moment before he could deliver it into his hands. Without the stickum, the ball would have bounced right off his forearm and been simply another incompletion.

The following week in Oakland, going through our pregame routine, I noticed Fred, a chain-smoking, nervous type, standing nearby waiting for his turn.

I motioned for Fred to come over and talk, as I peered over my shoulder as though I was afraid that someone might overhear us. Then I motioned him away, as though I had changed my mind and decided not to tell him whatever information I had originally intended to convey. Fred, clearly curious about what it was, beckoned to me, but it was my turn to take some snaps at linebacker.

I could see Fred out of the corner of my eye, pacing back and forth, impatiently waiting for me to return so that he could find out what I had wanted to tell him. After a number of rotations, just prior to our being called into the locker room, I finally walked over to Fred, glancing over my shoulder at my teammates as though I was worried they might see me talking with Fred.

"Fred, don't go near our bench."

"Why, what's the problem?"

"It just wouldn't be a good idea."

With that I turned my back to him and started to walk towards the locker room.

Fred followed me and grabbed my arm.

"Look, man, what's gonna happen if I go near your bench?"

I shook my head as though I had decided not to tell him, but then I stopped as we reached the edge of the field.

"Our guys know how much stickum you use, so they've put together a big container full of feathers, and when you go near our bench, they're going to tar and feather you."

I paused for a moment, watching Fred's eyes get bigger as he comprehended what I'd said.

"You'll look like a tar baby covered with snow."

"You've got to be kidding."

"No, I'm real serious. You'll look like a big white goose, and all that proud silver and black you Raiders wear will just disappear."

With that I turned and jogged towards our locker room, allowing Fred to imagine the moment.

Later, on the bus to the airport, while savoring our huge win, I remembered my bogus threat. I was sitting next to coach Bud Carson, our defensive coordinator, and I noticed him going over the defensive stats.

"Coach, how many deep comebacks near our bench did Bilitnikoff run?"

"That's strange, he didn't catch any, not a single one. In fact, he never even ran that route."

"Just demonstrates how much Oakland respects Mel and J.T."

Of course, maybe there was some other reason that Fred didn't run that particular pattern that day, but nevertheless I enjoyed my little ruse.

In our second Super Bowl, playing against Dallas, I used another ploy to get an edge on the bigger and stronger blocker I was about to face. On a key fourth and one, knowing that I had responsibility for penetrating through the gap to the inside of the tight end, I turned to Mel Blount just as the big tight end was nearing the line of scrimmage, knowing that he'd overhear me.

"Mel, I've got the outside; play the cutback."

Since I wasn't exactly the biggest linebacker and not even close to the strongest, the area of goal-line defense proved difficult. The job of this position is to get in a three-point stance and penetrate through the tackle/tight end gap, a particularly tough task when the tight end knows that that's what you will attempt to do.

I persuaded the coaches to give me the option of occasionally stunting on an outside loop, containing anything wide. I developed a quick outside move that enabled me to make some good plays on the outside. I figured that the Dallas tight end, having watched endless films of our games, would be prepared for that move.

As I got down in my stance, I could sense that he had heard me and that he believed that I was going to loop outside.

When the ball was snapped I easily penetrated into the backfield, hitting the fullback well behind the line of scrimmage. Unfortunately, the tight end had been quick enough, despite stepping to the outside, to pin my right arm behind me, and my left arm was caught against Dwight White's shoulder as he penetrated upfield also. Consequently, I could only attempt to spear the runner with my head and shoulders, in hopes that I might knock him off his feet. Despite my ruse, he was able to move the sticks.

Another trick I had used on passing downs when I had responsibility to cover the running backs was to fake a blitz. I had noticed that running backs, when not playing the role of primary receiver, often had blitz pickup before they released out into the flat. Often, linebackers seeing the back pause for blitz pickup would drop back and try to help another team-mate, assuming incorrectly that they no longer had to worry about the back. Those backs often would release out into the flat and make an easy catch in open field.

I had figured correctly that in instances like that if I faked a blitz, they would just stay in and pick me up, thinking I was really coming. It made for an easy coverage if they did release out to the flat late.

It is, of course, a lot easier to blitz than it is to cover a fast running back in open field. On a number of occasions, I noticed that if the quarterback was standing within a few yards with his back to me, I would be able to release from the running back's block and get a sack. It was an incredible feeling to get a sack when executing this coverage strategy. When I made a sack on pass coverage, it irritated Jack Ham and Jack Lambert, because we paid bonuses into the linebacker Christmas party fund for good plays and fines for bad plays. Sacks paid big. The Jacks preferred it when I funded the Christmas party.

On other occasions, I would utilize the opposite strategy, faking that I was dropping back into coverage by turning my back to the running back and taking a large step towards the secondary. This caused running backs who had blitz pickup to release to the outside. Then I would execute the blitz. I remember Floyd Little scolding me. "Russell, that's not fair, man," after I sacked Charlie Johnson.

One year early in my career, I was on the punt return team, and we were prepared to attempt a punt block. It was a game against the St. Louis Cardinals, and I thought I might be able to make the block. Early in the first quarter, I had to go in on the punt return team to execute a return right. My job was to prevent the right up-back, a rookie running back, from releasing quickly downfield. I worked very hard to stop him and prevent him from getting down the field early. I cut him on the next punt, and I could tell that he was angry, because he knew he wasn't doing his job correctly.

Our next punt didn't occur until early in the second quarter, and when the coaches called "the block," I felt a huge rush of adrenaline; this might be my chance to make a big play. So when the up-back approached his position, I turned to my teammates and yelled loudly, "Let's hold these guys up. Make sure you get a good jam; keep them on the line of scrimmage. We need this return."

I could see the up-back's eyes, and I knew he was thinking about those earlier punts. I could sense from his body language that he was thinking about how to avoid me, but when the ball was snapped I drove right at him. He actually leaped out of my way, trying to avert the jam, but he was my only blocker, and with him out of the way, I raced towards the punter, untouched. As I approached Jackie Smith, the Cardinal punter, I realized I was so early that I could definitely block the punt. As he kicked the ball, I put my facemask right down on it, and it ricocheted off my face mask. The ball hit the ground, bounced right back up into my arms, and I ran in forty-five yards for the score.

I had made a big play, one that could certainly help us win the game, but only because I had scammed my man. It was interesting to observe his eyes the next time they punted and a return was called. I could see that he didn't trust me. I yelled for my teammates to hold them up, and since he never moved from his spot, it was easy to block him. The next time I called for everybody to get a good break so we could block the punt, he was so confused that he actually backed up. I was playing with his mind, and he obviously wasn't reacting well.

On a number of occasions I cooked up a story and told Joe Greene that I had gotten a call from Bob Demarco, an All-Pro center first with St. Louis, a teammate of ours for a short period, and then with Cleveland, and that he had confided in me that he thought Joe was overrated and that he intended to block him all over the field. If Joe did get by him, he intended to hold him. Joe's eyes would get real large and I could see him preparing mentally to destroy Bob. Later, after a game in which Joe had hurt Bob so badly he was carried off the field on a stretcher, I worried that my little ruse wasn't so innocent after all.

Were such maneuvers unfair? I don't think so. In most sports, deception is just part of the game. As I became an older player, I needed an edge. Practicing tactics that fooled my opponent always seemed to be that advantage.

Although mind games are certainly fun, teams don't win games equipped only with such maneuvers. Sound techniques, good anticipation and a lot of effort are the fundamentals; there are no gimmicks that bring consistent wins.

CHAPTER NINETEEN

The Chief

M uch has been written about the Steelers' venerable founder, Art
Rooney Sr., known by his family, friends, players, and most of
Pittsburgh as "The Chief." According to local legend, the Chief, a long-
time sports enthusiast and stylish entrepreneur, won the money to buy
the Steelers in a card game. Whether or not that legend is true is anyone's
guess, but it only adds to the man's charm.

For the Chief, owning the Steelers made him truly happy. He loved the
action, the smell of liniment in the training room, the pressure-packed
atmosphere in the stadium, and most of all his rapport with his players.

He once told me that in the old days ('40s and '50s), he would drink
and play cards with his boys on the long train rides to places like Chicago,
Detroit and Cleveland. As the television revenues grew, salaries soared
and the game centered more around big business, I think the Chief missed
those good times with his players.

But Mr. Rooney rarely missed a practice, rain or shine, cold or heat.
Afterwards, he would walk through the locker room, smoking his big
cigar, consoling the injured, patting those on the back who needed it and
showing us that he really cared. The atmosphere made us all feel as though
we were part of a very special family.

When I came to the Steelers in 1963, it was a team that embod-
ied the Chief's spirit—rough and ready, aggressive and audacious. The
old vets took pride that teams feared playing the Steelers. Despite their

frequent losses, the Steelers were not a lot of fun to play, as they would often injure their opponents. In those days, the team established the definition of "tough."

Some special moments involving the Chief really stand out for me. The first occurred my rookie year when we practiced at South Park's field. It was a bitterly cold December day, and none of us, despite running hard for over an hour, could keep warm. In fact, it was so cold that Coach Parker drove his Cadillac down onto the field, right up behind the offensive huddle.

Parker, sitting in his car with the heater running, would roll the window down, blow cigar smoke into the face of Ed Brown (our quarterback), and give Brown the play he wanted us to execute. He'd then roll the window back up to watch the play. Apparently his defroster wasn't working, because he had an assistant get out and scrap the ice off the windshield every so often. But over on the sidelines, diligently supporting his boys, stood the Chief, dressed in no more than an overcoat and a scarf to keep him warm.

Later that year, we played the final game of the regular season in Yankee Stadium for the eastern division championship against the New York Giants. If we had won that game, we would have been in the NFL championship game against a Chicago Bears team that we had tied, 17-17, a few weeks earlier. Being that close to an NFL championship was new territory for his "stillers."

When we lost that huge game, some thought it was because we wore cleated shoes while the Giants wore sneakers on the frozen turf. The truth is that we were out-played. Afterward, in the silent locker room, we all sat, thinking about what might have been. Our miserable performance angered Coach Parker so much that he avoided us, afraid his legendary temper might erupt.

When the Chief entered the room, I tried to imagine how he was feeling. I only had been there for one year, but the loss felt horrible to me. How must the Chief, who had encouraged and supported his players and coaches throughout all those losing years, feel to finally come so close?

Mr. Rooney simply lit up one of his big stogies and walked around the room, speaking quietly to every player.

When he got to me, he put his arm around my shoulder and said, "Son, you had a good year, and I'm real proud of the way you played today and want to wish you a very good off season. Take care of yourself."

His statements and presence moved me. Though we had hugely disappointed this man, he still wished us well.

Once the Chief asked Ray Mansfield and me to join him at the Belmont Stakes to watch Nashua attempt to win the Triple Crown. The three of us flew to New York and then took a limousine to the racetrack, where he was recognized and fawned over by everyone from the parking lot attendant to the track manager.

Sitting next to Mr. Rooney and waiting for the big race, I could sense his excitement.

"You know, boys, at one time I was the best handicapper in the country. I won so much money here once they asked me to leave, and I did. I didn't want to bust them," the Chief said.

It was a statement conveyed without ego and in his just-the-facts sort of understated manner. The Chief was back in his element. Nashua lost that day, but the Chief had bet on the winner, a horse named Pass Catcher who was a 30-to-1 shot. He said he liked the name.

I think Mr. Rooney enjoyed dealing with his Steelers more than he did running his other businesses. Once Chuck Noll had turned us around in 1972, winning our first AFC central division championship, the Chief became determined to put together the team of the decade.

In early months of 1974, the Steelers drafted Lynn Swann No. 1, a potential superstar from USC who now holds a place in the NFL Hall of Fame. The Steelers were on a roll with No. 1 draft choices, having taken Joe Greene in 1969 and Terry Bradshaw in 1970, but the Chief felt they needed Swann to get to the next level—the Super Bowl.

Howard Slusher, Swann's savvy agent and lawyer, studied the draft and knew he possessed someone special in Swann. Finally, the Steelers relented (which was against the Chief's nature) and gave Swann the contract that Slusher wanted. After all the papers were signed, Howard met with the Chief for a few minutes before leaving for his flight back to L.A.

"So, you think you won, that you got our number, you took advantage of me," the Chief said.

"I just think Lynn got what he deserves."

"No, you think you took me to the cleaners. Don't you? Admit it."

"Based on Lynn's USC performance, it's a fair deal."

"Actually, I think we won. You settled too cheap."

"Why do you say that?" Howard asked, worrying that he might have missed something.

"You never overpay for a horse that wins the Kentucky Derby. I think this kid will make us Super Bowl Champions."

Of course that very year, Lynn's rookie season, we did win our first Super Bowl.

That first Super Bowl night, in New Orleans in January 1975, the locker room seemed quieter than one might expect. Chuck Noll, smiling in a calm and controlled manner, acted as though he had known all along that it was just a matter of time.

It was a tradition for one of the cocaptains to give away a game ball to the outstanding player. As I climbed up on the NFL awards platform, I spotted the Chief, standing in the background with the same expression he had many years earlier in Yankee Stadium, ever proud of his boys.

As I held the ball above my head, despite knowing that Joe Greene and Franco Harris had fantastic games, everyone in the room instinctively knew that the ball ought to be awarded to the Chief.

As I gave the Chief the ball with one hand and shook his with my other, I almost cried. The Chief calmly smiled, proud of his boys for finally climbing to the top of the ladder. We had all come so far. That was a moment I will never forget.

Our Life's Work

Chuck Noll, the only coach to win four out of six Super Bowls, often reminded us that we ought to "seek our life's work." It was almost as though he was encouraging us to recognize that point in time when our efforts would produce only diminishing returns. In effect, he hoped that it wouldn't be necessary for him to cut us; we'd cut ourselves.

There stands a time in the life of every athlete when the body grows too old and too weathered with injuries. A player's knowledge of the game increases every season, but all the while, his physical ability declines. Though the player is basically getting smarter with age, he also becomes weaker and slower, often from injuries.

For a linebacker, if lucky, the crossover year when one reaches the optimal point, a combination of experience and physical talent, is 30 years old. After that, the player's health goes downhill fast, but it's a great ride. When I reached the age of 35, I decided it was time to move on.

Since Chuck constantly reminded us to reevaluate ourselves, I became determined to make the decision myself. I retired when the time had come to focus 100 percent on business, rather than splitting time between business and football. I had worked seven-day weeks during the season for eight years, and I felt slightly burned out.

During the season, I attended meetings in my pinstripe suit, sold my DLJ real estate syndications at 6 a.m. breakfasts, and drove to the stadium at 8:30. Not wanting the coaches to know that something besides football took my attention, I'd throw an old beat-up leather jacket on over my suit slacks and take off my tie before entering the locker room.

After practice, I frequently went to the office to follow up with sales calls or to dinner meetings. I believed that my business pursuits actually helped my football, because if I were to focus only on the game, I would tend to overanalyze the opponent's tendencies and become unable to react, experiencing paralysis of analysis.

The Steelers offered me a two-year contract to continue playing. According to George Perles, even if I couldn't play, my leadership in the locker room would justify the contract. However, I figured that there were plenty of leaders in that locker room and that it was time for me to move on.

It was not a problem to find a way to make a living, since I already had my own business, Russell Investments, Inc. But issues arose as I attempted to replace football in my life, something that had dominated my life since I was a little kid. Ray Mansfield also retired that year, and we often got together to discuss how we felt about our post-football lives. Something was missing for both of us.

We decided that we needed to make our new endeavors as exciting and challenging as our football careers. Though difficult, it would be well worth the effort. I truly believe that it was good that I didn't make all that much money playing football and instead had to do so in the real world.

Can you imagine retiring from your profession at the age of 35 and having all the money you'd need to take care of your family forever? It might be a corrupting situation. There is a very real chance that you would never reach your potential, because you'd have no need to push yourself. Essentially, your life could be over. You might, unless you were very disciplined, spend the rest of your life living in the past. Not a good situation.

The players of the '70s had no such worries. We didn't make enough money during our playing days to be able to retire on that alone. A second career was mandatory. We had no choice but to develop an occupation on the side. I view this as a huge benefit.

Shortly after my retirement, my friend Walt Bent, the general manager of Pittsburgh Xerox, introduced me to Frank Zappala, a successful K-mart developer. Frank asked what Steeler I would recommend to help in marketing a financial product in one of the family companies. Despite knowing there were a number of very capable guys, I decided to recommend Rocky Bleier, knowing he was smart and hard-working.

After focusing hard on my syndication business and doubling my Steeler salary the first year out of the game, I still felt that I needed more products to broaden the base of my investment business.

I got a call from Rock in the fall of 1978. He urged me to meet with his new partners, Charlie Zappala (Frank's super-smooth and very smart youngest brother), and Don Rea, a savvy financial engineer. They had decided to start their own "investment bank," a bank that would specialize in tax-exempt bond issues for all kinds of projects—schools, bridges, sewers, highways, airports, and other infrastructure projects.

Charlie and Don asked Rock to join them, and he did. When they realized that they needed a security broker dealer who was licensed to execute transactions, Rock informed them of my business.

Obviously, receiving an invitation to work with a group of outstandingly talented, dedicated, driven, focused, and smart people proved to be a great break for me. I quickly agreed to grant the use of my license for a one-fourth interest in the company, with the understanding that I would continue to devote fifty percent of my time to Russell Investments, Inc. Russell, Rea, Bleier and Zappala ended up aligning itself with another broker dealer because my SEC license didn't allow the issuance of municipal bonds, but fortunately they didn't cut me from the new team.

They accepted my continued involvement with my original company, probably assuming that I'd drop Russell Investments once the new company became successful, and they were right. I put it on the shelf within a few years, but I did keep my involvement with Sam Zacharias, and our company, Realsearch International, which to this day we still use in our overseas investments.

The four of us started our new investment bank, executing financial assistance for fee income. As we provided services underwriting securities, we learned to understand the complexities of capital markets.

My transition into the business world wasn't always smooth as I charged ahead without much experience. I still found business every bit as challenging as football. Granted, there wasn't anyone trying to knock me down in the middle of a presentation, but I found this new arena can be very exciting in its own right, and we found ourselves traveling all over the world looking for investors.

The company grew as we added some of the smartest folks Pittsburgh had to offer, our best being Jeff Kendall, a lawyer who wanted to be a businessman. Jeff eventually earned full partner status and established himself as our superstar.

We worked hard and played hard. It was a good bunch of guys, and we were really on a roll for a while. We expanded into what we referred to as a super regional investment bank, with offices in Erie, Philadelphia and Charleston, West Virginia. We underwrote more than 30 billion dollars' worth of bonds. RRZ eventually replaced Goldman Sachs as lead manager of the Pennsylvania Turnpike bond issue and became a senior manager for the financing of the Pittsburgh International Airport.

Though different as night and day, our personalities complemented each other. We had too many strong egos to last very long, but we made a very good living and had a lot fun doing it.

Rocky and I tried our best to assist our new partners and not to live too much in the past, but, constantly asked to recite old Steeler stories, we couldn't help but reminisce.

Had we been more disciplined, we could have deflected the interest in our former business into our commitment to our new business. Our new partners were very understanding and were smart enough to recognize that the Steeler background occasionally gave our company an inroad, an opener that was not available to our competitors.

Pittsburghers, God bless them, tend to love their Steelers, particularly the teams of the '70s. Those of us who played in those days are astounded at the amount of attention people still give us after all these years. It seems that the longer today's teams go without winning a Super Bowl, the better we appear, at least in people's minds.

It wasn't very long before Rock decided to go full-time on his own as a broadcaster and motivational speaker. I told him he was crazy, but he did it his way, and it has worked out very well for him. Rocky succeeded as a motivational speaker and orates all over the country in front of huge audiences for big-time fees.

Since Rock's departure, RRZ&G has taken on many new challenges. We formed two new financial services companies, RRZ IMI (Investment Management Inc.) and RRZ Capital Markets, which acts as the general partner of an LBO fund. We eventually decided to sell the original company, known as RRZ Public Markets, Inc. to an employee group, headed by Greg Zappala, Charlie's nephew.

Charlie Zappala and Chuck Gomulka have stayed with IMI and the LBO fund, while Don Rea and I have teamed up with Jeff Kendall as equal partners in our merchant bank, Laurel Mountain Partners. Laurel invests its own money in LBOs, mergers and acquisitions, sometimes teaming up with other private equity sources, primarily focusing on integrated solid waste companies—about as low tech as you can get.

As I reflect back on my business career, I realize that, though many of my unusual experiences were successful and others were far from it, all made my journey more interesting and challenging. It has always been exciting and fun, and I have been accompanied by extraordinarily gifted and driven people.

CHAPTER TWENTY-ONE

Business War Stories

Working alongside my business teammates, I am constantly reminded of many principles I first learned on the football field. The need to be aggressive, to set goals high, and to practice hard all play important roles on and off the field.

I once heard a speaker who concluded his motivational speech by saying, "Think big, work hard and have a dream." These are thoughts so simplistic that they might not be taken seriously, but for some reason those words have stuck with me.

Here are just a few of the sometimes bizarre, and often humorous, business adventures that our group has experienced since starting RR&Z. They remind me of the importance to aim high and work hard for my achievements.

Don Rea and I, as part of our responsibilities at our investment bank, pursued private equity/ownership deals—transactions in which we could end up owning some of the asset without expending anything but our energy and abilities.

In the late '70s, Don, Sam Zacharias and I did a number of oil and gas drilling programs, but when the business dried up because of increased supply, reduced demand and falling prices, we got out—the cost just didn't justify the investment. But Don is stubborn, and he discovered that we could build and own hydroelectric dams with no cash investment and without any financial guarantees.

While building two hydro plants, one in Georgia and the other in South Carolina, we ran into an engineer who was also involved in power generation.

"You guys are missing the boat. You ought to be in the power business where they pay you to take the fuel supply," he said.

Our minds ran through the traditional power generation plants. Oil, gas and coal all cost money. The water was free, but no one would pay us to use it.

"And what is that?" Don asked.

"Boys, it's trash to cash—garbage incineration. That's all they do in Europe."

We knew about solid waste incineration, but we hadn't really thought about being the developer of such an enterprise because of the political nature of the permitting process. Reluctant to fight the "not in my backyard" mentality of nearby neighbors, we had focused on hydro—a "clean" power. Little did we know that the government had legislated such strict smokestack regulations that the smoke from trash incinerators is significantly cleaner than from the majority of big business manufacturing plants.

Don checked out the regulations and discovered that the government, in an effort to increase domestic power sources and lessen our dependency on oil, had granted the authority to do "prefunding deals," transactions that allowed the developer tax-free status, allowing him to generate a spread between his tax-free interest rate and the taxable rate received on his CD, generating money that could then be used to pay for the often exorbitant engineering and legal costs of putting the deal together. All you had to do was have a piece of property "under control" and have "discussions" with a reliable vendor and indications from a community that would welcome such a plant.

Don quickly put together the necessary ingredients and set out to put the financing together. It was late November 1981 and the federal grant to do prefundings expired at the end of the year, so we needed to move fast.

We first went to PNC and Mellon, asking them for letters of credit necessary to guarantee the bonds. But the banks dragged their feet, and by the time we gave up on our local banks, it was the second week of December. We called the Swiss Bank Corporation's representatives in New York and quickly set up a meeting for dinner at a posh restaurant.

On the flight to New York, Don Rea and Steve Frobouck, another partner working on the deal, finally focused on the amount of the financial guarantee they would request.

"How much do you think we should go for?" Steve asked.

"One hundred million dollars sounds good to me. It's a nice round number," Don said.

"Well, if you want a hundred, we'd better ask for one seventy-five," Steve said.

"Maybe one fifty," Don agreed.

After formulating their strategy, they proceeded to the restaurant and were treated to a very nice dinner, plenty of drinks and quality wine. The Swiss bankers seemed to be in a very good mood, and it wasn't until after dessert and a fine cognac that they even discussed business. As it drew later, our guys were getting nervous because no one had broached the subject of money yet.

"What is the size of this transaction?" the Swiss leader asked.

There was a pause, as Frobouck tried to decide how bold to be. Was it smart or insulting to ask for a lot more than expected?

"Three hundred million dollars," Steve said.

"Three hundred," the banker repeated quietly. "Yes, I believe I can get that approved."

They sat there stunned. Frobouck had done the unthinkable.

"Please wait a moment. I need to make a phone call," the Swiss banker said.

Steve and Don waited apprehensively, wondering who the man was calling. Could he possibly get approval so late at night? In just a few minutes he returned.

"Yes, three hundred is quite acceptable. You have our formal verbal approval right now, and you will have faxed written approval tomorrow morning," he said.

"Did you call Switzerland?" Don asked incredulously. "It's 4:00 a.m. over there!"

"Yes, for a deal this size I can wake up my boss," he said, smiling.

And to think that some people stereotype European banks as stodgy and unresponsive!

That deal influenced our business lives in a way we never would have anticipated. In putting together a waste incinerator, we had to understand the waste stream: where it came from, how it was transported, who presented any competition, and where to dispose of the ash. Of course it took six years of hard work, solving problems, getting permits and host community agreements, locating waste streams, and signing a joint venture agreement with our "partner," Westinghouse, before the plant became operational.

We soon discovered that landfills were far more interesting and profitable assets than incinerators, and, over the years, we developed a number of very profitable landfills and sold them to the major public waste companies.

The first landfill we developed was a bizarre experience. Again, Steve Frobouck possessed the vision to forecast the ultimate value of landfill enterprises.

"Come with me to try and buy our first landfill," Steve said.

"Is it profitable? Can we buy it at a good value?" I asked.

"Well, actually it's currently shut down for environmental reasons and needs to be repermitted, but my gut tells me it's a very undervalued asset."

By that time I had learned to respect Steve's gut.

So we travelled along a muddy dirt road to reach the deserted landfill in Steve's new BMW. The only person in sight was an old guy on a tractor. Frobouck pulled up, his tires skidding in the mud, and jumped out, his new Gucci loafers sinking into five inches of mud. He boldly strode over to the guy, as mud splashed up on the cuffs of his Armani suit, waving to me to follow.

"Excuse me, is Mr. Bruner here today? Steve asked.

"Who wants to know?" the guy asked.

"I'm Steve Frobouck, and this is Andy Russell."

"So?"

"We want to buy his landfill," Steve said.

"I'm Bruner."

"How about some lunch?" Steve asked.

"Sounds good."

Being the big spenders we are, we drove to the nearest Howard Johnson's for lunch, where we told Mr. Bruner about our business, stressing our financial capabilities. Mr. Bruner described his problems with the authorities as well as his difficulties with the political aspects required to renew his permit—issues that sounded formidable to me.

"So, you want out?" Steve asked.

"Does a bear shit in the woods?"

"How much?"

Mr. Bruner hesitated, and you could sense that he was judging how badly we wanted it—how high he could start.

"Five million bucks."

"How about eight?" Steve said.

"You want me to take paper."

"Some."

"How much?"

"Fifty thou up front with the rest when we solve the problems and get the expansion financed—trust me, we'll get it done," Steve said.

I almost turned the table over, not believing that our partner would up the ante when the guy was clearly in trouble and had started high, assuming we'd negotiate downwards.

Well, we bought that landfill for eight million, solved its problems, got that new permit, and borrowed 22 million dollars to reconstruct it to meet the new government standards and finish paying Bruner.

Two years later, we sold that landfill for more than forty million dollars.

One year later, after we had purchased another turnaround landfill near Albuquerque, New Mexico, Don asked me to join him on a trip to see if we could improve our competitive position there. Don explained that a Native American had proposed that we partner with the Indians, an endeavor which would allow us to circumnavigate the federal regulations regarding the disposal of certain wastes.

Don explained that the Indians could legally dispose of semihazardous waste, stuff like radioactive soils, on their reservations. Since the disposal would create no environmental problems and also triple the value of our investment, Don thought we should pursue this Indian enterprise. Their reservation was directly adjacent to our landfill, and they proposed to annex our property, which would effectively partner us with the tribe.

Don introduced me to the Indian spokesman, a well-dressed Wall Street type. But the two chiefs he brought, representing the two tribes that would be involved, were clothed in more traditional Southwest Indian garb. In fact, they were almost too perfect—something didn't seem right. We sat down in the coffee shop of our hotel.

Addressing the cocky leader, I said, "What tribe are you a member of?"

"My tribe is in Delaware, but I left there long ago."

I stared at the guy, thinking he was a bogus Indian, some shyster from "Dealsville."

Moments later, Don took the shark and one of the chiefs over to another table to discuss some of the details of the transaction, leaving me alone with the other chief. He sat there stony faced, staring at me but saying nothing. He was wearing lots of leather and fringe and had enough silver and turquoise jewelry to start a shop. I couldn't help but think that the deal guy had found this chief in a pool of extras at some movie studio. Feeling somewhat awkward, I figured that I should at least attempt to make conversation and qualify our prospect. .

"Where is your tribe located?"

"My tribe is in Tesuque—near Santa Fe."

"Isn't that near Rancho Encantado?" I asked.

"Yes, my father sell horses to Rancho Encantado."

"Is your tribe familiar with large financial transactions of this nature?"

"We do many big deals."

"Could you give me an example?"

"We sell water to the Santa Fe Ski Basin."

"Why is that so big?"

"We sell them water for snow-making in winter. In spring, we get the water back when it melts. Then, we sell the same water back to them. It's a very good deal."

The chief then smiled at me.

Ultimately, the deal fell through, but not for lack of trying. We eventually sold the landfill to Waste Management for a substantial loss—one of our few solid waste losers.

During this period, Jeff Kendall and I were assigned the daunting task of raising a $50,000,000 real estate investment fund, the prospects for which were mostly the major public and large corporate pension funds. After assembling a terrific group of "advisors" with very impressive track records (guys such as Peter Kalkus, Eddie Lewis, Myron Kerr, Ernie Buchman and Ron Puntil) we set out to raise the money from funds located all over the country.

On one occasion, in Sacramento to pitch CALPERS, our country's largest pension fund, Jeff would remind me that success is often in one's preparation. We were sitting in some crummy motel room, going over our presentation, trying to predict the questions that CALPERS board might ask.

"Andy, get up in front of that mirror and run through your opening speech."

"Why? I've been giving the same damn speech for months!"

"I thought you stumbled a few times last week to the IBM executives— we need this to be perfect, no fumbles."

"Hell, I've never practiced a pitch—don't want it to sound as though it's canned."

"Didn't Noll make you practice your techniques over and over?"

"Yes, but that was the NFL—nasty guys across from you."

"Believe me, CALPERS is just as tough—get up there in front of that mirror and rehearse your part."

So I got up and ran through the presentation, making a few small mistakes but correcting myself.

"Do it again," Jeff said.

Jeff would continue to remind me that success is in the details, that hard work will eventually pay off, and that overconfidence is often one's downfall. Unfortunately, our real estate venture would fail (we were only able to raise $21,000,000 of our $30,000,000 minimum) as the real estate markets fell dramatically during our two-year effort.

Upon returning home, admitting our failure, unwilling to expend any more money to chase this flawed concept in such a bad market, I met with Charlie Zappala, our key strategist.

"Russ, why don't you work with Don at National Waste?" Charlie asked.

National Waste was a development company focusing on the solid waste disposal business.

"Only if Jeff Kendall is willing to come with me," I said, knowing that Kendall, with his masters in labor relations and a law degree, was the brightest and most unrelentingly driven and fair businessman I'd ever known.

Kendall flourished at National, finding his groove, so to speak. He developed a construction and demolition landfill in Houston right under the noses of the big boys, BFI and Sanifill, who were based there. In fact, we had approached both companies to see if they wanted to partner with us, but they refused, saying there were just too many problems with the project for it to ever be successful. Jeff solved all those problems and financed the landfill with five million dollars in tax-exempt bonds. We then sold the project days before its opening to Sanifill for ten million.

In 1997, we purchased a small landfill and its largest hauler in south-central Illinois. Jeff believed that we could use these assets as the initial building blocks for a much larger and more fully integrated waste disposal company, Liberty Waste Services. It would consist of other landfills, hauling companies, and transfer stations. He also envisioned the possibility of railing waste down from Chicago, a huge waste-generating market.

So after confirming that Norfolk Southern was very agreeable to railing waste and providing us with a transfer station adjacent to the rail yard in Chicago, Jeff set out to purchase independent haulers in south Chicago, a group that had stubbornly resisted being bought out by the major waste companies that dominated most of Chicago's waste stream.

Jeff, knowing virtually no one in Chicago, used the Yellow Pages to find the numbers of all the independent haulers south of the city. Somehow he convinced all of them to meet at a restaurant to hear our presentation on why they should merge into a single company, precisely what they had been resisting for years. They probably just figured that they'd enjoy a free dinner.

After Jeff presented what I thought was a brilliant plan for the merger, they just sat there shaking their heads. Soon, everyone left, after telling us in no uncertain terms that they had no intention of combining. Jeff was hardly even disappointed and appeared energized by the opportunity.

"Jeff, nice try," I said. "Too bad they had no interest."

"No problem. This idea is just too good to ignore."

"The problem with mergers is that you have to treat everyone the same, value each company equally, and then you get into ego issues," I said.

"You're right, so we'll just buy them one at a time. It'll take a little longer that way, but we can get it done," Jeff said.

Six months later, after buying five of those companies, we felt strongly that we needed one more company on the team. The company we needed to join us in our development of a crucial transfer station, owned by an Irish family named O'Hare, had proven difficult to deal with, and Jeff asked me to join him on a last-ditch effort to sign them up. If we couldn't get them to agree, we were prepared to abort the development of the transfer station and come up with a new game plan, but that would mean losing a lot of money and wasting a great deal of hard work.

We arrived in Chicago for our 9:30 a.m. meeting with Tim O'Hare, the man in charge of the company's waste stream and the person with whom Jeff had been negotiating. It was frustrating because we had been waiting months for this company to respond and they had been dragging their feet. We walked into their modest offices and waited for the receptionist to get off the phone.

Slamming the phone down, appearing angry about something, she said, "What do you want?"

"We're here to see Tim O'Hare," Jeff said.

"He's not here—won't be back today."

"We had a meeting scheduled here at 9:30," Jeff said, looking at his watch.

"Well, you're outta luck. He's out and won't be back."

"What about Sean O'Hare? Can we see him?" Jeff asked, hoping to see Tim's older brother.

Looking perturbed, she got up from her desk and walked into the back office.

Moments later she returned, looking even more unhappy.

"He's busy—can't see you."

I walked over to her desk, trying to stifle my anger, and said, "Please excuse our persistence, but we've flown here this morning, all the way from Pittsburgh, just for this meeting, and we would really appreciate it if Mr. O'Hare could just give us fifteen minutes of his valuable time."

She again disappeared in the back, returning only moments later.

"Okay, he'll see you, but only for fifteen minutes."

After thanking this sweet receptionist, we walked back to Sean O'Hare's office, which was sparsely appointed and only large enough for two small chairs crammed against the wall. Mr. O'Hare, studying a paper, did not look up as we entered. We sat down and waited for him to recognize our presence.

After a few minutes of silence, he finally glanced up and just stared at us.

"So, what do you want?"

Jeff took a few minutes to explain the situation, stressing how important it was for us to have an answer that day.

"Can't help you. Tim handles all that kind of crap. Where the hell is he?"

With that, he picked up the phone and apparently called his brother. As he was listening to Tim's explanation, I could see his eyes tighten and his face begin to prepare for his delivery of bad news. I quickly glanced around the room, hoping to see anything that might help us connect with this tough old gentleman.

On his wall was a photograph of a younger Sean O'Hare, surrounded by a team of young Little League football players.

When he hung up the phone, I pointed to the photograph.

"Were you a coach? Looks like a group of Little Leaguers."

"Yes, you know anything about football?"

"Andy played fourteen years for the Pittsburgh Steelers in the NFL and was the team captain for ten years," Jeff said.

"I hate professional football—can't stand it."

"Well, I loved coaching my son's Little League team. In fact, it's one of my fondest memories," I said.

As Sean began to tell us the story of his coaching experience, clearly relishing teaching kids how to play the game and beaming with pride over their championship seasons, I again glanced around the room, hoping to find some other thing to talk about. My experience is that if things aren't going well in a business transaction, one must develop a good relationship with the principals before any propositions are made. Negotiations should always be win-win for both parties.

I was surprised to see a framed photo on his credenza of Mr. O'Hare standing with a canyon in the background. He had just finished his football story and seemed to be gearing up to reject our proposal.

"Mr. O'Hare, I couldn't help but notice that canyon photo. Where is that?"

"What do you know about canyons?" he snapped.

"Well, I've hiked most of the Grand Canyon's wilderness trails and just this morning I received a letter from the park's rangers rejecting my application for a permit."

Hearing this, Mr. O'Hare reached for his phone, dialed a number and waited.

"Fred, I need a hiking permit, today."

After listening a few moments, he looked at me and asked, "What's your name again? What trail do you want to go down and when?"

After answering him, I watched as he relayed the message. He then scowled and said, "Look, just get it done, now." With that he slammed the phone down.

"Mr. O'Hare, I don't understand. How can you get that permit for me?"

"We haul the waste for the Grand Canyon—nice contract."

That permit, gotten in such a bizarre fashion, would allow my best friend, Ray Mansfield, to go on the hike in the Grand Canyon with his son where he would tragically die of a massive heart attack. Ironically, Ray had told his son on several occasions that he loved the Canyon and it was where he wanted to die.

After securing that permit, O'Hare pushed back his chair and suggested that we join him for lunch over which we learned all about his interesting life. The guy had met with the Pope, Mother Teresa, former Polish president Lech Walesa, and been all over the world. He was quite the storyteller.

When we returned from lunch, Sean called Tim and told him to come out of hiding and return to the office. When he got there, they adjourned to Sean's office to make their final decision, while Jeff and I anxiously waited in the conference room.

Sean walked in, closed the door and sat down across from us. Appearing very relaxed and apparently at peace with what he was about to say, he stared directly at us with his icy blues. Both Jeff and I were on the edge of our seats, praying that months of hard work were not about to go down the drain.

"We are going to accept your deal, but I want you to know something. If this deal we are entering into with you hurts my family in any way, you will not like what I will do to you."

He sat there, smiling at us.

"What are you going to do, Mr. O'Hare?" I asked.

"I'm going to cut your balls off."

With that, holding out his hands in a way that suggested he didn't want any response, he pushed back his chair and said, "Maybe you want to think about it for awhile." He then got up from the table and left the room.

Jeff and I looked at each other, not knowing how to react to this outrageous statement. Was he kidding? Or was he really making a serious threat?

"So, what to do you think, Partner?" Jeff asked. "I think we should go for it. There's no way that delivering a guaranteed amount of garbage to our transfer station is going to hurt his family."

"Yes, but what if the project doesn't go well? What if this guy is truly a wacko?" I asked.

"No way, he's bluffing."

Later, the O'Hares reneged and refused to honor their contract, claiming that the prices had changed. Fortunately, despite the O'Hares' withdrawal from our agreement (granted, there are always two sides to every dispute), everything worked out extraordinarily well for us when we sold the company to Allied Waste.

CHAPTER TWENTY-TWO

Making Mistakes

If you haven't made mistakes, haven't failed, haven't lost, haven't been humiliated, embarrassed, or devastated to the core of your being, then most likely, you haven't taken big enough risks. You may have played life a little too safe. If we haven't failed, and sometimes on a frequent basis, can we really ever know the sweet exhilaration of success?

I think it is important to recognize our mistakes and to deal with them, face them to the best of our ability, learn from them, and then, accepting that we're not perfect, move on from that experience to be a better person and, perhaps, a better performer or achiever in whatever it is that we do.

I made a lot of mistakes playing for the Steelers, far more than I really care to admit. Some were simple errors in execution of technique (missing tackles, dropping interceptions, missing blocks, etc.); others were due to the devil ego getting in my way, trying to play the hero and make the big play that might turn the game around. Some were caused by relying too much on my understanding of the opponent's tendencies, totally confidant that a certain play was about to be run but then being fooled by the opposition. Yes, I got outfoxed, and entirely too often.

For some reason I remember the mistakes much more than I remember the successes. The humiliation of getting beaten, of giving your opponent the satisfaction of ever knowing he could outperform you, of letting your teammates down, was greater than the exhilaration of making a big play that helped the team. Here are some of my major bloopers during my Steeler career.

My first big mistake relative to strategy (I had lots of small ones) occurred in our final game my rookie year (1963) against the New York Giants in Yankee Stadium, in a game that was essentially a playoff game. If we won that game we would have been in the NFL championship game against the Chicago Bears, a team we had tied in Forbes Field 17-17 a few weeks earlier.

Very few Steeler fans remember that the team was that close to a championship ring way back in 1963. We had beaten those Giants in Pittsburgh 28-0, but they had been without their star quarterback, Y. A. Tittle.

Late in the game, still in the hunt, my responsibility was to drop back to the strong-side hash mark, about 12 yards deep, and prevent anyone from catching a ball in my zone. Frank Gifford, the great Giants running back/receiver, had hooked up to my left, close enough for me to easily cover him, but I looked back at Y. A. Tittle to see if he would try to go to Gifford. This was a mistake, because by taking my eyes off Gifford, I didn't see him drift behind me to my right. Still thinking Gifford was hooked up to my left, leaning that way, I was unable to react to Tittle's throw to Gifford, a huge first down that kept the drive going that ultimately beat us.

My mistake was looking back, hoping to intercept, to make the big play. Instead, I should have just covered Gifford and made Tittle go somewhere else, or if he did throw it, just let the ball hit me in the back of the jersey or helmet—just put myself between Tittle and Gifford; the rest would have been easy. If they hadn't completed that pass, we could have forced them to punt, gotten the ball back and perhaps won that game.

I believe coaches often teach zone defenses incorrectly. They instruct you to drop to a specific point, like ten yards deep at the hash mark, and check for receivers entering your zone but then go back to observing the quarterback's eyes and break on the ball (go to the reception point) when it is thrown. This worked for me in college (I had ten interceptions my senior year at Mizzou), but the problem in the pros is that they throw the ball much too fast to react in time. I found it much better to just cover the man in my zone and make the quarterback go somewhere else. If everyone would do that in each zone they'd have to punt.

Coaches would probably say that my theory isn't sound because the offense might flood the zone (bring more than one player into that zone and if you focus on one of them you can't cover the other), but typically offensive coordinators do not have two receivers in the same zone. Therefore, don't worry about it. They also might say that I should have been able to glance back and forth, from quarterback to receiver, but this frequently doesn't work because you still lose the receiver (who may drift away) when your eyes go back to the quarterback. Better to just cover the man in your zone, man to man, and do not look back at the quarterback, because it will cause you to fail more often than it will allow you to intercept.

In the '70s, executing the above strategy, receivers in my zone rarely caught a pass because I concentrated on the receiver rather than the quarterback. Bud Carson, our defensive coordinator, and Woody Wodenhoefer, our linebacker coach, didn't really teach my theory, but I just did it anyway. Apparently it worked, because they never asked me to change what I was doing. Granted, you won't get many interceptions that way, but you'll do a better job for your team. Of course, my theory of zone defense was easier to execute in those days because we could reroute, jam, chuck receivers, often just stopping them from coming across our zones as long as the ball wasn't in the air. Today's players only get one jam in the first five yards.

Another mistake I made too often was to assume that the quarterback would not throw the ball to my man when I assumed he could see that I was in position to intercept. In our big loss to the Miami Dolphins in the AFC championship game in 1972 (the game after the immaculate reception) on a key third down late in the game, I dropped back to my zone, seeing Jim Kick hooking up within five yards of me. I could see Bob Griese, a very smart quarterback, looking at Kick, but assuming he could see that I was in position to intercept, I looked inside to see if there was a receiver crossing. That little glance inside was a big mistake, because Griese surprised me and threw it to Kick, picking up a key first down. Had I just gone over and covered Kick, Griese would have been forced to go somewhere else and perhaps we would have forced them to punt. So one mistake I made too often was to assume that the quarterback could see that I had someone covered (because of my proximity) and then he still threw it to my man. The reason could have been that our defensive line was about to sack him and he was forced to go there at that instant.

Another humbling mistake I made was in a game against the New Orleans Saints in Pitt Stadium in the late '60s when I failed to cover a wide receiver deep in my zone because I slipped on the wet turf. I remember that it was a crucial long yardage situation (third and 20) and the fans were quite unhappy with me for falling and allowing the Saints to move the sticks.

In fact, they booed me, and it was the first and only time I was ever booed by the Pittsburgh fans. I remember at first being hurt by their reaction and then becoming angry, both at the fans and then at myself, but then channeling that anger to perform better the remainder of the game—you can't stop using your brain. Hey, if you are out there, you have to deal with the situation, whether it be bad weather, slippery field, injuries, or angry fans, stop making excuses and get the job done, so maybe I deserved to be booed. It happens!

But the worst mistakes are the ones that are caused because you let your ego get in front of your brain. Once, playing a critical game against our archrival Cleveland, we found ourselves up by three points late in the fourth quarter with the Browns on our 25-yard line, successfully moving the ball down the field. I thought that we desperately needed to make a big play, to throw them for a loss and get them out of field-goal range. It was third down and the game was on the line.

I lined up and read the formation, a full-left setup that showed every reason to believe that Cleveland intended to run a sweep to our right, towards Dwight White, Mel Blount and myself. I knew that the tendency charts showed that the sweep was their predominant favorite from that formation and from that down and yardage, and I could sense from the Browns' alignment and body language (the guard was leaning back and ready to pull) that they were highly likely to run wide to our side.

In fact, I was so sure that I decided to take a chance, change the defense, and jump into the guard-center gap and penetrate upfield, yelling to Dwight at same time that I was executing a stunt where I would go inside and Dwight would swing outside with responsibility to contain the play.

The problem was twofold. One, Dwight couldn't hear me because of the noise of the crowd, and two, he would never even have anticipated the call, because I didn't have the authority to make that call under the circumstances. I was freelancing.

I certainly can appreciate that Dwight had his own problems, trying to avoid the block of Doug Dieken, a Pro Bowl tackle, and certainly couldn't be criticized for not anticipating a call that wasn't normative under the circumstances anyway, coming from his crazy right-side linebacker who had decided, unknown to him at the last second, to go it alone, more or less, trying to make the big play that might turn the game around—not exactly my style. Not a good idea to freelance in a team game like football.

Well, I was right about that play. The Browns did run the sweep, but the problem was that I took the wrong angle, driving too straight forward and not angling enough outside, forgetting that the fullback would take a fake handoff, filling the hole left by the pulling guard. Out of control, overextended, with too much forward body lean, I was easily cut down by the fullback who clearly saw me penetrate after only a few yards into the backfield.

Meanwhile, the halfback easily ran around our end because there was no one there to contain the play, since it was my responsibility.

The Browns scored a touchdown, and all of a sudden we were down by four points, all because I made a bonehead play, trying to be the hero. The devil ego will get you every time.

What I also didn't realize was that had we only given up a field goal, that there was still enough time for our offense to move down the field and kick a field goal of our own to win by three, had I not gone brain-dead. Our offense did get into field-goal range but were forced to go for the touchdown, and we lost. I had cost us a crucial game and felt ashamed and, frankly, pretty stupid.

On Monday, as I sat in the whirlpool for treatment of my sore knee, Chuck Noll approached, shaking his head. I knew he would have seen the films by then and figured he'd be furious.

"What were you thinking?" Chuck asked.

"I just knew they were going to run that sweep, and I thought I could penetrate upfield and take them out of field-goal position, but I forgot about the fullback."

"Don't ever freelance, and don't guess. Read your keys."

His comment made me feel like I was back playing in junior high.

"Sorry, Coach, I really screwed up," I said.

"Get healthy, we've got a big one this week."

He looked me in the eyes, shook his head, chuckled quietly to himself, patted me on the back and then just walked away with a wry smile on his face.

I sat there with my hyperextended elbow and sore knee in the whirlpool (all pro players are constantly nursing some injury), watching him depart the room, thinking that there is a man I want to play for. I had monumentally screwed up, and he just smiled, knowing that no one felt worse about my mistake than me, and he was already focused on the next game.

It was one of the good lessons that Coach Noll taught us. It doesn't do any good worrying about past mistakes. Learn from them and move on, doing whatever it takes to win the next game. Of course, he would remind me again during that next week to not guess and certainly never freelance. Football is a game of risk, and Coach Noll liked to play the odds—play those defenses that had the highest probability of stopping the opponent. High-risk strategies were not part of his game plan.

One of my problems was that when I felt certain what was coming, what play the opponent would run, my tendency was to overreact, to try and make the big play. My logic was simple. If I knew what the other team was going to do, I ought to be able to stop it, either by penetrating so quickly or so far up the field that they would be unable to run what they planned. Sometimes I would be wrong and they'd run something else, and sometimes I would forget some little detail, like who might be there to block me, or some other deception involved with the play, such as my ignoring a fake handoff to someone before running what I thought they would.

Hey, I'm not saying that I was unusual in this sense. I'm sure a lot of my teammates often fought the same impulse, wanting to play a well-calculated hunch and sometimes discovering that it got them in trouble.

Late in my career, we were playing a big game in Houston (Monday night television) and the Oilers had brought in a tight end who really wasn't a tight end. He was an agile, 6'5," 275-pound tackle whom they used only on short yardage running plays. I was hugely out-sized and had realized on previous plays that my normal technique (controlling the tight end by grabbing his shoulder pads beneath the armpits and getting low enough to prevent his block) wouldn't work with this guy. He was huge and ripped from a lot of weightlifting. I figured I'd have to beat him some other way, like using my brain, being deceptive, faking one way and going the other, or beating him with quickness.

So when they lined up near our goal line, in a formation with the big dude on my side, I had a very strong sense that they were coming my way. I think after playing so many years, a player often just subliminally knows in some intuitive way what the opponent is going to do, making it almost unnecessary to check each presnap key or run through the tendencies in your head, sensing the body language of key players. That was one of those times.

So I turned and yelled to Mel Blount that I had outside containment (I did) and that I would be looping outside to prevent getting hooked, all the while knowing that the big dude was listening as he lined up. At the snap of the ball the giant leaped to the outside, clearly trying to hook me, anticipating my quick outside move, but I just ignored him and drove straight forward, coming completely free, unfettered as they say.

I drove towards the halfback, expecting to see the pitchout, but when I didn't see the ball coming to him instantly, I made the mistake of pausing to look back towards the quarterback (always a mistake) to see him finishing a fake to the fullback and then pitching the ball to the halfback with me just standing there, totally unblocked but frozen in place, unable to react to the halfback. Fortunately, Mel Blount threw him for a two-yard loss, but I still had blown a play that I had properly anticipated but, again, forgot a detail—the fake to the fullback. Success is in the details.

Already mentioned is my horrible game against the Oakland Raiders where I never found my groove, fighting my own brain as much as the Raider players. You hate to be big contributor to a team loss.

I realize, reader, that you may not be able to sympathize with these mistakes, and I am sure that I never really had them in a proper perspective. After all, it's not like football is a serious business like heart surgery or running a major business, but to me these mistakes were devastating at the time. If I had been alone out there I doubt they would have had the same impact, but I was playing a team sport and I had no right to go off and do my own thing. I had let my teammates down and found the experience humiliating, embarrassing and painful.

Well, we are all human, prone to making mistakes, sometimes because we are just plain stupid, other times because our technique is flawed or we are trying too hard, and, of course, sometimes because those other competitors are pretty good and we have to give them some credit.

The key, I think, is how we react to our mistakes. First and foremost is to not make excuses, to be accountable and accept the fact that we screwed up. Frankly, I've had a hard time with that one, often seeking some outside reason, not under my control, that caused me to fail. This caused me to sometimes argue with the coaches, to find some other fault and try and pass the blame to them, making the case that the game plan was flawed. I was wrong to do that.

Late in my career, under Chuck Noll, we were allowed to have input with regard to the game plan that eliminated any excuse-making. Sometimes the players would want to reject something in the game plan, feeling that the strategy might look good on the blackboard but would never work on the field. But we would have the opportunity during the week to practice it our way and the coach's way. Of course, each practice was filmed and watched after practice, so you could see clearly what worked best. Rarely would we still be debating a strategy as late as Friday or Saturday. Chuck used to say "Don't surprise me on Sunday." In other words, don't do it the coach's way all week and your way in the game. Bottom line was that we all wanted to execute the best possible strategy that would prevent the opponent from being successful.

Second, it's important to learn from our errors and to try and not repeat the same mistakes. I know, the old joke is that the one thing we learn from experience is that we don't learn from experience, but of course, we should and must.

Finally, and of equal importance, is that we cannot be so afraid to make mistakes that we render ourselves useless. The fear of making a mistake can be paralyzing. So we must force ourselves to relax, realize that no one is perfect, be willing to take chances, not fear failure, and visualize success.

Celebrate the Heroes of Pittsburgh Sports

in These Other Acclaimed Titles from Sports Publishing!

Myron Cope: Double Yoi!
by Myron Cope
6 x 9 hardcover, 300 pages,
eight-page photo section

2002 release!

Honus: The Life and Times of a Baseball Hero
by William Hageman
6 x 9 hardcover, 235 pages,
16-page photo section

1960: The Last Pure Season
by Kerry Keene
6 x 9 softcover, 216 pages, photos
throughout

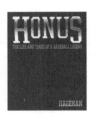

Honus: The Life and Times of a Baseball Hero (leatherbound edition)
by William Hageman
6 x 9 leatherbound, 235 pages,
16-page photo section

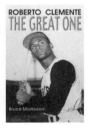

Roberto Clemente: The Great One
by Bruce Markusen
6 x 9 hardcover and softcover,
362 pages,
16-page photo section

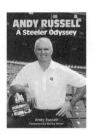

Andy Russell: A Steeler Odyssey
by Andy Russell
6 x 9 hardcover and softcover,
272 pages,
eight-page photo section

Reflections on Roberto
by Phil Musick
8 1/2 x 11 softcover, 128 pages,
300 color
and b/w photos throughout

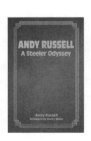

Andy Russell: A Steeler Odyssey (leatherbound edition)
by Andy Russell
6 x 9 leatherbound, 272 pages,
eight-page photo section

To order at any time, please call toll-free 877-424-BOOK (2665).

For fast service and quick delivery,
order on-line at
www.SportsPublishingLLC.com.